This book is dedicated to all those who have suffered
at the hands of the "righteous."

"But know now that our present sufferings are not worthy to be compared to the glory that will be revealed to us."
—Romans 8:18

Homecoming

R uth's mind was full of thoughts, yet none of them made sense. She was known for her wisdom, her ability to articulate herself in a way that shed light, that broke through the confusion in the lost souls of those around her—that saved lives. What an incredible moment to witness the spark return to someone's eyes when they grasped the hope she was attempting to impart to them, when they understood the piece of truth that would help them dig their way up out of some impossible situation. Unfortunately, now, when *she* needed the breakthrough— nothing.

There was no one to help Ruth. Everyone had turned their backs. Not at first, of course. No, they had taken their time, made sure the fall was certain and the claims could be substantiated. Then they had disappeared like ghosts. Not that she blamed them; everyone was in shock. She had left them all behind too: the turncoats, the gossips, the supposed faithful. But it was more than just her fellow believers, she had left everything behind, either packed up and put in storage or given back to the church from which it had come, including the house—*her* house! Suddenly, there was a needle in Ruth's throat, pinching her windpipe like a fishbone, and her lungs seemed paralyzed, keeping her from breathing the deep breath she needed so terribly.

In flashes, Ruth saw the history of 41 Morning Lane. There was the day she and Sam first looked at the four-thousand-square-foot residence in the gated community of Havenhurst Estates just outside Charleston. "A short bike ride from the dunes," they were told by the realtor. Ruth and Sam grasped hands in the hollow, freshly constructed rooms and whispered their thoughts to each other about what the kids would think. There were the color swatches she happily pored over for hours on end to make a sanctuary of beauty and peace for their children, their family, their friends, and even their congregants. There was the laughter they had shared over BBQs, pool parties, birthdays, and anniversaries in the years that followed. There were the tears for the pets lost and found, the flesh wounds and the Band-Aids, the emotional wounds and the apologies. There was the food Ruth cooked—the endless dinners and lunches and breakfasts—that scented the air with powdered sugar and olive oil and infused the walls with her love and care. There was the sound of the sprinklers waking her up each morning before the sunrise—before anyone else—when she would sit on the overstuffed couch in her small home office with a view of the roses in the backyard, read her Bible, and pray God's will for the day ahead, especially for her children.

And it was her children that kept her going now. If it hadn't been for them, in the face of the indelible pain she was experiencing, Ruth would have ripped off her seatbelt, unlocked the door, and thrown herself from her and Sam's Escalade out onto the road. Even if she didn't die from the fall, even if she only mangled her body, at least she would feel something other than the hole inside her that seemed to grow more unbearable with each heartbeat.

Father God, please give me strength. Show me your endless love and wisdom. Yea though I walk through the valley of the shadow of death. Please help me not to fear it. Help me. Oh, God. Help me! As she thought out her prayer, a tear slipped down Ruth's cheek. She subtly brushed it away and adjusted the air conditioning vent so that more cool air blew against her face. Ruth felt her life shouldn't be playing out like this. She was in her prime—thirty-eight—and by any standards, she was beautiful: supple skin, blonde hair, azure eyes. She was also smart and capable. She dressed well, and despite never having braces as a kid, she had a toothpaste-commercial smile—at least that's what she had been told. She was a good person with a generous soul who had never done a thing to hurt anyone. So, how had she ended up here being suffocated by the reality of her own existence? Once more, Ruth forced herself to struggle for the oxygen she needed so badly, and she looked out the tinted glass window of the Cadillac at the forests and fields flying by.

Missouri. The Ozarks. The Mormons believed this was where the original Garden of Eden had been created before Noah's flood wiped it from the face of the earth. They still believed this was the place where Jesus would return. Paradise. It was dazzlingly lush, especially apparent at this time of year—the end of June—when the chlorophyll in all the flora had started up its frenzied production. The fields, trees, thickets, and even the ponds and streams were plump with life they would store up over the summer to get them through the harsh, white winter that would inevitably come. It was supposed to be a calming color—green. That's what Ruth's interior decorator had claimed when Ruth was settling on paint samples for her and Sam's new house all those years ago in Charleston. And maybe it was true. Looking out at the emerald spectrum whipping by, Ruth was reminded of life still to come, unfurling endlessly out from her current situation. It was a mere blip in the radar of existence—this pain. Suddenly, she was able to suck in a deep breath. That was precisely what she needed, a million more of those.

Ruth relaxed back into her seat and closed her eyes, the confused panic of her incessant thoughts quieted for a moment. She could hear the soft hum of the Escalade's engine, the whisper of the air conditioning, the calming conveyor belt sound of the rubber tires on the pavement pulling the SUV along the asphalt. In ten more minutes, they would be at the farm—Sam's parents' place—their hideaway for the next few weeks or months or however long it took for them to gather the truth of themselves together and figure out a plan to move on. It would be a misery for everyone, and honestly, Ruth didn't know if she would be able to take it more than a few days. And maybe she shouldn't have come this far. Maybe when the truth was revealed about Sam's transgressions, she should have walked away immediately—game over. The fact was, she loved Sam, still wanted to be with him—even as she hated him, despised him, felt ripped apart by every atom of her husband's existence. But mostly, she was still in shock. There was no making any decision when just thinking and breathing felt like the greatest chores she had ever endured.

The real knockout punch was what Sam's actions had done to her children. As the news broke one month and a different life ago, Ruth watched each of her offspring go from radiant beings of youthful bliss to vacant shells of innocence lost. There was a color gone from her babies' cheeks nowadays, a benighted hollowness that had formed in what had once been their engorged fortunate existence. She wasn't sure who was more affected, Rachel, JD, or Timothy. The truth was they had all been impacted in their own ways, though how that crash into this new reality would play out would probably not be seen for years, and at this point, Ruth didn't know what to do to blunt the trauma. Maybe that was why she stayed with her husband. Perhaps that was why she hadn't yet walked away from their marriage.

Rachel—a gangly but fierce fifteen-year-old with pale, velvet skin and pouty lips—had been at color guard practice when the Associated Press began disseminating a news article—ripped from the *National Enquirer* of all places—about Sam's involvement with a male prostitute and drug dealer named Red McCrory. Ruth couldn't even imagine how awful it must have been for her eldest child to hear of her father's shame as it spread across social media while she stood on that Charleston football field doing the only thing she would admit to loving at her age. If she had been anywhere else, maybe it wouldn't have been so awful. But right there in the middle of the high school football stadium, her Havenhurst color guard flag at the ready, the shell-shocked looks from the sidelines had caught Rachel's attention. And when her coach, paled-faced and uncertain, called her into his office, Rachel believed she had imagined the worst when she suspected a terrible car accident or death.

It made Ruth's stomach turn to think of how Rachel had worked so hard to get on that color guard team only to be torn from it in such an embarrassing way. Two years before, she and her four best girlfriends made a pact to get on the team together, and they did. Rachel could barely sleep the night before tryouts. Then, waiting for decisions from the coach, she could scarcely eat. Ruth worried about her daughter's obsession with color guard, but she was also glad to see Rachel excited about something in life at her age.

As the eldest of Sam and Ruth's three kids, Rachel had naturally assumed the mantel of exemplar child, except when it came to intrusions on her personal property. Anything past her bedroom door was off limits to everyone—"KEEP OUT!" Still, even when her own space had been invaded, whether deliberately or inadvertently, ultimately Rachel was always more subdued in her reactions than Ruth expected. But then, that's the way Rachel had always been—unexpectedly easy.

From inception to delivery, Rachel hardly gave Ruth a surprise and never a worry. Even the way Rachel grew in Ruth's womb was elegant. Her birth was painful, yes, but not the ugly, screaming kind of pain Ruth was told to expect. Instead, it was more of an elongated, exhaustive, pressure-fueled discomfort. Then, there she was, a perfect loaf of flesh, big dark eyes, and light blonde hair. Rachel hadn't cried when she was placed in Ruth's arms. She had merely stared at Ruth as though perplexed at this vision before her, and Ruth looked back at Rachel the same way.

Ruth barely managed to potty train Rachel by the time JD came along. JD was Ruth's little man. Rough and tumble, according to JD nobody was having a good time if somebody wasn't scratched up and bleeding. Jonathan David was the kind of boy Ruth dreaded raising, one who could find a snake or spider or frog anywhere he looked, and who was always the first to climb a tree or jump into the deep end of a body of water or take any dare. Even before he could walk, JD wanted to throw balls and catch balls and hit balls. She knew JD would be an incredibly successful athlete, and he was. From T-ball to junior league, from football to baseball to basketball and soccer, JD was the star of every sport he played, and he was adored by his teammates and coaches for his talent and passion. He was the most vocal of her children when Sam and Ruth told them they were moving back to Sam's parents' farm "for a while." Ruth was quite sure, at thirteen, JD understood what Sam had been accused of, and it was clear he didn't want to leave the opportunities he had to play sports in Charleston to hide out in some Podunk town whose football team was barely large enough to even pass as a team. It almost scared Ruth the way JD could fly off the handle so quickly when he was tested, what with his size double that of most boys his age and his green eyes able to sear her to her soul with hate when he wanted to show it. Yes, JD was Ruth's greatest worry, the masculinity coursing through him so raw and robust it terrified her, especially coming on at this early stage in his life. But then, when she became pregnant with JD, she wasn't ready for another child. It wouldn't have mattered what sex he or she was.

JD had been an accident, the result of a romantic weekend Ruth and Sam had been gifted by one of their parishioners after the congregation of their small, nondenominational church discovered they'd put off their second anniversary plans because they couldn't afford to do anything special. The getaway was to a resort in Hilton Head, and everything was taken care of: meals, drinks, spa treatments, horseback riding on the beach—*everything*. All Sam and Ruth had to do was drive down. And that's what they did, in Ruth's ramshackle minivan because it had less chance of breaking down than Sam's rusted-through truck.

Even now, Ruth distinctly remembered how the bed in their hotel room on the island felt so plush and cool against her back. One day, she would have a bed like that, she'd thought—one covered in new, white sheets and feather pillows that fluffed up when you lay your head on them instead of wilting into flat pallets of musk like the ones she'd owned at that time. Back then, Ruth wanted to sleep, wanted to melt into the peace of that quiet, cool room and forget the bills and the burdens and the demands of her and Sam's lean years in South Carolina. Sam, too, had seemed to relax the moment they arrived. When he reappeared from filling their ice bucket, he smiled at her, "Well, somebody made themselves at home." He disappeared into the bathroom.

Ruth said nothing. She could hear Sam pee and wash his hands. Then it was quiet again, and Ruth imagined all worked out, six-foot-one of him feathering back his short cut, chestnut hair in the mirror, cocking his head to the side, an earnest expression on his absurdly handsome face. When Sam appeared again, he stopped just shy of the bed.

"What?" She asked.

Now it was Sam's turn not to say anything. He went to her, climbed onto the bed, and wrapped her in his arms. She buried her face in his neck where the smell of his cologne and deodorant mixed with the humidity of the day creating a scent that out of all the billions of men in the world, she imagined only *he* had. She felt the muscles of his arms and the thick fingers of his hands holding her, and she felt not just at peace, but safe. Despite how meager their life was at that time—he was *always* her safety.

They had lain cuddled together for five or six hours before they both woke up. He was hard, and she wanted him inside her. So, she backed into him, grinding on his crotch until he was awake and pushing against her. Then, almost dreamily they had undressed, and she turned to face him, let him hold her legs out in the air as he thrust. They hardly ever kissed when they made love. But who cared? Sam's penis felt perfect inside Ruth, like it was made for her, and she had no comparison, being as Sam had been her one and only. Who was she to suspect intercourse should be any different? The important thing was they always came, both of them, and they always seemed satisfied, both of them. However, this night was different. Instead of each of them finishing themselves off with side by side masturbation, this night Sam came inside of her. It was something he usually couldn't do. And after, she knew she was pregnant. She didn't say anything, of course, but later when she got up to use the bathroom and caught her reflection in the hotel mirror, she knew her body chemistry had changed. Her lithe features were flush with life in the way she became during pregnancy. Her hair seemed extra shiny as it cascaded over her shoulders and her nipples were extra rosy and taught. More green was shining through her azure eyes than usual, and her skin was glowing. Either the hotel was magic, or she would have another baby, she thought.

The next day, Ruth still went horseback riding out on the beach and ate the freshly caught grouper that was on the menu that night.

But she took in the soft white sands, the ice-blue salt water, and the blood-orange sunset with an extra bit of reflection.

"I love you," she whispered into Sam's ear as he held her in one of the hammocks tied between palm trees near the beach. "I love you so much."

Ruth was knocked out of her reverie by the slowdown of the Escalade and the pop of rocks under the tires as Sam turned down the gravel road towards his parents' farm. Then Ruth saw her first glimpse of the farmhouse in the distance, and suddenly she couldn't breathe again.

Familial Tableau

To anyone but Ruth, Sam's parents' farm would have seemed like the ideal escape, tucked back amongst mature white and red oak trees, no neighbors for miles. The two-story farmhouse looked like a calendar photo. White siding, a sweeping front porch, and gables on top of a slate grey, aluminum roof, the farmhouse stood sternly at the end of the long gravel driveway. Just a stone's throw to the north was the old hay barn that had been transformed into a cabin back when Sam was a young boy. To the south was the *new* barn, a massive metal building that looked more like an airplane hangar than a traditional farm building. The hangar housed all of Sam's father's farm equipment and tools, and it had an office area in the back where he could nap on a beat-up leather couch when the inevitable heat of certain Missouri summer afternoons became too unbearable for farm work.

As the Cadillac made its way down the gravel road, leaving a cloud of chalky dust in its wake, the farm dogs—a grey Australian shepherd and a beagle—came racing towards the SUV barking excitedly. Ruth suspected the two canines, Holly and Potato, were the most excited of all the parties involved in this visit. Even her youngest, Tim, who at six years old loved all things four-legged and could usually be counted on for animated exposition at the sight of even the lowliest cow, remained silent in the very back seat. But then he hadn't said a word since two nights before when she told him to pack everything important to him in two suitcases and prepare to leave his bedroom and their life in Charleston permanently. Initially, Tim packed nothing he would need, his bags crammed with stuffed toys, a microscope, a few trophies he had won for being top of his first-grade class, and all his favorite picture books about nature and animals. Upon learning what Tim had filled his bags with, Ruth then forced him to pick out only three items he deemed absolutely necessary. Everything else would have to go to storage. Tim's tiny shoulders shook as he silently cried, selecting with much thought the microscope, a coffee-table-sized book with photos of the cosmos, and a cheap, stuffed toy lizard he'd won at the boardwalk after spending a fortune playing a carny shooting game with Sam.

Sam put the Cadillac in park, and all the dread Ruth hoped their non-stop fourteen-hour drive to Missouri had left behind came rushing in on her, making her feel like she might vomit. For a moment, everyone sat silently as dust from the road wafted past the windows of the Escalade and settled. Then the screen door on the front of the farmhouse opened and out onto the porch stepped Naomi, a tiny woman with grey hair pulled back into a strident bun. Naomi had a dull, crinkled face that was aged from too much sun and negligible skincare. She wore a full-length, floral apron over a pair of denim overalls and a cream-colored T-shirt with a pair of green rubber Crocs. As she stepped off the porch heading for the Cadillac, Naomi beckoned with a broad smile and a two-handed wave, as though she had no clue as to the real reason her son had uprooted his family and dragged them halfway across the country, with what little they could carry, to hunker down. Ruth wasn't even sure she could look Naomi in the eyes. After all, Naomi was Sam's mother, the woman who raised him, who had taught him to be the man that he was (or wasn't). Ruth suspected, however, Naomi would blame *her* for Sam's indiscretions just as quickly as she'd blame him.

If he had been taken care of, he wouldn't have been looking for distractions elsewhere, she could hear Naomi say.

Distractions indeed, Ruth thought.

Sam was the first to open his door, "Hey, Mom."

Naomi opened her arms to Sam, "Well, you're here. Welcome home." They hugged.

"Where's Dad?" Sam asked.

Naomi ignored the question and moved past Sam to Rachel who

had just stepped out of the Escalade into the hot, white sun. "Give your grandma a hug," Naomi demanded.

Rachel acquiesced, though without any of the enthusiasm she would have usually shown her grandma.

"I swear you've grown two feet since I last saw you," Naomi said.

Rachel forced a squeamish smile, "I'm not *that* tall."

"Oh, you are. You're tall as a building. And skinny too. Look at those legs!" Naomi insisted.

Tim and JD made their way out of the Escalade and were petting the dogs when Naomi turned to them. "Get away from those fleabags and give your grandma some love."

The boys sheepishly moved over to Naomi and gave her hugs.

JD looked around, "Where's Grandpa Joe?"

Naomi dimmed a bit, "He's out cuttin' some trees. He'll be back for supper." Naomi then turned to Ruth, but didn't offer her a hug, kept her arms around the boys' shoulders and motioned with her chin in the direction of the old hay barn turned guest house. "Got the cabin all cleaned and ready for you. There's enough beds for everybody, but y'all will have to figure out who takes what."

Ruth smiled, not quite meeting Naomi's eyes, "Thank you."

Naomi turned to the kids, "You kids come with me and see the garden. I got the best due on my strawberries this year."

Rachel, JD, and Tim solemnly followed Naomi as she headed around to the back of the house, prattling on about how their grandpa cut down the tire swing over by the new barn because the limb on the tree where the tire was hanging started to rot.

Sam looked at Ruth, "Dad always takes off to cut trees when he wants to avoid something."

Ruth stared at the guest house wearily, "Guess we should start unpacking."

The renovation of the old timber frame hay barn was modest and had been the undertaking of Sam and his father, Joe, back when Sam was in high school. Cream-colored linoleum pressed with images of daisies boxed inside square ropes of crab stitch was now firmly glued to the concrete slab that used to be a dirt floor. The walls were hopelessly hung with wood paneling that had faded to an unnatural orange. In the drive bay where the tractor had once set, there was now a kitchenette and a picnic table. In the old horse stall, the only bathroom had been built out. The living room held a heater the size of a small car and two velvet couches, one orange and one green—both remnants of the seventies. A steep set of stairs descending from the old hay drop led to two bedrooms up in the loft. One room held bunks for the kids. The other was set with a queen-size bed.

Ruth looked at the sad, sunken, queen-sized mattress knowing it was meant for her and Sam to share. Naomi had covered it in an old quilt and two flimsy, Polyfill pillows. It was nothing like the lush pillow-top, body-foam, king-size bed she and Sam had slept on back in Charleston. But Ruth didn't have the energy to despise it properly. Instead, she simply laid down on it and closed her eyes.

The first time Ruth and Sam visited the Christianson farm after getting married, it was Christmas. However, unlike before their nuptials when they had been sequestered to separate bedrooms of the farmhouse, once they were lawfully wed, Joe allowed Naomi to make up the cabin for them. Naomi left cinnamon scented potpourri in the bathroom and bedroom and hung stockings with Ruth and Sam's names embroidered on them over the heater. Ruth remembered romancing the idea of her and Sam staying in the cabin all Christmas long, running around naked and making love on every available surface while it snowed outside. She was pregnant with Rachel at the time and was easily aroused by even the rub of her own jeans between her legs. Unfortunately, it didn't snow at all, and Sam spent most of his time with Joe plumbing a burst pipe at the nondenominational church where Joe had been pastor since before Sam was born. Even if Sam had been available to cuddle, Naomi involved Ruth in baking desserts and casseroles for neighbors as well as their own Christmas Day feast, which was due to include Joe and Naomi's dearest friends Bob and Karen Dowling and the Dowling's recently divorced daughter, Kayla.

For as many times as Ruth attempted to steer Naomi away from talk about Kayla, somehow they inevitably ended up back on the subject of Kayla's awful divorce. According to Naomi, Kayla's ex had left her with nothing but two broken ribs, a fractured hip, and a mountain of gambling debt. This was not the problem, however. The problem, according to Naomi, was that the Bible clearly stated divorce was off limits—Luke 16:18—*thank you very much*. Yet a divorce was exactly what Kayla had asked the government to give her, and by having Kayla at their Christmas dinner table, Naomi believed it was tantamount to dining with a bona fide harlot, which could not have scandalized Naomi more even if the encounter *hadn't* been planned on baby Jesus's birthday.

Kayla's own parents had confided in the Christiansons they believed their daughter was now unredeemable. But what did anyone expect? Kayla had always been an odd girl, very artsy and not very talkative. Everyone was surprised when Kayla's now ex-husband found an interest in her at all, what with the way she wore heavy black eyeliner and hardly ever smiled. "She was a real problem for her parents in high school," Naomi whispered to Ruth. Then she added that Karen believed Kayla had lost her virginity at the age of fifteen to a foreign exchange student. "He was French and wore a rat's tail—*clearly satanic!*"

According to Naomi, more than once, Bob and Karen had hauled teenage Kayla up to the altar of Conway Nondenominational so Joe and the other deacons could cast the demons from her. It seemed the more they tried to lead her down the straight and narrow, the more she rebelled. So, it was no surprise Kayla now found herself in such a slough of despond. It was only with Christ's abounding grace Bob and Karen had taken her back in to their home, and it was with the Lord's exceeding mercy they would all somehow make it through Christmas dinner with Kayla in attendance. Naomi said Joe was already preparing a prayer geared to incite the much-needed repentance of Kayla for her vast transgressions, and he would deliver it before the turkey was cut and the fixings were shared.

Ruth had a hard time believing that Naomi could really think of Kayla's plight in such a dire manner, and she wondered if Naomi's heightened righteous indignation was meant to scare *her* in case she should ever consider the possibility of divorcing Sam. But at the time, the idea of such an act seemed ridiculous to Ruth; why would she ever in a million years want to leave Sam?

Interrupting Ruth's thoughts, Sam walked into the cabin loft where she was lying down. He was carrying her two Louis Vuitton suitcases. "Where you want me to put these?"

Ruth said nothing.

Sam moved over to the bed, sat down, touched Ruth's shoulder, "Babe?"

Ruth recoiled, "Ruth. My name is Ruth." Then she rubbed her shoulder tenderly as if massaging the remnants of Sam's touch away like some slight sting.

Sam nodded, "Thank you for coming here with me."

Ruth stared into space, "I've never seen your mother hate me so much."

"What can I do?"

Ruth wanted to scream that Sam had already done enough—too much! She wanted to slap him, beat him, kill him. Almost simultaneously, she wanted to feel his touch, taste his mouth, push his hand between her legs. Instead of doing any of that, she quietly stood up and moved over to the window at the far end of the room that had replaced what was once a hay loading door.

From the vantage point of the window, Ruth could see Naomi with Rachel, JD, and Tim out in the garden. Naomi was right about her garden doing well. It was magazine cover beautiful. And if the situation had been different, Ruth herself would have relished moving between the long, healthy rows of heirloom corn and okra, strawberries and cantaloupe, snap peas and green peppers, picking and eating the abundant fruits fresh off their plump stalks. As it was, Ruth simply admired the tableau of her children with their grandmother, imagining for a moment that everything would turn out all right, that her children would be fine, that her mother-in-law would come around to treating her like the daughter she'd never had, that what Sam had inflicted on their family was nothing out of the ordinary. Then Ruth had another thought: *What if she was the guilty one in her and Sam's relationship? What if, as Naomi's tone had suggested, Ruth was the reason things had turned out the way they had for her and Sam?* Before this new notion could paralyze Ruth, she turned away from the window only to find Sam still sitting on the bed, hands folded between his legs. He was watching her with careful eyes, clearly scared of what he had done to her and what she was now capable of doing to him.

Mack & Dorsey

By sunset the Escalade had been unloaded, and the essential accoutrements of Ruth's family's life had been folded into drawers, hung in closets, and tucked into cabinets. The kids were not happy about sharing a bedroom, so Rachel moved into the farmhouse where she could sleep in Sam's old room. Joe had still not been heard from.

The brass hues of the evening sky and the joyous orchestra of cicadas and whippoorwills heralding the oncoming night serenaded Ruth as she made her way from the tidied cabin to the farmhouse where Naomi had insisted on cooking dinner, with the help of the grandkids of course. Lightning bugs transported themselves like dust motes knee high above the scarred farmhouse yard calling to their lovers in bioluminescent code, and almost imperceptibly bats dive-bombed any invertebrates that dared rise above the tree line. The air smelled ripe with a truffle-like musk of aged pollen, wet bark, burned grass, and crisp tree leaf, and the scent cut through the numbing brume Ruth had felt lost in with the explicit and strange notion that perhaps life was sweet *because* of ruin, not in spite of it.

Awash in the salubrious ideal of the moment, Ruth was reminded of the autumn olive trees that lined the back pasture. Years before, she, Sam, and the kids had spent a magical afternoon laughing at anything and everything as they devoured the tart, crimson berries that clustered on the autumn olive branches. However, when the kids had joyously informed Joe about this adventure, he assured them the trees were worthless, and he was planning to cut them down. That seemed like an eternity ago, back when their nondenominational church in Charleston was on the verge of finding its footing, and for the first time, they were able to pay their bills without worry, back when Ruth still agonized over spending two hundred dollars on a silk blouse, and Sam worried if trading in his Toyota and driving a new SUV would seem too flashy to his burgeoning congregation.

Ruth deliberately sucked in a steadying breath as she stepped up onto the porch of the farmhouse. Inside she could hear Naomi instructing Tim on how to set the dinner table while simultaneously schooling JD on how to correctly fill the dinner glasses with iced tea. Ruth opened the screen door and was hit with the smell of grease and flour, hot butter, and boiled greens. The house was the same as it had been seventeen years ago when Ruth first visited the farm—each ding and scuff on the hardwood floors and plaster walls occasionally painted over but mostly present and accounted for.

Wanting to steer clear of Naomi for just a little while longer, Ruth stepped into the parlor where there was only one lamp glowing in the corner. It was a faux Tiffany lamp, at least that's what Ruth suspected. When she looked at it closer, she realized perhaps it was authentic, its stained glass shade clearly the elaborate workmanship of ages past. On the walls behind the lamp were old black and white photos of Sam's grandparents who started the farm in 1945 when Sam's grandfather, Mack Christianson, returned from his service in the South Pacific with a neck wound still healing from a piece of enemy shrapnel. Over the years Ruth had come to learn how hammering and sawing away for almost a year, Mack slowly erected the farmhouse for himself and his wife Dorsey.

Mack raising a home of such magnitude was considered luxurious, and it was quite the undertaking for a simple farmer with no previous construction experience. But Mack and Dorsey wanted babies—*whole armfuls of 'em.* So, Mack took his time to build big and make it right. Every beam and joist was leveled and bolted down as solidly as Mack could manage, his only architectural knowledge coming from a book he'd checked out from the local library and never returned, *Building Your Dream Home in the Twentieth Century.*

The Christiansons' land, which was at least fifty flat acres and two hundred hilly acres, was half forest and half fields run through by two creeks, two ponds, and one fresh, cold spring. The whole territory had originally been part of the Kickapoo or Osage tribal lands, depending on which old timer was asked about it. Either way, the natives had long ago been banished from the sumptuous hillsides and out of the misty hollers, leaving their arrowheads for European settlers with muskets and ruthless ambition to find years later. Deer and turkey were still plentiful, as were rabbits, squirrels, dove, and the occasional duck. But the more abundant species which had once called the fields and forests home—elk, boar, bears, wolves, and cougars—had all been killed off by the mid-1900s around the same time Mack and Dorsey discovered the area themselves.

According to the stories handed down to Ruth, Mack and Dorsey met one night in Cape Girardeau, Missouri. Dorsey was a small, blonde-haired sixteen-year-old with good posture and a shy smile. Mack was a tall, brown-headed nineteen-year-old with a physique of sparring tendons and muscle which he'd acquired working on various barges up and down the Mississippi. Dorsey was visiting her older sister who worked as a waitress at The Steamboat, a local diner popular with river rats like Mack. Sitting at the Formica counter waiting for his steak and fries, Mack struck up a conversation with Dorsey about the best song to come out on the radio as of late when a tune neither of them liked began trilling from the jukebox like a feral cat. Dorsey admitted that she leaned towards the easy listening Hollywood crooners like Bing Crosby. Mack liked good ol' pots and pans and fiddle-filled country. They agreed on the rambling folk number, "You Nearly Lose Your Mind," by Ernest Tubb, which had recently debuted and was just about as perfect a love song as either of them had ever heard. But come to find out, there were all kinds of things Mack and Dorsey agreed on, and after a few more voyages up and down the Mississippi, Mack and Dorsey got engaged. Four months after that, they were married.

As they engorged themselves on the plump fruit of one another, Mack became keenly aware of the responsibility, financial and otherwise, he had brought upon himself in taking on a wife and potential mother of his children. To address this new and important duty, Mack determined it would be wise if he joined the Navy. If not for his country, he told Dorsey, they could certainly use the G.I. Bill to help them settle down properly when he returned from service. Dorsey was keen to change Mack's mind, but even she had to admit the meager living Mack scraped by on, working the barges, wasn't enough to acceptably raise a family. So, despite her fears that he would leave her a young widow, she went with Mack the day he enlisted.

The reality of how much he was going to miss Dorsey caught up with Mack the weekend before he left for basic training. He took Dorsey, in his buddy's car, on a last minute trip to the White River deep into the thick of the Ozark Mountains. This was Mack's favorite place to go fishing with his father back when he was a kid, though Mack assured Dorsey the Ozark Mountains weren't really mountains. "They're more like huge, rolling hills," he said.

They never made it to the White River. On their way, they passed through the tiny town of Conway, Missouri, and Dorsey begged Mack to pull over at a particularly scenic lookout that yielded an unobstructed view of a gleaming chartreuse valley that yawned out a half mile in either direction and was bordered on one side by vaulted rock cliffs and on the other by a grove of peeling birch trees. Dorsey said the place reminded her of the French countryside she'd seen in photos before the war had rained devastation over all of it. Mack agreed Conway was, indeed, picturesque. When Dorsey suggested they pitch the tent there instead of driving on, once again, Mack couldn't say, no.

As they corresponded during the great war, the one thing they found comfort in was their mutual love of their last weekend together and that particular part of the world where they spent it. Conway was theirs alone so far as they were concerned. And when Mack returned to Dorsey after the US had brought a successful end to the Japanese invasion, they decided to settle down not far from the scenic overlook where Dorsey had once enthused over the scenery.

The stillness of the Ozarks, its untouched nature and rural geniality, was something Mack needed after the carnage and devastation of the Pacific. The land he and Dorsey found to build their farm on was also luckily in the middle of nowhere, and that meant—even for an area that was already a steal—it was cheap. In fact, at one point only fifteen years before the Great Depression, Dorsey and Mack learned Wright County had given land like theirs away. "If you can pay the taxes on it," the county assessor told people, "it's yours!"

When they first arrived, Mack etched a dirt road over two miles from the main highway out to where he planned to build their farmhouse in a large clearing just up the hill from a good-sized creek. Then he had to dig his own well and pay a fortune to have electricity run out later after he and Dorsey had been settled a few years.

Mack's initial plan was to plant corn in the fields in front of the homestead and leave beef cattle to graze the back hillsides. Then Mack read up on the supposed value of crop rotation and realized perhaps cycling the cattle from pasture to pasture might make more sense. This meant more work, of course, but the natural fertilizer the cows left in their wake more than made up for the need to hoe new cornrows every other year.

Despite their planning for armfuls of babies, five days after their seventh wedding anniversary, and only four years since they'd founded the farm, Dorsey was diagnosed with stomach cancer. Mack knew gentle Dorsey would never survive the monstrous brute ravaging her insides, and so did she. Instead of wringing their hands and worrying about out running from death, they accepted Dorsey's fate early on—choosing home-cooked dinners and porch swing sunsets to hospital rooms and mind-numbing medications. Dorsey had only one request as the time for her passing drew near; she wanted to be buried back behind the house, down by the creek that ran through the holler. As with pretty much everything she had asked for since they met, without hesitation, Mack gave his assurance that her wishes would be granted.

As she stood, over seventy years later, in the very farmhouse Mack had constructed out of love and devotion to his wife, Ruth could only imagine the crushing blow of Dorsey's fate to Mack's existence being as there must have been a memory for every nail Mack had driven and row of soil he had hoed. Only when all the lights were turned out at night, with just the cicadas to mask the sound, Ruth imagined Mack taking hold of Dorsey's pillow and breathing in the last vestiges of her smell before crying into it uncontrollably. She also imagined he hated himself for this weakness, but that frustration would only make him cry harder. Did his fits last like Ruth's own, from the moment he crawled into bed until the grey of morning began to slip through the windows from another unwanted day? Did he wonder if he would ever be happy again?

It was three months to the day after Dorsey's death that Moriah Mc-Kinney dropped by the Christianson farm in her mint-green Packard, dressed up like a Sunday ham. The smell of Moriah's treacly perfume was wholly different than that of Dorsey's powdery flesh. But no matter the difference, the fragrance was welcome in Mack's house of pain and suffering. Moriah had come, she stated matter-of-factly, to invite Mack to a tent revival at Conway Baptist Church the week after next. She would be happy to pick him up if he were to agree to come hear the good news of the Lord. Mack was from second generation Danes, and Dorsey had been born of third generation Irish. So, by birth, they were Lutheran and Catholic respectively. Though living out in the middle of nowhere, they hadn't attended any kind of religious service in years—the closest Lutheran church being twenty miles away and the nearest Catholic church being over ninety miles from the farm. Mack knew precisely how far the Catholic church was given that the priest there had disclosed the distance with clear vexation when he arrived at the farm to give Dorsey her last rites the afternoon of her death. Regardless of any past religious associations, Mack agreed to attend the Baptist revival mostly because he longed for company and figured a night or two away from the painfully quiet farm would be good for his spirits. So, as promised, Moriah picked Mack up on Monday, the first night of the spiritual gathering.

The usual suffocating humidity of August in the Ozarks had been tamped by the arrival of a cool breeze that cleared the skies and ruffled the flaps of the circus tent turned house of God where the revival was being held. Throughout service, Moriah and Mack, with their Bibles spread across their laps, stared straight ahead to the booming voiced evangelist, Reverend Dale Ellis, who spoke of God's wrath, Satan's trickery, and Jesus's soon return without seeming to stop and take a breath. The night after that, and the night after that were the same— hell, fire, and eternal damnation! Mack wasn't particularly fond of the eager crusader or his zealous services, but Moriah couldn't get enough of just how magnificently Reverend Ellis painted such a vivid picture of life (and death) without Christ. Truth be told, Moriah's husband of five years had recently left her for a woman he met in St. Louis, so Mack could understand Moriah's appreciation of any man who spoke of moral duty and Biblical virtues with the conviction of the devout gospeler.

And maybe it was the chastity Mack imagined Moriah so steadfastly aligned to, which was why he was thoroughly taken aback when Moriah lunged at him, smashing her lips against his, as she dropped him off following Saturday night's service. This was not an unappreciated ambush as far as Mack's body was concerned, but it was a confusing one to his mind. After she pulled away, clearly surprised by the shock she could read on his face, Moriah began apologizing. Mack assured her that she had nothing to be sorry about, and instead of allowing her to carry on about how ashamed she was, he took her face in his hands and kissed her back.

In truth, Mack and Moriah's attraction to one another may have been based on their each being the other's respective crutch, both emotionally on life support from their previous romantic entanglements. That's why it wasn't exactly a surprise to Mack when, after barely two months of seeing one another, Moriah appeared in a somber dress, scant hair and makeup, and perfume non-existent, to demand Mack ask her to marry him. After her ex-husband left her like he did, Moriah admitted she was wary of men. And at least a marriage certificate—though not eternally binding as she had clearly learned—did give a woman a bit of insurance of sorts.

Being as not many people around the area knew much about Mack, they weren't particularly surprised or interested to find out he was getting re-hitched. Although because he was wedding one Moriah McKinney, who was much more well-known—or at least thoroughly gossiped about—word of their marriage spread quickly.

The ceremony itself was a quiet affair, just Mack, Moriah, one of her girlfriends, and the pastor of Conway Baptist Church. The service was held in the parlor of the house, and afterward, Moriah served coffee and angel food cake with fresh strawberries and cream to the attendees.

The day after her and Mack's nuptials, Moriah moved into the farmhouse for good. She insisted on relocating her belongings alone, and when she appeared at the house with her one and only carload of clothes and a few knickknacks, Mack realized he had never actually seen where Moriah lived or even knew where her former residence was. The curtains with which Moriah replaced Dorsey's were far too ornate for a farmhouse, so were the gaudy oriental rugs and gold gilt-framed paintings of English countrysides. But how could Mack complain? Moriah had claimed the house as her dominion and was happy to acquiesce the rest of the farm to him. And on the upside, Moriah was a perfectionist. The house had never smelled so fresh, the crooks and crevices had never been so free of the dust and dirt that proliferated farm life. On the downside, there were countless things Mack and Moriah hardly knew about one another. And with their lives divided off into their seemingly appropriate roles—Mack the farmer/breadwinner, Moriah the housekeeper/cook—it appeared maybe they never would know much more than that.

There was a shuffling of feet behind Ruth. She pried her eyes away from a photo of Mack and Moriah which had so vividly jogged her memory of their romance. Sam was standing behind her in the darkness of the parlor doorway.

"I think this is a real Tiffany lamp," Ruth said, admiring the antique lamp once again.

Sam stayed where he was. "Probably from my grandma."

"I'm dreading going in there for dinner," Ruth whispered.

"Yeah. I still haven't seen my dad."

Ruth could read the trepidation on Sam's face even in this low light. She imagined this is how he must've looked when, as a little boy growing up on this farm, he had failed his father. Part of her was glad he was going to be forced to sit at a table with the man who raised him, who was a die-hard small-town preacher, a man who had railed against, abortion, Islam, socialism, and most of all homosexuality his entire adult life. Then she softened thinking about just how hateful and unforgiving Joe could be. "Maybe he won't show up for dinner tonight," she offered.

"I heard the tractor coming up the back hill. He's gonna be here."

Ruth turned to the photos, ran her fingers along one of the thick, gold gilt frames engraved with roses. "You think life seventy years ago was as black and white as these photos?"

"You put your wedding ring back on."

Ruth took the hand bearing her wedding ring and hid it in the palm of her other hand. "I couldn't deal with the repercussions of not wearing it. Your mom, you know."

"Maybe it will remind you—"

"Can we not?" Ruth interrupted. Then she sighed, "Let's just get through dinner. Okay?"

Sam gave Ruth a half smile. It was the same smile he'd been giving her for weeks now, the smile he made when his heart was breaking over hurting her, and he knew there was nothing he could do other than allow her space to forgive him. This time, however, she wasn't sure she could forgive. And forgive what exactly: a lie, the truth? Theirs was not some marital spat of simple cross purposes. Unlike the photos of old that hung on the sitting room walls, the betrayals that had occurred between Ruth and Sam were beyond mere shades of grey, and though the answers of how to deal with them seemed to be almost within reach, they currently remained doggedly indecipherable.

Ruth gave Sam a weak smile back, the same one she had used for years, the one which said she loved him but she didn't know what to think of their current circumstance. And she pushed past him for the dining room that was now steaming warm with food.

Little Joe

Naomi called over her shoulder to JD as she moved into the dining room from the kitchen, "Get those okra in here!" She sipped a glass of iced tea that she held in her hand and cringed. "Rachel, how many saccharin did you put in the tea?"

"Um . . . four, I think."

"My heavens above—sweet tea!" Naomi whistled as she sat her tea glass at one end of the table.

Rachel winced as she finished placing a fork on the right side of one of the place settings. "Grandma, did we set the table right?"

Naomi ignored her, which meant they had done well enough she wouldn't complain. "Timothy, what did you do with that butter dish I gave you?"

Without uttering a sound, Tim pointed to the butter dish in the middle of the table, slightly hidden by a basket of hot rolls.

"He hasn't said a word to me since y'all got here." Naomi shot in Ruth's direction without looking at her. Clearly, Naomi had seen Ruth's approach out of the corner of her eye but didn't want to acknowledge her directly until she had something to toss out that would remind Ruth of her current and very low status in Naomi's internal hierarchy of deplorable people.

"I told you. He stopped talking before we left home," JD said as he entered with the bowl of fried okra.

"Well, that's silly. Timothy, tell your grandma you love her."

Tim said nothing, just looked down at his feet.

"Timothy!" Naomi demanded.

"Momma, leave it be. Ruth and I have tried everything." Sam entered the dining room behind Ruth.

"It's the seed of rebellion, I can feel it?" Naomi said, finally looking at Ruth, determined to show her complete and utter astonishment at the state of Ruth's hapless children.

"Where do you want us to sit, Naomi?" Ruth said as she steered herself over to the table, not taking the bait.

"Joe is at the head of the table. Sam, you sit next to me down here. The rest of you can sit wherever."

The screen door on the back of the house swung open and slammed shut. Everyone froze in place for a moment, even Naomi. They waited as Sam's father, Joe, could be heard removing his boots and washing his hands in the mudroom before all six-foot-five of him finally emerged into the dining room.

Being a distraction from Mack and Moriah's marriage of exigence was initially a wondrous thing for Little Joe. He was always graciously received in the kitchen and on shopping trips into Conway with Moriah and out on the tractor or in the barn with Mack. It was apparent as he grew that Little Joe would hardly be little, however. By the time the next Christianson, Asher, was born, Little Joe—who was only four—was already taller than children twice his age. And this was undoubtedly why, as he grew older, he seemed to imbue authority on those around him simply by default of his immense physical presence.

Moriah attempted to inspire Joe to take up sports as a result of his strength and size. She never ceased to remind him how he could be "a force!" But Joe preferred singularity over society. This reclusive attitude wasn't because of Mack's influence, but Moriah would always see it that way. To make herself feel as though she had an impact on her first born that was equal to her husband's, Moriah demanded Joe's utmost devotion to Christ and the holy scriptures. She bought a pocket-sized New Testament for him to carry out in the woods so he would have the word of God by his side whether he was mending fences, clearing brush, hunting squirrels, or gigging for suckers down on the river.

And she would take him to countless revivals around the area in the summertime.

While reading the Bible made Joe markedly literate, as he entered high school his grades declined. He assured Mack and Moriah this wasn't because he couldn't learn what was being taught, he simply wasn't interested in anything his instructors were teaching. Why did he need to learn algebra? Why did he need to learn biology? He knew how things worked enough to run a farm, and that's all he wanted to do besides being a preacher. And all he needed in order to preach was right there in his pocket—in the Bible.

Mack had no animus for Joe's theological aspirations considering Joe's younger siblings, Asher and Mary, balanced out his rectitude. They were typical of their contemporaries—regular attendees of high school dances and admirers of geographical attractions far outside their small town. But as they grew older, the differences between Asher, Mary, and Joe ballooned until they threatened to burst the tranquil world of the Christianson farm apart.

Arguments over morality between Joe and his siblings became increasingly virulent until every date or social function Asher or Mary attended was followed by a seemingly unending barrage of questions that attempted to trip them up and expose some lapse in their virtue. Things became so hostile, even Moriah began to worry about Joe's bitter fundamentalism. And that's why, as soon as they were old enough, Moriah and Mack co-signed the loan papers for Asher to attend business school in Chicago and let Mary go to art school all the way out in Rhode Island, measures which were seen as disappointing, almost unforgivable transgressions by Joe who stayed behind to tend the farm. Surely, out in the world, both Asher and Mary would become fully ensnared by the temptations of Satan, being as they were both already clearly inclined to his trickery.

Even as Joe was determined to stop time on the Christianson farm, elsewhere life evolved. Dirt roads that once powdered the hills and hollers with dust were paved by the county. And Conway, which had once boasted hardly more than a post office and a single church, became a thriving township with harvest festivals and Fourth of July picnics for all. Fields that had never been more than salad bars for local wildlife were harrowed and sewn with crops, even as dairy and beef cattle filled all the other available green space. More and more exposed by the thinning of their forest havens, wildlife seemed abundant and ripe for the taking. Crime was practically nonexistent aside from one or two fights that broke out at the local tavern on a Saturday night. What was once feral had been tamed, and what was once separated from the world had joined it in almost every way. And everyone agreed this was a good thing . . . *almost* everyone.

With Joe there to assist him, Mack's farm turned a profit with ease, allowing him to buy up more acreage and expand his herd of beef cattle to over a hundred. Joe took a small salary for his trouble, and he continued to stay on in his old room in the farmhouse. However, not long after Mary moved out, Joe stopped going to Conway Baptist Church with Moriah and Mack because he felt the church was a mere social club where members imbibed freely on alcohol, tobacco, and gossip throughout the week and washed those sins down with a laughable dose of sermonizing on Sunday. Even worse, they shamefully ignored the gift of the second baptism—the Pentecost—a divine act in which the Holy Spirit gifted Christ's followers with the ability to speak in tongues and the art of translating those tongues into prophecies. This deviation of Joe from his parents' traditional beliefs and their church circle concerned both Mack and Moriah because it meant Joe would have even less interaction with folks around town—interaction that, in his case, was already scarce. However, this worry was dwarfed a year later when Joe disclosed he had enough money to build his own church—a *true* house of worship that would embrace *all* of God's word, not just that which had become the socially acceptable norm.

Joe purchased land and began work on a modest, white-steepled building on the outskirts of Conway. The church would operate under no official denomination, and this—Joe claimed—would allow him and his congregation to worship the holy trinity and follow the word of God without the shackles of "religion" binding them to watered down beliefs that had come into vogue under the auspices of the Baptist, the Lutherans, the Methodists, etc.

People around the area weren't exactly appalled by Joe's decision to construct another house of worship, but they did wonder if he was right in the head regarding his hardline legalism. Still, Joe toiled, grading the land, pouring the footing, and erecting the timber walls by himself, at least until one afternoon in late summer when a seventeen-year-old girl appeared at the bottom of his ladder in overalls and work boots. Her red hair was pulled back in a handkerchief. She stated without the slightest sign of nerves that her name was Naomi Levitt, and she was there to help.

Joe knew who Naomi was. Her family owned the Good Times grocery store at the edge of Conway—the only supermarket for twenty miles. The Levitt's were well to do. Her father, David, who drove a Lincoln that was always washed and waxed, was one of the friendliest people Joe had ever met. Her mother, Susannah, was constantly heading up a committee for some town parade or festival "to bring the community closer together." Naomi had an older brother named, Elliot, who had gone off to fight in the Vietnam war a year prior with just about every other guy in his graduating class. Naomi herself had graduated that spring and been promoted from cashier to assistant manager of Good Times as part of her graduation present.

At first, Joe told Naomi her help wasn't needed, but she assured him even if hard labor was not in her wheelhouse, it was clear Joe could use someone to assist with bringing fresh supplies up to the roof upon which he was currently perched or even a cup of water on the treacherously hot, humid days, which were sure to come that summer. Furthermore, Naomi told Joe she believed in his cause. Organized religion had become—just like the war and everything else in America—a monster that had gotten out of control. Religion was a business created so those at the top could control those at the bottom. And she wanted to be a part of breaking up the establishment, to shake up the system, to find the truth in all the lies. From the way she spoke so passionately, Joe saw himself in Naomi. He found in her someone who looked at the world as he did. So, almost as quickly as he had made up his mind to dismiss her, he agreed to allow her to be the first to join his flock.

Together that summer, Joe and Naomi toiled side by side constructing every last nook and cranny of Joe's church. And as they did, they shared their minds and souls with each other, never realizing they had also inadvertently shared their hearts.

It wasn't until October, when Joe was installing the first set of pews he had carved out of old oak trees from his parents' farm that he realized he wanted to marry Naomi. Naomi's father, Mr. Levitt, had come to visit him one afternoon under what at first glance appeared the most casual of circumstances. Mr. Levitt said he wanted to see the church Naomi was always going on about—the church she had missed so many days of work to help complete. Joe happily showed Mr. Levitt around the small building, sharing a few construction highlights as well as describing a few hardships he had faced in making the house of worship the sturdy building it had become. Mr. Levitt smiled appreciatively and listened carefully to Joe's words. Then Mr. Levitt touched Joe on the shoulder and looked him in the eyes.

"My daughter has fallen in love with you," Mr. Levitt said.

Joe could only look down at his muddy boots, unsure how to respond.

"We're Jewish. We don't go around talking much about it around here, but we are. Surely you must know that."

Now, Joe met Mr. Levitt's eyes. If this was about to be an argument over religion, Joe would wipe the floor with Naomi's father. "I know that's what you are, Mr. Levitt."

"It's what my daughter is too," Mr. Levitt said.

"Is that what she told you?" Joe asked.

"It's by birthright, Mr. Christianson."

Joe smiled. "Do you want your daughter to die and go to the fiery pits of hell, Mr. Levitt?"

Mr. Levitt swallowed back the sudden rush of adrenaline that spiked through his veins. "I don't think you and my Naomi are right for one another. I would kindly ask that you tell her she's not the one for you so that she can move on."

Joe took in the church around him, the labor of love, a physical expression of the beliefs of his heart. "No."

Mr. Levitt nodded, still managing to keep his cool. "Look at this place. You have your future set for you. But Naomi, she was born to a different path." Mr. Levitt paused, then lowered his voice. "I won't ask you again."

"Do you really believe that Jesus has yet to return to this earth? Do you truly believe he hasn't yet died for your sins on Calvary's Cross?" Joe asked.

Mr. Levitt said nothing.

"If you don't repent of your sins and ask Christ into your heart, you will suffer the fiery pits of hell for all of eternity, Mr. Levitt—while your daughter and myself wear crowns of glory in heaven."

Mr. Levitt took in Joe's conviction, his straight back, his unwavering gaze. There would be no arguing with this man. After a beat, Mr. Levitt nodded in resignation. Then he turned and walked away without another word.

As Joe watched Mr. Levitt pull out of the church driveway in his shiny Lincoln, he knew he would have to marry Naomi immediately, if anything to save her very soul. And marry, they did—one week later. It was the first event held in the finished church.

A Woman of God

Sam closed the door to he and Ruth's bedroom in the cabin. "Well, that was wonderful," he said with sarcasm. "My dad didn't speak to me once during dinner. He wouldn't even look at me."

From where she sat on the edge of the bed, Ruth didn't look at Sam either. Instead, she focused on removing her watch and earrings. In truth, Ruth more than agreed with Sam's sentiments; dinner with Naomi and Joe that night was one of the more dreadful moments of her life—painfully stilted and utterly embarrassing. Second only to the stomach-churning terror of eternal judgment from God had to be the judgment from her in-laws. On a certain level, Ruth felt pitied by them. She felt like a leper who had stunk up their dining room with her presence, spreading her rot as she handled the green bean casserole and fried okra and lifted the tea pitcher to refill her glass. It was clear Joe and Naomi held their antipathy for Ruth relatively in check because of the kids, but that didn't mean it wasn't thick in the air, ready to boil over, choking the whole room with its acrid miasma.

"You want the light on?" Sam asked as he peeled off his shirt?

Once again, Ruth remained silent. Instead, she slipped the soft cashmere sweater she was wearing over her head and unbuttoned her jeans.

Sam turned off the light and moved over to a chair where he dropped his polo shirt before removing his jeans and draping them there too. Ruth knew what he looked like in the moonlight without turning her head to see him. She knew his tall, handsome frame would be sexy nearly naked in the dark. She heard him scrape off his socks and leave them on the floor. He was standing there in only his underwear now, some dark colored briefs that fit him tightly and showed off his muscular rear as well as the endowed, uncircumcised extremity between his legs. She heard him unclasp his watch and lay it on the chair like he used to rest it on the nightstand. Then she thought of his underwear again. Most men didn't care what kind of undergarments they wore. She knew some men didn't even wear underwear, but Sam had always been particular about his undergarments. He was interested in picking out name-brand "skivvies," looking over the packaging diligently, often paying more attention to what he had on under his suits than what kind of ties he wore with them on Sunday mornings. Ruth had never suspected such behavior might not be normal until now.

Ruth sloughed off her jeans and left them piled on the floor next to the bed, along with her sweater. Before, she would have folded them up and made sure Sam's clothes were folded properly too, or put away in the delicate's hamper to be washed. But she didn't have the strength to think about such details, not anymore.

Sam stepped over to the bed and slipped under the flimsy, floral print sheets, but she remained seated on top. She could feel his eyes on her. She imagined herself in the moonlight now, her pale, delicate skin draped over her soft shoulder bones and toned back muscles, her breasts cradled in the lace bra that gently pinched at her vertebrae, her hair silky and partially askew from removing her sweater.

She suddenly flashed on a memory of long ago. "Do you remember the first time you brought me here?" Ruth asked without turning to Sam. "You took me on that float trip down the river, and I told you we were gonna end up in the water because you didn't know how to steer a canoe."

"Yeah, I remember," Sam said. "We didn't end up in the water though."

"That's 'cause we changed seats. You let me steer," Ruth said.

"I never had a problem letting you take the lead when you wanted it."

Ruth sighed and rolled back onto the bed, but didn't slip under the sheets. "I always thought that was weird. How could you not know how to steer a canoe?"

Sam looked up at the ceiling and sighed. "My dad was busy saving the souls of Conway. We only went canoeing a couple times in all the years I was growing up."

"It's not like I'd been on float trips any more than you," Ruth said.

"What are you trying to say?" Sam asked.

Ruth was silent. What *was* she trying to say? Was she *trying* to emasculate him? Was she *trying* to assign blame to herself for not knowing the truth that now separated them?

"Well, whatever the case, we didn't end up in the water." Sam sighed.

Ruth turned to look at Sam, and he looked back at her, his brows smudged together right over his nose in that way that made him look so adorable and innocent, so keen to be forgiven. In the quiet darkness, staring at his boylike face, Ruth could almost forget her mouth wasn't the only one he had kissed with lust. She could almost remember that she was still a young woman who liked having sex with her husband, who liked seeing him naked and having him reach between her legs with his nail-bitten fingers, to get her wet before entering her with his beautiful cock.

Since Ruth's world had lost its center of gravity weeks before, and everything had been upended and now floated unanchored to space and time, Ruth wasn't sure she had looked at Sam, really studied his face like she used to do in order not to forget a line or imperfection, a blemish or a hair. Now here he was before her in the flesh like he had always and only been, and she loved him so much.

Ruth reached out and took hold of Sam's hand. She guided it across the mattress and pushed it beneath her panties, down deep between her legs. Sam stared hard at Ruth as she did this, worry in his gaze. But she was insistent, determined to make him erase all that had come before by making her come now. She closed her eyes to feel him, to escape into the fey experience of an orgasm. After a moment, Sam took over. He repositioned himself closer to her on the bed, angling his hand so he could use his middle finger to enter her and his thumb to massage her clit.

Ruth sighed. This was what she needed—to get off, to release the tension damned up inside her. And it was working. She hadn't climaxed for two weeks before the news, and she certainly hadn't orgasmed since. But being lost in this backwoods cabin, a million miles away from the world, only the forest and fields for miles around, Ruth wanted to reconnect to herself or disconnect, as it were. She wanted to feel something that wasn't anchored to what Naomi would have labeled a slough of despond.

With each thrust deeper into her with his finger, Ruth's heartbeat grew faster, and her breathing became sharper. She opened her eyes and found Sam's face hovering above her, watching her like an EMT would watch a lifeless body he was giving CPR, waiting for it to come alive. When Ruth made the slightest moan, Sam used his free hand to slip off his underwear. Then he rolled Ruth onto her back and moved on top of her. She could feel his penis dangling against her thigh, growing thicker with each beat of his own heart. His dick would be just the thing to finish her, to bring her to climax. But as Sam slipped off her panties, suddenly Ruth imagined *him* as she *was*—lying on his back, ready to be entered. Then she imagined the man—the hustler who Sam had paid to fuck him—above her. And suddenly, Ruth was sick.

"No," Ruth whispered as Sam lifted her legs.

Sam leaned down to kiss her, to calm her.

"No," Ruth whispered, louder this time. And she pushed Sam off her, sitting back up on the edge of the bed.

"Ruth—" But Sam was interrupted by a quiet sob that erupted out of Ruth, her back trembling in the moonlight. She knew she must seem crazy.

After a moment, he slipped on his underwear, grabbed his pillow, and left the room.

In the silence, Ruth continued to weep. She cried for everything that night—all her shattered hopes and dreams, all the injustice in the world, the refugees and orphaned babies, the cancer patients and the drug addicts. She cried for the unfairness of life, the lies that brought on war and the wars that brought on more lies. She cried for her children and all they had been through and all they would yet go through.

And she cried for herself, for her body that was no longer as young as it used to be and her choices that had brought her to this place. She cried for the sinner she was and the sins she had yet to commit. And she cried for the comfort of her mother's womb and heaven, which seemed so elusive on this earth.

At dawn Ruth found herself shivering and alone, curled up on the bed, still naked and uncovered. She felt as though she had slept a million years, deep and soundly, waking up in another time, on another planet. And for a moment, she felt rested. Then she was hit by the chill on her skin, an ache in her back, the unrelenting raw of her emotions still splayed. She stood and walked over to the window to look out at the world. Mist lumbered like cotton over the fields of alfalfa and slipped lightly along the fresh cut green yard in front of the farmhouse. Overhead, pinks and grays clamored for space, cutting streaks against one another through the sky. At this time of the morning, the farm was at its most quiet, the feverish concert of the night dwelling invertebrates complete, and the birds and dragonflies and bumble bees of the day yet to take over with their frenzied songs. Ruth felt sick to her stomach; this was still the same time and still the same planet, and she was still in the same predicament that she had been in when she fell asleep the night before.

Back at the Christianson house on Morning Lane, Ruth relished dawn—her time—when no one was demanding answers to the plethora of questions that seemed to abound for her all other hours of the day: "Where is my tie? My tie. The blue one." "Did you wash my green sweater? You better not have shrunk it!" "What happened to the orange juice? The carton is empty." "I can't find my phone. I laid it right here!"

From dawn until at least seven-thirty (seven-forty-five on the weekends) there was no thumping of music or screaming of voices or running of water or slamming of doors. There was just her, padding around her home in her bare feet, no lights turned on, the scent of fresh coffee flowering the air. In those moments, she would find herself again, the woman who got lost in the shuffle trying to be the perfect wife and mother.

Even when the kids were off at school and Sam was at church, Ruth was still caretaker of the house, calling repairmen for everything from broken sprinkler heads to a rabbit that got stuck in the dryer vent (no less than three times). How could changing car insurance and canceling a credit card, questioning a gas bill and folding laundry take up so much time and energy? And when it wasn't simple house maintenance, it was buying groceries and returning clothes and making sure everyone made their dentist appointments and doctor appointments and sports practices and birthday parties. There was the PTA and fundraisers and luncheons and homeowners' association meetings. On and on it went, the endless barrage of duties. Ruth suspected she only made things harder on herself by wanting to do everything flawlessly, but she refused to shy away from being kind, patient, loving, and looking the part of a put together housewife whether it was when she was talking to a phone operator at a call center in India or a postal worker delivering mail. In fact, this was a code of conduct Ruth implored other women of faith to take on like badges of service to God when she wrote her first book, *The Christian Woman Next Door.*

It was not Ruth's idea to write a book. She and Sam's church had grown so large, and she had become such a source of inspiration to so many, she was approached by the editors at a Christian publishing imprint. They wanted to offer her money—quite a lot of money— if she would write a book about being the wife of Sam Christianson megachurch pastor extraordinaire. She instead pitched them the idea of writing a book about showing the world you are Christian simply by the way you exist within it. No handing out tracks. No big displays of religious superiority. "Would you know if the people next door are Christian if they didn't tell you?" She asked in the book. "Would their behavior make you want to become a Christian if you weren't?" In particular, Ruth took on mothers whose leadership within the home re-flected exponentially out into the world by extension of their families. "If one can put a thousand to flight and two can put ten thousand to flight, how many people do we reach with the ideals we instill within our children?"

Ruth's first book had landed on the New York Times Bestsellers List —albeit at the bottom of the list under Religion, Spirituality and Faith. Still, it was enough for her to be offered a subsequent book advance ten months later, and another two years after that. In fact, she was writing book three when everything in her perfect world had imploded weeks earlier. "Why We Go to Church" was the title of the chapter she was working on when news of Sam's reckless and unsavory behavior began blasting across every known news outlet and blazing across various social media platforms like a firestorm. In the chapter on church, Ruth wrote about her favorite day of the week—Sunday. All throughout the week, Ruth told her readers, she gave to everyone else; she depleted her resources of hope and love and grace. But on Sunday, that was the day she was refilled again.

And now, it was remembering this truth that spurred Ruth to find her toiletry bag, don a T-shirt and shorts, and make her way down to the tiny cabin bathroom. They would go to church—her family. It was Sunday, after all. Yes, Joe would be preaching, and that might be uncomfortable. Yes, everyone in Joe's small congregation would know who they were and would know more details of the exodus they had taken from South Carolina (and why) than potentially she even did. But attending church service might also be the thing everyone in her family needed, a return to normalcy of sorts.

Being up early allowed Ruth the bathroom to herself, and she took her time primping. If she was going to be judged, Ruth figured she could cushion some of that criticism with star power, and in the world of modern Christianity, she knew she still had a bit of that at her disposal at least in rural areas like Conway where even in her diminished state she was still someone whose presence was capable of wowing others.

Appearing and feeling fresh after her shower, a blowout, and the careful application of makeup, Ruth made her way back upstairs where she selected the least wrinkled Sunday morning outfit she had—a navy pencil skirt suit and turquoise floral silk shirt. As she was pinching on a pair of pearl earrings to round out the look, Sam entered the room.

He stood there in his mussed hair, underwear askew, and bags under his eyes. "What are you doing?" he asked.

"It's Sunday. We're going to church." Ruth replied.

"No," Sam said definitively.

Ruth didn't respond, marched past him towards the room on the other side of the hall. She opened the door and looked in. "Guys, get up. We have church in an hour." Then she moved back into the room where Sam was still standing, though he was now much more alert.

"Ruth, please—" Sam started to say, but Ruth cut him off.

"If you think this is any easier on me, any of this . . ." But she didn't finish. Instead, she took in a breath to steady herself and quickly left the room.

Sunday Service

When Ruth knocked on the front door of the farmhouse to announce she and Sam would be attending church, Naomi—hair in pink foam curlers—did her best not to give away how pleased this surprise made her. Instead, Naomi maintained her policy of not smiling at her daughter-in-law and suggested Ruth have the boys ride into town with her, Joe, and Rachel. Ruth knew that Naomi believed the more the kids were around her and Joe the better off they would be. In Naomi and Joe's presence, they would learn *real* Christian values that clearly Ruth and Sam had long forgotten. Instead of bristling against this implied rebuke, Ruth told Naomi she would send the boys over as soon as they finished brushing their teeth. It would be easier to drive into Conway alone with Sam anyway. Even in their current state of estrangement, it was more comfortable to sit in silence with him than endure the shocked quiet that seemed to overtake her children when they were around their parents nowadays.

In the seventeen years that Ruth had been visiting Conway, it had changed very little. There was still just one stoplight. And the acorn-brown brick county courthouse still stood sentry over the town square. Yes, a Chinese restaurant was now located in place of what was once an old shoe store, and a women's boutique had now become a gun emporium, but otherwise not much else had been altered by the fortunes, or in some cases misfortunes, of time. Even Naomi's parents' grocery store, Good Times, still stood out on the edge of town as it always had, though it was now owned by middle-aged transplants from the East Coast and had become a chain with two other stores in nearby whistle-stops. Keeler's Bank, the Masonic Lodge, and Sleep Tight Inn still claimed the same real estate and look they had when they had first been built. Even the metal sign welcoming visitors to Conway didn't look like it had been updated since it was first planted by the county over fifty years ago. In well-faded paint, it read: Conway, Missouri, pop. 325.

Surprisingly enough, one of the most significant changes around Conway was Joe's church which, with the expansion of the farms around it and the transformation of so many forests into fields, seemed much closer to town than in the early days of its existence. Conway Nondenominational had been modified only three times over the years: once to expand the sanctuary, once to add a nursery and a classroom for children's church, and once to create a church office. Yet, despite being modernized and enlarged, it remained honest to its roots in every other way, a small rural house of worship with gleaming hardwood floors, painfully rigid wooden pews and bare whitewashed walls. It was such a throwback to simpler times, Joe was regularly asked to rent it for weddings from out-of-towners and locals alike, but unless the engaged couple were members of Conway Nondenominational, Joe would turn down any offers no matter how profitable to transform the church into a photoshoot for "heathens." Joe's congregants liked this strident attitude of his; it gave them a sense of power they otherwise lacked in their everyday lives. By going to Conway Nondenominational, they were unique and privileged. It was the traditional look of the church that Ruth suspected reinforced in his congregants a comfort that what-ever was being preached behind the large pulpit at the front of the sanctuary under the oversized stained cross was good because it was from a bygone era that embraced notions and ideas that the small town of Conway had otherwise been helpless to fend off.

By the time Ruth and Sam arrived, service had already begun. Ruth knew this was the way Sam wanted it. If they came in late enough, he could avoid the majority of the awkward hellos and contrived small talk. In order to assure their tardy entrance, he insisted they drive by the old flour mill down by the Piney River to see if it was still operating. Then he did two loops around the town square going on with great admiration about the upkeep of the courthouse grass and flower beds. Before he could split off down to the high school for a look at the new gym, Ruth calmly asked that they reminisce another time. Being late for song service was one thing. Arriving in the middle of Joe's sermon would be quite another.

The faithful were on their feet singing as Ruth and Sam entered the main doors of the church and made their way down the side aisle to the front where Naomi had planted herself with Rachel, JD, and Tim. There was no avoiding the stares or unhearing the sudden rush of whispers. Up front, Joe stood behind Patty Jewel, the song leader, a soprano with a prematurely silver bob, a face of dry leather, and lips that seemed welded on with frosted pink lipstick. When the song was over, Patty turned to Joe. He stepped up to the pulpit and asked the congregation to take a seat. It was always a master class in authority to watch the way Joe commanded the utmost attention and respect from his congregation, and Ruth suspected this had only served to cement Joe's pastoral ambitions over the years. "An iron hand gets things done," Joe had once told her. He was living proof that maxim was true.

Joe took a moment behind the podium before gripping both sides of it and clearing his voice. "I had a sermon prepared for you today. But, this mornin' I got to thinkin' about who all was going to be here, and what they needed to hear. And a scripture struck me sure as if a lightning bolt from God himself. 'Let anyone who thinks he stands, take heed lest he fall into sin.'" Ruth could feel Sam shudder next to her even as her own heart seemed to skip a beat at Joe's words.

"'But resist the devil, and he shall flee from you.'" Joe continued. "That is our only hope—to resist the devil, to take heed." Joe took a pause as if he were genuinely thinking over what he was about to share. "You know when I was a kid, my daddy caught me and a buddy of mine smoking cigarettes out in the ol' hay barn one day. Now, my daddy was a good man, not much of a temper to speak of. But on that day, my daddy got fired up. I'm not sure if he was more upset 'cause we were smokin' or 'cause we had the genius to do so in a hay barn." There were a few chuckles in the crowd. After another beat, Joe continued. "Point is, my daddy took me out back after he'd run off my buddy, and he wore the dickens out of me 'til he was certain I wouldn't be able to sit for a month. See, my daddy knew I needed to be taught to always be on my guard against sin. And thank the Lord above he did, 'cause after that day, my lips never touched another cigarette." Once more Joe paused. "God wants the same for us. And sometimes He punishes us harshly for the sins we commit. He'll wear you out, just like my daddy did, to keep us in line—to teach us to always be on our guard." Suddenly, Joe looked right at Sam. "To teach us never to do that thing again."

Without realizing she had done so, Ruth grasped Sam's hand in solidarity with him, against the anger that burned out of Joe's eyes in Sam's direction.

When church let out forty minutes later, instead of feeling refreshed, Ruth was exhausted. She had sweat through her silk shirt, and she couldn't wait to get back to the cabin where she could be alone. First, she would have to make it past those in Joe's congregation who were more interested in being able to say they'd had a conversation with the now infamous Christiansons than being afraid of any wickedness that might rub off on them from such an encounter.

These small kindnesses post-service had always been something Ruth looked forward to at her and Sam's church. It was never a surprise if she wasn't on her way home until at least an hour after service had ended, because she was pulled into dozens of different conversations from staff who needed to ask her opinion on matters church-related, newcomers who wanted to meet her, or dear friends who wanted to share a small joke or forgotten grace they had failed to mention the last time she spoke with them.

For as independent as the kids were at Ruth and Sam's church in Charleston, here at Conway Nondenominational, as Ruth led the family out of the small sanctuary, they stayed huddled between Ruth and Sam like skittish ducklings. The Crawfords were the first to say hello. Lilburn and Dollie were elders in Joe's church, some of the first to join back when he had initially opened the doors. They had watched all the Christiansons grow up and had been at Sam and Ruth's wedding. They were softer than Joe and Naomi and relished giving a warm hug and sweet smile to the extended Christianson clan. They were no different today, squeezing each member of the family and assuring them it nice was to see them—*all* of them. Next were the Hollands. Then the Presleys. Then a young couple Ruth didn't know who seemed not to realize who she and Sam were either. Then she was at the double doors of the church, which had been swung open wide to release Joe's congregation back out into the wicked world. Ruth winced at the sunlight but welcomed the fresh air. Joe was standing next to the doors, as always, shaking each parishioner's hand, bidding everyone a blessed Sunday. Instead of offering Ruth his hand, however, he bent over and picked up little Tim.

"How's my boy?" Joe asked.

Tim said nothing and struggled to be relieved of Joe's grip. Clearly annoyed, Joe released Tim back to the ground.

"Sorry about that, Joe," Ruth said.

"Boy's traumatized, plain and simple." Joe pushed past Ruth and Sam into the church.

Sam looked at Ruth hurt; *why had she brought him here this morning?*

Ruth shot the same stare back; *coming to Conway was Sam's idea.*

Sam made for the Cadillac at the far end of the parking lot, a parking lot which after all these years was still just gravel, dust, and the inevitable dandelion popping up here and there.

JD looked at Ruth nervously. "I wanna ride back with you and Dad."

Rachel conceded. "Yeah, me too."

Ruth nodded assuredly. "Okay."

Tim and JD hurried after Sam before Ruth could change her mind. Ruth and Rachel were about to follow suit when Mike Murray, a stout, gray-haired cowboy with twinkling, blue eyes stepped up in starched, indigo Wranglers hitched up to his navel.

"If it ain't the prettiest two ladies south of the Mason Dixon," he said.

"Mike." Ruth smiled.

"Hi, Mr. Murray." Rachel echoed.

"What? What?! You call me Mike, just like your momma," Mike commanded. He grabbed Rachel up in a bear hug that Ruth was sure Rachel would complain about later, though it was something he'd done since she had known him.

"It's so good to see you!" He said and released Rachel once again. He turned to Ruth and opened his arms wide with a hug for her as well. It was nice to feel Mike's strength as she let him envelop her.

"Connie is gonna die that she missed you today," Mike said as he released Ruth.

"Is she alright?"

"It's her momma up in Champaign. Had to go into the hospital yesterday. We knew it was happening. Heart valve replacement." Then Mike stomped his foot excitedly. "Which reminds me . . . I need some help with my bees tomorrow mornin'. You wouldn't happen to be free to help me out would you?" Mike asked Rachel.

Rachel looked at Ruth, uncertain.

"I'll give you twenty bucks and a jar of my finest honey."

Rachel looked at Ruth again.

"You might as well, sweetie. You've got nothing else lined up around here right now."

Rachel nodded. "All right, then. I guess."

"Woo-hoo," Mike said. "Ain't it amazin' how God answers prayers. Here I was needin' help and look who shows up?" Mike leaned into Ruth and lowered his voice. "How's everything else going?"

Ruth forced a smile. She appreciated that he didn't pretend there wasn't some massive elephant in the parking lot. "We're working through it."

Mike put his arm around Ruth. "That's good. That's *real* good. You let me or Connie know if you need anything, all right?"

"Thank you, Mike."

"I'm serious now. Anything at all. We're here for you kids." Mike released Ruth and headed across the parking lot just as suddenly as he had appeared. Halfway gone, he called back to Rachel. "Ten o' clock tomorrow! We don't wanna keep those bees a'waiting!"

Both Ruth and Rachel watched Mike go, then Ruth put her arm around Rachel to walk with her to the car. Instantly, any softness that Mike's presence had imbued in Rachel was gone, and she sloughed off Ruth's arm gruffly. "Mom, don't."

Ruth watched Rachel stomp to the car. Should she get upset with her daughter? Should she be understanding? Was Rachel acting out because of their circumstances or was she just being a teenage girl with a million different feelings vying for attention inside her all at once? Did it even matter, especially considering the fact all of her children had clearly sided with Ruth over Naomi in their choice of a ride home? Before Ruth could celebrate her small victory against her mother-in-law, she was distracted by something else. A tall, handsome man with a blonde beard and mustache leaned against the Cadillac chatting up Sam. A month ago, she wouldn't have noticed. Well, she would have noticed the way the man's tree trunk legs filled out his jeans and the charming features of his romance novel face, but she would have quickly pushed those thoughts out of her mind. And she wouldn't have given two whits about him talking to Sam. Now however, she was suddenly on the move.

Ruth knew full well that her hurried pace gave away her the teenage girl insecurities over Sam's proximity to this attractive male. And she tried to act casual even as she swiftly and determinedly moved in on their conversation.

"You about ready?" She asked Sam brightly.

Sam smiled casually, and along with the man, turned to face Ruth. "Ruth, this is Delmer Green. Delmer, this is my wife, Ruth."

Ruth shook Delmer's hand. "Nice to meet you."

Delmer had an unhurried quality about him. He was one of those deep, contemplative men who seemed to stand unwavering like a thousand-year-old Redwood in a forest of saplings. Instantly, Ruth felt calmed by his smile and the way the light glinted off his iceberg grey eyes. She was embarrassed that she had allowed herself to think of

Delmer as competition or anything other than a man merely having a chat with her husband. And what a man he was. Delmer's hands were rough and looked like they were no strangers to hard work. His chest was full, and little wires of blonde hair poked up around his neck from under the white T he wore beneath his plaid, collared dress shirt. And once again, Ruth was feeling like a teenage girl, this time fantasizing about Delmer, giving him all the attributes she could ever want in a man, but most importantly the attribute of someone who liked women, who could never in a million years lust for a lover of the same sex.

"Delmer's a realtor, and he's got a few rental properties he'd like to show us," Sam said.

"Oh, that's great." Ruth smiled.

"There's a new house out on Hassick Road that was built for a Fort Leonard Wood family. About the time it was all finished, though, they got a transfer to Germany. It might be perfect." Delmer's voice cooed.

"I told Mr. Green we'd be around tomorrow morning to give it a look, if that's alright with you?" Sam asked Ruth.

"Well, we're barely settled at your parents' house." Ruth countered, flustered at the thought of packing up and moving everything again.

"Take your time." Delmer fished a business card out of his pocket and handed it to Sam. Once again, Ruth had a stroke of jealousy shoot through her body as she imagined Delmer and Sam's fingers touching ever so slightly in the exchange of the small piece of parchment.

"Really appreciate you saying, hi," Sam said, and he shook Delmer's hand.

"Nice to meet you both. Look forward to helping you if I can." Delmer nodded a farewell to Ruth before heading across the parking lot to a large, shiny truck.

"Nice guy," Sam said, flipping Delmer's business card between his fingers.

"A little predatory if you ask me, jumping on us before we're even settled." Ruth countered.

Sam refused to engage. "Do my parents know we're taking the kids with us?"

Ruth looked back at the churchyard, which was mostly empty aside from a couple stragglers. She didn't see Naomi or Joe anywhere probably because they were inside tidying up. Ruth lied. "Yeah. They know."

Trudy & Dexter

The leaves and needles of the mature oaks and pines of the Mark Twain National Forest that framed the town of Conway glowed translucent green under the nurturing summer sun as Sam drove the family along the two-lane blacktop back to his parents' farm. Ruth was grateful to see so many of the silver barked sentries left untouched, markers from another time that had witnessed so much or perhaps so little over the years depending upon how you looked at it. She thought of Sam's grandparents again, how they had come to Conway and settled down in this sylvan setting, how they had such great hopes for their life and the lives of all who would come after them. Could they ever in a million years have imagined the seemingly unique circumstances Ruth found herself in now, seventy-something years later, wife to a man— an internationally renowned preacher—who had not just abandoned their vows in the most egregious way possible but had debased their entire family through his affair with another man—a hustler—an affair that was even this very moment making national headlines? And once again, the question came to her as it had been appearing in her mind for weeks. But each time it was clearer and more explicit: *What was she supposed to do with her life now that the truth of it had been revealed?*

Ruth closed her eyes to clear her mind. But the moment she left the present, she was enveloped by the past, and while so much of the farm had reminded her of Sam and made her question what had brought him to this point in his life, in actuality it was her own history that was flickered through her mind with more and more frequency these days, causing her wonder why she'd made the choices she had made and how she'd managed to end up here in this awful nightmare of a moment. Ruth only knew the bits and pieces of Sam's family history that had been shared with her by Sam and Naomi, and her own family history was just as frustratingly vague. Ruth's mother's side of the family—the Kuhns—were lumberjacks who had felled the great Black Forest of Germany, and after deciding to try their hands with the mysterious and vast woodlands of the new world, arrived on the shores of Boston from Amsterdam in 1743 via a ship called *The Bloemvelden*. All this according to the names and dates of birth painstakingly transcribed in the front pages of a family Bible that had been passed down from generation to generation, and was now packed away with all Ruth's belongings in a storage facility in Charleston. Other than that, Ruth knew very little of her heritage. Then again, wasn't this the case of most Americans, that they remembered only as far back as the faces they had seen with their own eyes: mothers, fathers, grandparents, great-grandparents? Still, the past seemed to claw at Ruth's mind, begging her for attention. *What had happened that had brought her to this place? How could things have been different? Was it all her fault or was it something else that had occurred long before her, which was to blame?*

Ruth's earliest recollections were not her own memories but stories colored in by her grandmother, Trudy Munson. They were about her grandfather, a man named Dexter Kuhn. As with Sam's grandparents, perhaps the stories of Dexter and Trudy's love had become more romantic with time, the warts and blemishes sanded down and painted over. Either way, Ruth relished them.

According to Trudy, Ruth's grandfather, Dexter, was a tough-minded boy who grew up in a far different world than the one he had been born into. By the time he was a young man the Great Depression had swept over America, starving a country that had once been plump with life. And this stripping away had revealed a truth, that in the land of the free and home of the brave even after a bloody Civil War and over a half a century, not all were equal—not by a long shot.

When he met Ruth's grandmother on New Year's Eve at a Washington, DC, jazz club in 1957, Dexter Kuhn was a journalist for *The*

Washington Post, reporting on the very national racial inequity he saw so clearly, hoping against hope to reverse the course of the grave future America was hurdling towards. Dexter was white—if not downright pale, and Trudy was Black—umber skin burnished to perfection. Trudy owned a restaurant for "colored people" off Florida Avenue where she invited upstart jazz musicians to play on Tuesdays and Thursdays, and she dared Dexter to drop by, imagining there was no way a white boy would darken the doors of her "ghetto" establishment. But show up, he did. And the performances, not to mention the food, were electrifying for Dexter.

Almost every Tuesday for two years Dexter appeared after work and stayed until closing, watching the bands, chatting with other patrons, and devouring Trudy's homemade, southern delicacies. His mere existence gave Trudy hope that indeed good would win out and equality for all people would one day be the law of the land, and he assured her more people felt like him than the opposite. It was just a matter of time before the truth would rectify the lies made up to hold people of color down.

"Nothing good ever came easy," Dexter would say.

Trudy would smirk. "Well, it's been hard for so long, whatever is comin' better be more than good."

Yes, from the stories Trudy relayed to Ruth, it was clear Dexter gave Trudy hope. He also made her laugh. Maybe it was his white boy drawl or the seriousness with which he took his jokes, but whatever it was, for Trudy, he made the world sparkle and shine as though the word hallelujah had come to life.

Being a woman of color, Trudy never assumed Dexter might be interested in anything other than her cooking and general charm. Then one night she realized it wasn't that Dexter *wasn't* interested, it was that for over thirty years he'd never *had* a woman and didn't know what that kind of relationship would even look like. So, she made a bold move as she was closing up; she kissed him.

Dexter took to Trudy's love like sugar to chocolate, and soon, he asked her to marry him. Trudy laughed him off heartily knowing he was aware anti-miscegenation laws abounded, but Trudy also knew Dexter was the love of her life, and that indeed his request was genuine. So, she said she *would* marry him *in her heart*, if he married her in his.

Despite trying their best to avoid it, Trudy soon became pregnant, and Florence Abigail Kuhn was born on a frigid October night in 1960. She had brown eyes like her momma, but in every other sense, she was white like her daddy. Trudy hated herself for being relieved, and Dexter despised himself for being slightly disappointed. Either way, Dexter and Trudy were parents and connected in a way that not one of man's laws could ever undo. So, they quietly moved in together.

For Florence, life would be as Trudy feared—turbulent. Few Blacks appreciated Florence's appearance on Trudy's hip in the restaurant. And few whites treated Florence with the affection a white baby born to white parents would have been afforded. Even as a young girl Florence noticed these slights, and the only thing that could sooth the marginalizing pain of this spurn were the affections of Dexter who doted on her as though she was the last angel in all of heaven. If Dexter said everything was okay, it was. If he was crying, so was she, but if he was laughing, she was too. Dexter was Florence's God, and she was his.

Florence and Dexter's relationship was a comfort to Trudy. It made her feel like perhaps her and Dexter's coming together hadn't been a mistake. Maybe it was right and good—their love. Then riots broke out after the assassination of Dr. Martin Luther King Jr., and Dexter was bludgeoned in the head while attempting to report on the chaos. When he died a week later, he didn't just leave Trudy a widow, he left Florence seemingly abandoned in what had thus far been a forbidding world to her.

Florence never recovered from Dexter's death, and she and Trudy fought terribly over her determination to be a part of the counter-culture that had sprouted up as a result of the civil unrest with flower crowns, free love, communal living, and socialist leanings. Then at fourteen Florence ran away with a group of bohemians from New York City whom she met while at a Vietnam War protest. And the next time Trudy heard from her, Florence was almost a woman. What a woman she had become too. She exuded the flagrant independence of her father, able to talk about the world as though she owned it in her crocheted tops, bellbottom jeans, and dirty bare feet. There was always a cigarette in Florence's mouth or a joint pinched between her fingers, a twinkle in her eye, and a smirk of cynicism on her face. Later, Florence would shy away from talking about her most hippie years, her feminist marches with breasts bared, her trips to New Mexico to drop acid, or the time she became pregnant during an orgy out in Montana and disappeared completely from her love child's life for a half-dozen years.

Yes, Ruth was the product of Florence's devotion to free love. And from the look of Ruth's skin and hair, it was a white man with whom Florence had apparently worshiped quite fervently. For Ruth bore no traces of the African heritage of her grandmother. Though it was Trudy who would be tasked with raising Ruth in the absence of her derelict mother. And so, like Florence before her, the first years of Ruth's white life were spent on Trudy's dark-skinned hip, though Trudy had given up the restaurant business and now worked part-time as a clerk at a neighborhood grocery store. And maybe it was because Trudy found herself a woman of color raising yet another white baby that she wanted so desperately to dig back in time and learn all there was about the white last name her daughter, and now granddaughter, had been bequeathed —Kuhn. Maybe, she hoped, it would give Ruth a sense of belonging in the white world that would inevitably bookend the other side of this Black middle mark. But Dexter's parents had long ago passed away and the only vestiges of Dexter's heritage were names written in a family Bible. So, Trudy passed the Bible into Ruth's care, and otherwise simply regaled her with stories of Dexter from his and Trudy's time together, stories that she hoped would prove useful for Ruth when she inevitably found a soul mate of her own.

As for Trudy's family history, she promised herself she wouldn't spoil Ruth's young life with all the violent complexities of her own upbringing, brutal convolutions that even Trudy herself could barely comprehend. As for Ruth's transient mother, Florence, Trudy swore she knew as much about her as young Ruth did. She encouraged Ruth not to dwell on Florence's absence. Trudy was certain one day Florence would return for good, and at that time, Ruth would come to know her mother well. Of course, what Trudy couldn't know was that when Florence did reappear in Ruth's life, she would at once steer Ruth towards and away from the truth that was buried deep inside Ruth's marrow. She would change Ruth's life both good and ugly. She would destroy her and save her all at once.

Suddenly, the novella of the past, diverting Ruth's attention away from her current circumstances, was cut short by the slowdown of the Cadillac on the long driveway leading to the Christianson's farm.

"What the hell?" Sam said.

He hardly ever cursed. When he did, Ruth paid attention. Through the windswept dust encircling the Cadillac, a figure appeared at the end of the Christiansons' driveway leaning on the hood of a rented Chevy Malibu parked in front of the house. *What the hell, indeed?*

Two-Faced Preacher

Ruth and Sam both knew the woman at the end of the driveway. She was a pretty girl in her late twenties with a burnished, chestnut mane, spectacular breasts, and a pair of snakeskin boots.

Ruth touched Sam's arm instinctively. "Turn around. Let's go back into town. We'll do some grocery shopping. We've barely got anything to eat at the cabin anyway."

Sam stared down the driveway unflinching. "I'm not leaving her to mess with my parents."

The tone in Sam's voice grabbed the kids' full attention. "What's going on?" Rachel asked as she leaned against Ruth's seat squinting to see out the windshield.

Ruth tried again, "Let's call your parents, tell them we want to take them out. She can't stay here forever. We can call the sheriff. She's on private property."

"My dad hates eating out. You know that. And I'm not sure he'd be any more thrilled to get the sheriff involved," Sam huffed. He took his foot off the break, letting the Cadillac creep forward.

Ruth shook her head. A confrontation was a bad decision, but really, what other choice did they have? They could run, but clearly, they couldn't hide.

Sam didn't take his eyes off the woman who waited like a vulture, pushing her designer sunglasses up her smug nose and standing up straight as the Cadillac pulled into the far side of the drive. "Ruth, take the kids and go to the cabin."

"I'm not leaving you alone with that woman," Ruth stated matter-of-factly.

"Please." Sam threw the Cadillac into park.

Ruth turned to the kids. She gave them her best don't-argue-with-me look, the one they understood meant that whatever she was about to say was in their best interest as much as it was in hers. "All of you go to the cabin."

Rachel asked again, "Mom, can't you at least tell us what's happening?"

Ruth flexed the strength in her voice. "We'll talk about it later. Go. Now."

As the kids filed out of the car and headed for the cabin, Ruth turned to Sam, but before she could encourage him to stay cool, he stepped out of the Cadillac. Knowing any attempt to calm the situation was futile, Ruth, too, exited the Cadillac to face the woman whose name it seemed would now until forever be bound to her and Sam's life.

Lillian Monroe was a communications major from Florida State who received her master's degree in journalism from the University of Texas but looked like she had her doctorate in cheerleading, what with her perfect smile and smooth skin. Ruth knew all there was to know about Lillian because she was the reporter who broke the story about Sam's affair. It was as surprising for Ruth—as it seemed to be for everyone else—to discover, Lillian didn't work for one of the major newspapers or news media outlets like CNN, MSNBC, *The New York Times*, or *The Washington Post*, liberal powerhouses Sam had occasionally railed against in his preaching and who had taken him to task just as mercilessly. No, Lillian was a writer for the wildly unscrupulous and laughably unreliable *National Enquirer*. Ruth would learn, on the myriad of cable news shows Lillian visited following her earth-shattering revelation that one of America's most trusted and influential evangelicals was a closet homosexual, that Lillian had worked her way up the ranks at the 90 year-old gossip rag with stories that had always seemed as sensational as any other headline placed on the front page, but which happened to somehow be based in such unequivocal fact, she had actually earned the tabloid a Pulitzer nomination within her first year of working there.

Lillian's Pulitzer nomination was the result of a story she uncovered about birth defects plaguing a half dozen newborns in a rural Kansas town. After tests of the air and water supply turned up nothing questionable, locals began to believe they were the target of a government conspiracy or an experiment by aliens gone awry. The alien theory gained traction after strange lights appeared over a particular farm each night, then disappeared without a trace. Lillian's investigation discovered the truth was nowhere near as supernatural but was just as sensational. A local, QAnon-following nurse practitioner was found giving animal hormones to pregnant mothers in place of prenatal vitamins believing they would produce healthier children, children worthy of their white, nationalist heritage.

Ruth and Sam's first brush with the media came just two months after their young assemblage of like-minded Christian brothers and sisters began meeting in the empty storefront of the Twin Corners strip mall on the south side of Lynchburg, Virginia, over sixteen years before the arrival of Lillian. The small, two-thousand-square-foot room with concrete walls, stained acoustic ceiling tiles, and a single bathroom closet had been offered to Sam as a place of worship by the owner of the strip mall whom Sam had led to the Lord after a chance encounter with him at a gas station. The way the owner put it, he needed a tax write-off more than he needed the rent. And so, a deal was quickly brokered for one dollar a month rent on a month-to-month basis for essentially as long as Sam and his church required the space. The upside was that most of the shops in the complex were closed on Sunday morning, so there was ample parking for the twenty to thirty followers who had joined Sam's flock over the last year. The downside was that even after repainting and recarpeting, the air inside the former Off the Leash Pet Supply was still tinged with the chemical smell of tick and flea collars and crusty fish food. Nevertheless, to Sam it might as well have been the Holy of Holies. Of course, not everyone was thrilled a church had planted itself in a commercial lot, including a liquor store owner across the street who believed the presence of Holy Light Ministries was driving away his business.

It was on a Sunday morning three months after setting up their small congregation, just as Sam and Ruth were arriving to turn on the lights and tidy the folding chairs, that they were confronted by a reporter and his camera crew who were waiting outside the storefront like hyenas eyeing prey. The balding, middle-aged correspondent of a local CBS affiliate wore a green tie and sports coat up top and stonewashed jeans and sandals down below. Almost conspiratorially the reporter relayed the news to Sam and Ruth that "some neighborhood businesses" were complaining about their presence, and he asked if Sam was aware that local building codes might possibly forbid them from having a church in the small corner of the plaza they currently occupied. With the camera rolling and trained steadily on Sam, expecting a reaction that would play perfectly in a soundbite to an audience skeptical of dollar-store preachers, Sam smiled his "Jesus smile," as Ruth secretly called it, and invited the reporter into the church for service. Sam then encouraged the cameraman to record all he wanted of the church and the service. After, Sam promised, he would sit down with the reporter for a full, in-depth interview. Surprised by Sam's offer, the reporter and his cameraman indeed stayed for all of Sunday service and waited until the last parishioner left. Then Sam did exactly what he promised. With shirt sleeves rolled up and tie loosened around his neck, Sam explained to the reporter that he was simply following the call of God on his life, to reach the world and fill the broken with hope and remind the lost of God's love. Sam said if Holy Light Ministries had broken some law of man's in moving into the strip mall, just like Jesus told the Pharisees to give to Caesar what was his, Sam, too, would follow man's law and move out. But Sam also pointed to a placard on the wall just inside the small storefront that read "Capacity Limit: 80," which Sam said he suspected meant there was no code violation taking place given the current size of his congregation was less than a couple dozen. Ruth remembered the zealous delight Sam offered the correspondent as the same prepossession he had shown her when they first met, his perfect teeth glistening beneath his valedictorian smile and his green eyes trained with bona fide attentiveness to the unsuspecting reporter's every question.

Instead of driving Sam out of the Twin Corner's strip mall, the reporter's segment—which played on both the five o' clock and the ten o' clock news the next night—attracted more people to service the following Sunday than the church had folding chairs to accommodate. Even the liquor store owner, who played prominently in the story and seemed to be the *only* "neighborhood business" tormented by the church's presence, darkened the door of their strip mall house of worship and made nice with Sam, who he admitted was clearly a "good guy."

For the most part, that's how it had mostly gone with reporters and the media when it came to Sam and Ruth and Holy Light Ministries. The former would show up with cameras and tape recorders and questions meant to trip up and force admission of some human error that inevitably played a part in organized religion, only to leave spellbound and sincerely interested in whatever had been shared by Sam, magnetized by his warmth of spirit and captivated by the heart he wore on his sleeve. Ruth believed in many ways the reason Holy Light had proliferated over the years was thanks as much to badgering media as it was to Sam's ability to wield that biased exposure into sterling publicity for himself and his church.

Two years after they opened the doors to their strip mall sanctuary, Holy Light made the big move to Charleston, South Carolina, because, just like with the shopping complex, they had been offered an opportunity they couldn't turn down, a massive, old movie theater in Charleston's downtown. Asking price: one dollar. It was a hard decision to make, leaving their friends and most of their congregation behind, but Sam knew once they renovated the theater, it would provide space for at least a three-hundred-member church, and that was a lot closer to his megachurch dream than the strip mall could ever be. So, move to Charleston they did. Six years after that, they moved into an abandoned elementary school they spent almost a million dollars refurbishing. Yes, it was a lie, what so many Christians had been taught to believe. The news media wasn't out to get anyone *per se*. They were out to find a story. Give them a good one, and on their way they went. Hold back, treat them like scum, defend, divert, dissuade, and they would make you pay tenfold for wasting their time. Neither were they necessarily liberal. But they did depend on communicating mostly from a place of reality and fact, not the unicorns-and-rainbows speak so many Christians had fallen prey to. Even when Sam had gone after the news media here or there for what he felt was a lopsided view of some aspect of American life, he was never one of the ridiculous conservatives who railed about the use of "Happy Holidays" instead of "Merry Christmas." And he could never be accused of throwing a tantrum because the Ten Commandments were taken out of the statehouse. He got it—the way the world worked—and so did Ruth. They both understood that society was made up of many points of view, religious beliefs, and types of people, all of whom deserved love and acceptance. This universal embrace Sam so effortlessly offered was—Sam liked to remind skeptics—the embrace Christ himself offered others when he walked this planet two thousand years ago. And this secret weapon Sam had commandeered from his Holy Father was the thing that had seduced all the media, both liberals and conservatives . . . at least until the day Lillian Monroe slipped unknowingly into their lives.

From what Ruth gathered, Lillian's interest in Sam started many months before she ever began to write a word of the *Enquirer* feature story that would rip apart the Christiansons' world. Apparently, she was visiting her parents, who lived forty-five minutes West of Charleston in Summerville, when they kept going on about the wonderful work Holy Light Ministries was doing for the poor of Charleston. So, Lillian decided to visit the 11 a.m. Sunday service and see if it could really be as good as all that.

The energy of the place was palpable, the smiles on everyone's faces seemed genuine, and Lillian would admit later that Sam's persona truly was beyond magnetic. But there was also something about the place that bothered her. It was too perfect, she would say. Maybe it was simply her liberal inclinations, she laughed, but not long after her first trek to the Holy Light campus, Lillian began digging into Sam's life, even tailing him in her mom's brown Camry, documenting his movements outside the walls of his sanctuary. She began asking around if anyone had ever heard any negative gossip about this man of God who seemed to be a regular pied piper of the modern-day Christian movement. Why did Lillian think Sam was hiding something? Maybe he *was* the second coming, just like everyone seemed to believe. But if he was human, didn't he have at least one sin he kept hidden from the world, one immorality that was his Achilles heel?

For months Sam became Lillian's obsession, and for months she uncovered only good, only facts that fell in line with his public persona. Then one fateful weekend, during the time he was usually practicing his Sunday sermon, Lillian caught Sam making an odd stop on the north side of Charleston at the Blue Sands Motel & Diner.

Later, when Ruth would ask Sam how many times he'd met up at the Blue Sands with the "massage therapist" whose name was Red, Sam would tell Ruth he'd only met with Red a dozen times total over the course of three years. According to Lillian, this was the same story she received when she approached the muscular, ginger-haired man who exited the hotel room Sam had entered three hours before and then exited with a bit of a drunkard's wobble two and a half hours later.

At first, Red—with his military haircut and hyper-masculine demeanor—was resistant to informing on Sam. Even after Lillian offered him more cash than he could make giving twenty massages, he still refused to admit he knew who Sam was or that he might have been involved in anything untoward with Sam. Lillian persisted, however. This was her strength. She was like one of the snapping turtles Sam had pointed out to Ruth when he first brought her back to the farm. "Once they get a hold of you, they won't let go 'til lightning strikes," Sam told Ruth with a twinkle in his eye.

Despite successfully dodging Lillian the first time, Red was easy to track down. He was listed along with a fifty or so other male "massage therapists" on a website that featured them muscled and shirtless and willing to meet up anywhere around the Charleston metro area for a "full-body rubdown." Clearly geared towards homosexual men, Lillian was surprised at how succinct the website was, like a menu, with each man priced anywhere from a hundred to a couple hundred bucks for an hour.

Posing as just another male client, Lillian scheduled an appointment with Red via text, but when Red showed up at the Hyatt hotel room she booked for the "massage" and saw her standing on the other side of the door, he immediately turned to go. Lillian chased after him and doubled her first monetary offer, then tripled it. And then, waiting for the elevator to whisk him away, she appealed to his sense of justice. Why should someone be allowed to stand behind a pulpit and rail against sodomy only to indulge in homosexual activity himself unbeknownst to the thousands hanging on his every word? Why should Red be sub-jugated to the shadows of Charleston society while Sam walked around its hero? Red admitted he knew Sam was a well-to-do pastor. Then again, Red had clients from all walks of life—many of whom despised the act Red helped them indulge in. The way Red saw it, he was doing them a service—relieving pressure that otherwise might have killed them or sent them spiraling out of control to the detriment of others. Why shouldn't he help those most in need like Sam? After all, he was blessed with looks, a large cock, an unquenchable desire for sex, and a charmer's ability to adapt to whatever company he found himself in?

Lillian cooed that she understood Red entirely, that she didn't see him as a rent boy or a hustler or anything filthy, but instead she looked up to him as someone who was indeed assisting, like a wet nurse, cer-tain members of society by giving men of a particular bent something they might be too shy or too uncomfortable or too scared to otherwise seek out. But Sam Christianson, Lillian assured Red, was not someone to knowingly protect—not like Red's other clients who did nothing more than privately go about their lives as soon as they left Red's arms. No, beyond preaching against homosexual behavior, Sam's church held day camps for men and boys struggling with their homosexual desires where they promised with enough supplication and devotion to God those feelings could be cast out like demons, where they promised that if these soldiers of God cried out for healing from their homosexual persuasions, only then would they be worthy of God's eternal heaven. Red himself had been raised on a rural farm in Georgia, beat hard at first by his daddy, then by the military, then by life. For the longest time he had believed this torture was good for him, would make him straight. As life passed and his feelings for other men remained, he realized the pain he had allowed himself to endure had only managed to bend him into something unnatural, someone unable to love normally, someone so hurt the only men he could feel something with were his clients, strangers over whom he always exerted the control his daddy had exerted over him.

Red agreed to help Lillian expose Sam as the two-faced preacher that he was, but Red wanted much more money for his help than she had offered. And he wanted Lillian's assurance that in the article she wrote exposing Sam, she would talk about the ex-gay ministry being run out of the Holy Light Ministries' basement. Lillian agreed to Red's terms. Within weeks, along with a ten-thousand-dollar down payment, she had given him a small X-pro Hi-def camera to record his next tryst with Sam so there would be no question of the truth even in the face of the inevitable denials that came with the disrobing of such an encounter.

"You need to not be here," Sam said, as he crossed the gravel driveway towards Lillian.

Lillian smiled casually. "Just back from church?"

"This is private property." Sam gestured to the Christianson farm all around them.

"I know what you must think of me, but I wanted to reach out and see if you were ready to share your side of the story?" Lillian asked. "As I've said before, I want to be the first to interview you about your side of things."

"How did you find us?" Sam asked.

"It wasn't that hard." Lillian looked past Sam to Ruth. "Ruth, happy Sunday."

Ruth returned only daggers.

"I'm gonna tell you one more time. Go." Sam said, beyond perturbed.

"Actually, I'm gonna wait for your parents, if it's all the same," Lillian said. She leaned against her rental car again.

Suddenly, Sam lunged for her, "Get out! Get out of here now! You have no business being on this property!"

The way Sam handled Lillian was shocking to Ruth who had never seen him behave violently towards anything. Sam grabbed Lillian by her hair and forced her around to the driver's side door of her car. Instantly, Lillian began screaming in terror and pain.

Ruth screamed out too as she sprinted into the middle of the situation, "Sam! No!" But Ruth couldn't manage to get between Sam and Lillian as he shoved Lillian into her car seat so viciously, Ruth feared for Lillian's life.

"Let go of me, you psycho!" Lillian screamed.

"Get the hell out of here! And leave my family alone!" Sam yelled back, his face flushed, the veins protruding from his neck. He slammed the car door on Lillian, and Ruth half expected to hear the crunch of bone.

"Sam!" Ruth shouted to bring him back to his senses. But Sam couldn't hear her or didn't want to.

"The next time you show up here, you're gonna wish you hadn't," he growled through clenched teeth.

Up by the highway, Naomi and Joe's truck was turning down the road.

"I'll sue you! I'll have you arrested for battery and assault!" Lillian screamed.

"Good luck with that. You're on my turf now. Around here the law doesn't look kindly on reporters or troublemaking cunts!"

Both Lillian and Ruth were taken aback by Sam's words.

Sam kicked the side of Lillian's rental with such force he left a dent in the door. "Now get the fuck out of here!" he screamed.

With Joe and Naomi quickly approaching, the odds for Lillian's safety were falling ever more quickly out of her favor. She started her rental and peeled out of the driveway in a cloud of dust.

Sam wiped foamy spittle off his chin as his parents exited their truck wide-eyed and clearly suspicious of whatever had just taken place.

"Sam?" Naomi asked.

Sam looked at Naomi and Joe unresponsively. Then he looked at Ruth and took off around the house towards the back pasture.

Naomi stared accusingly at Ruth. "What on earth?"

Ruth let out a breath she hadn't realized she'd been holding. "I gotta take care of the kids." She turned to head for the cabin where she was sure her children had watched the entire episode unfold through the kitchen window.

Naomi persisted, calling after her, "That's it? No one is going to tell us what's going on?"

Ruth turned back to Naomi, shook her head, "Don't worry. We're gonna go look at some properties for rent tomorrow. We'll get out of your hair." Ruth turned away once more. She was done. She literally had nothing more to say to Naomi, to Joe, to Sam, to her children, to anybody!

Tally the Mason Jar

S till to this day, Ruth remembered licking molasses off her grandmother's finger. It was a humid, summer night in Trudy's canary-
yellow and leprechaun-green kitchen. Potatoes were steaming in a large
pot on the stove, and flour dusted the Formica counter where biscuits
had been rolled out and cut only minutes earlier. Ruth remembered
Trudy's laugh, her grand lips and large, white teeth that seemed to
stretch into infinity. Ruth had never loved anyone more than she
loved Trudy—her real mother in many ways. Trudy's touch was like a
warm blanket fresh off the line, capable of sending an electric comfort
through Ruth's body that made her believe everything would be okay.

In the beginning, Ruth had no sense that the color of her skin was
different than Trudy's or that their life together was a trying one. Their
small, two-bedroom craftsman just off French Street in DC had been
built on the cheap many years before. The ballet slipper colored tiles in
the only bathroom were scarred with chips and hairline cracks where
they had been broken from use and the settling of the house over the
years. Where wallpaper covered the plaster in the dining room, some
of the out of reach seams had begun to unfurl. The hardwood floors
had warped and split, and the varnish on them had long since been
sanded away by countless scuffs from shoes and boots and the movement of furniture. It was too cold in the wintertime and too hot in
the summer. When it rained Trudy prayed the roof wouldn't leak, and
when it snowed, she prayed it wouldn't cave in. Throughout all this,
Ruth had no idea that her life was any different than any other young

girl's, and she was blissfully ignorant of how hard Trudy worked so that perception wouldn't change.

Just as they would be in her adulthood, Sundays were Ruth's favorite day as a little girl, for she knew Sunday was the day she would have her precious grandmother all to herself. No job to report to. No bills to be paid. No errands to run. On Sundays, Ruth would wake up with all the thrill of Christmas morning. She would wash her tiny, pale face and brush her thin, dishwater-blonde hair. She would dawn her gauzy, peach Sunday dress with the lace ruffles and her black patent shoes, and she would wait and watch while Trudy, dressed in a peacock blue dress suit, lightly scented her ebony neck with an atomizer that Ruth knew was a gift from her grandfather.

Six mornings out of the week, since she could remember, Ruth and Trudy walked to Foundry Methodist Church hand-in-hand, summer, spring, winter, and fall—seven blocks each way. Monday through Friday, Trudy would leave Ruth in the care of the lovely women who ran the preschool there while Trudy went off to work. But on Sunday, Ruth and Trudy would make the pilgrimage to attend Foundry Methodist's ten o'clock service. Along the way, Ruth and Trudy would discuss all the beautiful things in life, the interesting things, the things Ruth was certain others around them couldn't possibly understand the way she and Trudy did. They were both amused by how fast hummingbirds zipped through the sky and how easily those same thimble-sized birds blended into the leaves of the nearby lilac bushes. They couldn't understand why squirrels seemed to always be so agitated about everything and pigeons seemed so mindless. They imagined how certain flowers would make beautiful prints for a skirt or curtains or a bedspread. When it rained, they debated whether the rainfall was actually the teardrops of angels or God flushing his toilet, and they laughed pretending thunder was the Almighty moving the furniture around in heaven or perhaps bowling on his solid gold bowling alley. Sometimes, Ruth would ask Trudy to tell her about Dexter, and Trudy would smile a faraway sort of smile and reminisce about Dexter's wild hair that stood on ends just like Ruth's when he woke up from sleeping, or she'd tell Ruth what a gentleman Dexter could be, always patient, always kind, even when he was the one who had been slighted. "That's the kind of husband you're going to have," Trudy would tell Ruth. "You're gonna marry a sweet, *sweet*, loving man just like your grandfather. And he's going to buy you chocolates and perfume and take you to the movies and hold your hand 'til the day you die." Sometimes Trudy would read Ruth old newspaper articles that Dexter had written, which she had saved. The best ones were stories about "Black folk" Trudy would say, accounts that humanized them to a world that saw them as less than. Ruth didn't always understand why the stories would make her grandmother cry, but they were beautiful nonetheless, and Ruth never tired of hearing Trudy read them to her.

In many ways, Foundry Methodist Church was Ruth's second home, and she loved it there—the way the polished wooden banisters smelled like lemon and salt, the way the whitewashed classrooms held the promise of fascinating Bible stories, the way the cavernous sanctuary, with its ominous pipe organ and stained glass windows, allowed her to imagine what it might be like if she were a princess and the church was her castle. Ruth believed the water from the drinking fountains that bedecked the hallways was the coldest and sweetest she had ever tasted, and she relished every opportunity to be lifted up for a lengthy sip. Beyond that, everyone was nice to her at Foundry. They seemed to have a special appreciation of her that she couldn't discern from the rest of the world. Later in life, she would realize this was because they knew— knew about her famous reporter grandfather who had died in the riots, knew about her infamous hippy mother who had left her to be raised by Trudy, knew how hard life must be for an orphan of sorts from a biracial family. Yes, Ruth delighted in the comfort of such a place, never understanding the politics she and Trudy's existence actually stirred up for those in charge. It wasn't until she and Sam had their own church that she would look back at her time at Foundry Methodist differently, almost wishing she could know more of what had gone on behind the scenes, what debates might have been involved in caring for an old, Black woman and her young, white granddaughter.

After church, there was always fellowship. Ruth felt a deep keenness for the word "fellowship." It seemed so nice and soft and loving. During "fellowship" everyone was happy and smiling and amenable to one another. In the large common room next to the sanctuary, everyone gathered to drink creamed coffee and eat fresh frosted donuts. Ruth was allowed a single donut from one of the pink boxes set out on the long folding tables. Then Ruth and Trudy would make their way over to the multicolored fiberglass chairs set up around the perimeter of the room. Trudy would sit with a cup of coffee and nod to certain members of the church who nodded back to her. Ruth would relish each bite of her donut until all that was left was the icing that coated the tips of her tiny fingers.

Often Ruth and Trudy were offered rides home with other parishioners, some with very nice cars and very kind smiles, but Trudy always waved the offers away. She preferred to enjoy God's gift of nature, and Ruth suspected she enjoyed their conversations walking to and from church as much as Ruth did.

Sunday lunch was usually leftovers from the night before melded into some new fashion. Fried chicken and biscuits would become chicken sandwiches with ranch dressing. Boiled green beans and corn would become cold green bean and corn salad with a touch of relish for a kick of flavor. Sometimes, after lunch was devoured and dishes had been washed and put away, they would turn on the TV and watch baseball, especially if the Detroit Tigers were playing—"Grandpa Dexter's team," Trudy would remind Ruth. Sometimes, they would go see a movie at the theater off 9th, if there was something worth seeing. Whatever it was that they did, Trudy made sure they would rest. After all, Sunday was the Lord's day and enjoying it was how man honored Christ's gift of life to them.

If Ruth didn't have many friends as a young girl, it wasn't because there weren't children around that were her age. It was more that she found kids her age exasperating and silly. They were always crying or complaining or flailing wildly about. Teachers at the Foundry Methodist pre-school praised Ruth for sharing with others and never pushing or shoving to get her way. Mostly, Ruth didn't want to be bothered by the other children and preferred to let them have their way as long as they left her alone in return. Indeed, she was often more interested in the adults around her like Peggy Pengrasse, the song teacher, who wore floor-length ruffled dresses and had long, mahogany hair.

Miss Pengrasse, as all the kids called her, seemed to be ever breathlessly smiling when she entered a room, as though she had just come from some wondrous place that had left her in a state of ecstasy. Somehow, she always made singing fun, whether it was playing games with the kids to get everyone to belt their hearts out or sharing a story that would inspire them to perform a song with real emotion. Ruth's favorite memory of Miss Pengrasse was when she brought a quart mason jar to song service. It had two eyes and a smile glued onto one side of it, and she said its name was Tally. Well, Tally—filled with a clear liquid that Ruth believed to be water—would rest on a small podium next to Peggy as she was directing her young choir of voices. The better the kids sang, the more colorfully Tally would react when Miss Pengrasse stirred the water inside with a silver spoon she carried in her purse. Orange. Green. Blue. Purple. All were great reactions. But red was supposed to be the color that meant Tally was *really* impressed. Each week the kids sang with all their strength trying to get the clear liquid inside of Tally to turn red, and for weeks they got closer and seemingly closer. But, still no red. Then one day, Miss Pengrasse told all the kids that at the upcoming Sunday service their little choir would perform their best song before the church. She said that she really wanted them to give their all this practice because it was the last opportunity they would have before the concert. They sang the song she had selected for them to perform, and they sang well, but when Miss Pengrasse stirred the clear liquid inside of Tally, it didn't change colors at all. She beseeched the kids to sing the song again, this time with even more gusto. Surely this time, Tally would react. Once more, they sang their hearts out. Once more, when Miss Pengrasse stuck the silver spoon inside of Tally to stir the water and change its color, nothing happened. Miss Pengrasse didn't know what the matter was with Tally. Maybe, she posited to the children, they needed to sing again, the way they would sing on Sunday morning for all their friends and family. So, they sang the best they had ever sung. Ruth remembered their chorus of voices reverberating off the walls of the small classroom where they met, filling her ears with what sounded like the way singing was supposed to sound. With breath held, Miss Pengrasse took her spoon and stirred the clear water inside Tally. But this time something happened they were never expecting. Not only did the water inside Tally turn red, but it also began bubbling up and erupting over the sides of Tally. Miss Pengrasse seemed as surprised and excited as the kids at this unexpected development.

"Wow!" she exclaimed. She had never seen Tally react like that in all her years teaching song service. She implored the kids to sing as well as they just had that following Sunday.

It wasn't just the games Miss Pengrasse would play with Ruth and her classmates that engendered such affection from Ruth. It was also the way Miss Pengrasse told Bible stories about the songs they were singing that meant a great deal to Ruth's young heart. Even the story of baby Jesus meant more when Miss Pengrasse shared it while helping her students to understand the meaning behind certain Christmas carols. Ruth could sense the fear Mary must've felt when she learned she was pregnant with a baby while not yet married to Joseph, and the trepidation she must've felt carrying God's only son. *What might have happened if something went wrong? What if she were caught pregnant without being married to Joseph?* In Mary's time, they stoned women for being with child and unwed. The fate of the whole world rested on Mary's shoulders, and the salvation of mankind was dependent on her bearing baby Jesus without complication. How terrible it must've been to only be able to find shelter in a stable on the cold night baby Jesus was born. But how glorious to give birth to the Savior of Men no matter how humble their accommodations.

At the end of Sunday school service, Ruth's teachers always asked the kids to bow their heads so they could say a final prayer to send the kids off back to their lives. Before they said a prayer, each time her teachers asked if there was anyone in the room who wanted to be saved.

Ruth knew "saved" meant "asking Jesus into your heart" so you could go to heaven and be with Him when you died. Beyond her teachers, she had also heard Trudy speak about the need to "become a Christian" and very quickly in her young mind Ruth began to put together the fact that she had never done this thing—asked Jesus into her heart. So, one song service when Miss Pengrasse told the kids that Jesus had come to earth from His place in heaven to teach men about His Father and die on a cross so that they might be saved, Ruth knew what she needed to do.

Even thirty years later, Ruth remembered asking Jesus into her heart like it was yesterday. Weekday song service had just ended, and everyone was heading for the large community room next to the sanctuary where lunch was served. Ruth hung back, however. And when Miss Pengrasse finished putting her songbooks away, Ruth approached her to see if she would help Ruth ask Jesus into her heart. Miss Pengrasse beamed and sat down on the piano bench nearby. She took Ruth's hands in hers and said she was so happy Ruth wanted to be saved. She said it was simple to ask Jesus into her heart. She need only close her eyes and ask him to come in. And that's exactly what Ruth did. She closed her eyes and with all her heart asked Jesus to save her so that she could one day, when she died, go to heaven and live with Him. There was no grand explosion of feeling in Ruth's heart, no trumpets or choir or angels that heralded Ruth's salvation. But when she opened her eyes, it was like the world was new. Even Miss Pengrasse looked different than before— more beautiful, if that was possible. As she walked to lunch, Ruth felt as though she were walking on air, and Ruth's heart felt lighter than it had ever felt before.

When Trudy picked Ruth up that afternoon, Ruth was giddy with excitement to tell her grandmother what she had done. And just like Ruth knew Trudy would, when she heard the news, Trudy mouthed a little prayer to heaven and wrapped her arms around her grandbaby. "I'm so proud of you," Trudy whispered in Ruth's ear. It was the greatest moment of Ruth's young life. And being saved truly was Ruth's salvation many times as she grew older and learned more about the world she had been born into.

But like so many things, the salvation Ruth had experienced was more complicated now that she understood so much more, like the fact it wasn't water in Tally the mason jar but vinegar—vinegar that when mixed with a little baking powder resulted in the explosion she had witnessed with all the other choir children on that fateful Friday afternoon before their big Sunday concert. And it was dye—a couple drops—dried overnight on Miss Pengrasse's silver spoon that changed Tally's color when she pulled the spoon out of her purse and dipped it into Tally's clear liquid innards. Yes, so much magic from her childhood was lost as Ruth grew older. Now, for the first time, even the idea of salvation from damnation being as easy as closing your eyes and saying a little prayer gnawed at Ruth's guts. Even the idea of such simple concepts as heaven and hell seemed childish. But what to do? If she stopped believing in such things, the foundation she had built her life on would be gone in an instant. Then again, considering her current circumstances, perhaps it already was.

The Back Pasture

Naomi insisted on fixing Sunday lunch for Ruth and the kids, and really, what choice did Ruth have but to concede to Naomi's will? They had brought their clothes and a few snacks with them on their exodus from Charleston, but neither she nor Sam had yet bought any real sustenance for their family to eat. So, sup with Joe and Naomi, Ruth and the kids did. It was as stifled and awkward as the night before but now gilded with the images of Sam and Lillian's violent encounter, not to mention Joe's chastising sermon. As soon as she could, Ruth made a selfish escape, telling the kids she was going to look for Sam who had never shown up for lunch, and they should help Naomi put away the food and wash dishes.

The sticky summer air outside the house was only slightly cooler than the oppressive heat inside. Joe and Naomi had installed central air years ago, but Joe was opposed to using it unless absolutely necessary, which seemed to be never. Ruth crossed the yard to a wooden gate that led out towards the back pasture. The field had recently been mowed for hay and the sharp stubble of the alfalfa needled her ankles with each step she took through it. She wasn't sure if she would find Sam down by the autumn olive trees, but that's where she decided she would look. Maybe the autumn olive trees wouldn't be there either, finally cleared by Joe. If Sam wasn't roaming the fields and forests, maybe that meant his head had cleared, and he had made his way back to the cabin while everyone was eating lunch. Even now, he could be taking a nap on one of the old, musty couches, and Ruth wondered if she should have checked the cabin first.

As much as Ruth was wounded by him, disgusted by him, irritated by his very existence, Sam remained—at least at this point—her kindred. Almost from the day they met this had been the case, their souls connected in that way of bosom friends. And existence, even as hurtful as it currently was, felt confusing without that alliance she had come to rely on, that she and Sam had enjoyed for almost half her life. So, she walked on, determined to find Sam, to make sure he was okay, that he wasn't hanging himself from a tree somewhere. Suddenly the thought of Sam hurting himself sent a jolt of fright through Ruth's body, and she quickened her pace. She knew how badly he beat himself up when he failed at anything. How hard must he be pulverizing himself right now? Yet because this latest development truly was a failure of almost unimaginable proportions, Sam hadn't requested any sort of sympathy from Ruth. Of course, he had been raised by Joe. So, even when he made *honest* mistakes, Sam expected no pity. Everyone knew there was no room for error in Joe's world. You were either on the same page with Joe, and he approved of you, or you were a deviant. Heaven or hell. Black or white. Sam had learned achingly well how to hate himself for even the slightest of his shortcomings, and Ruth grieved for the mental anguish she knew he suffered as a result. Then she stopped her line of thought. No! NO! Mistakes were mistakes. They could be forgiven. What Sam had done to her, to their children, to their friends, to their congregation, to the Christian community at large—that wasn't a mistake! What he'd done was deliberate, a knife into the gut of all she had shared with him. Maybe if he had simply asked permission to stray, maybe they could have figured something out, something that wouldn't have landed them here like this—her, nauseous as she strode across a barbed pasture to make sure Sam wasn't, well . . . killing himself.

Another twenty yards and Ruth would navigate around the small peninsula of trees that hid the far east corner of the pasture. For a moment, it felt good to Ruth, not obsessing about herself, to be lost in the care and concern of Sam like she had grown accustomed to over the course of their almost twenty years together. She felt the familiar chemicals rush through her veins—the ones she was inclined to, the hormones that made her feel good because they accentuated her natural ability to be a caretaker and wife. Yet, even as she felt this second of normalcy, it evaporated like rain on hot concrete. No. NO! She was angry at Sam. Maybe he *should* hang himself. Maybe that *would* be justice. Maybe she and the kids deserved the freedom and instant sympathy that would come with his passing. Maybe they could go back to Charleston, and she could pastor Holy Light Ministries herself. It wasn't *her* sins that had driven them into exile, after all. It wasn't *her* lies. It was Sam's!

When she rounded the hurst of trees, Ruth was slightly disappointed to find Sam sitting against the base of an old white oak, nonchalantly twiddling a piece of grass between his fingers. She instantly slowed her pace and secretly hoped he didn't see that she had mere seconds before held certain concerns for him—cares that he didn't deserve. Almost as soon as she saw Sam sitting there, still in his slacks and dress shirt, his sports coat and tie draped over a nearby sapling, Ruth wished she hadn't found him, hadn't come looking for him, didn't know him, didn't feel a stirring between her legs for his sweaty body and the smell of the hair by his temples.

"He cut them all down," Sam said, nodding to a fence row nearby.

Ruth didn't want to understand Sam, but she knew he was talking about the autumn olive trees. Indeed they were all gone, the small ornamental shrubs with their soft, velvety leaves and tiny, crimson berries.

"He cleared the back forty, as well. Not a tree in sight." Sam stated.

Ruth stared at the ground in front of her. It was crawling with life: ladybugs, gnats, crickets, spiders, etc. all participating in a microscopic community like humans in a town square going about their daily tasks without realizing their infinitesimal place in the universe. Every blade of grass was a different shade of green, thousands upon thousands of virescent colors too numerous to even begin to catalog. Above, where the stalks of alfalfa and weeds and grass and wildflowers had recently been sheared by Joe's mower, they were toasted yellow, scorched by the sun and dead, but down below, near the earth, they were vibrant and wet with life still circulating through their veins, making plans to regrow, to reach for the heavens once more.

"Did you and the kids eat?" Sam asked, interrupting Ruth's thoughts.

Ruth wanted to be nice but couldn't help growling sarcastically. "We ate with your parents. It was wonderful."

"I was sitting out here trying to figure out what to do, trying to come up with a way to make things better," Sam said. "I'm so tired, Ruth. I feel like I haven't slept in years—my whole life maybe." But he couldn't go on, and Ruth knew he was choked up, the outline of his eye sockets suddenly red, the bulbs inside watery and bugged out. He was suffering.

"I hate you," she said. "And I hate myself for hating you, especially right now when I know you need me. But you deserve it, every bit of pain and embarrassment you're going through. Me and the kids, I was just thinking how I wish you were dead so we could go back to our lives. We didn't do anything wrong. You did."

"You want me to end it, maybe that's what I should do."

It was beautiful when Sam cried over things like their kids' accomplishments, the power of the Holy Ghost, and special moments between the two of them once every few years, but this . . . his self-indulgence disgusted her.

Ruth hissed. "You know what hurts the most? You're supposed to be my best friend. You're supposed to be the one person I can talk to about anything. And I have never ever kept anything from you. Never. I've told you all kinds of things—secrets I haven't told anyone else." Ruth wiped a tear from her cheek.

"What was I supposed to say, that I . . . fuck men?" Sam asked.

"You're disgusting!" Ruth spit out. She instantly regretted her words. This is how all their private conversations went nowadays. Outbursts. Regret. More outbursts. More regret. Tears. Always tears.

Sam stood up. "Don't you think I know that—how repulsive I am to you, to everyone? I get how insane this all is. I feel like a crazy person, Ruth. I feel like I want to die! I really do."

Ruth whispered, "No, you're just upset because you can't have both that life and this one anymore."

Ruth's statement sobered Sam up. He shook his head as if to deny Ruth's words, but he didn't say anything to contradict them. Then finally, he sighed. "Is it over between us?"

"We have to think about the kids," she said. "That's the agreement we made when we decided to come here. We have to do what's right for them."

"But us," Sam said, "we also have to think about us too. We have to make some decisions about us, so we're not stuck in this perpetual state of torture. Us hating and hurting one another is not going to help the kids either."

"So, what do you want to do?" Ruth asked, staring at him defiantly, daring him to say he wanted to be with her, yet hoping at the same time that's what he wanted, more than another man, more than cock. She wanted him to want her, to want her lips and breasts and the glory of all life clasped softly between her legs.

"All I know is I love you. I truly do. And knowing how deeply you're hurting because of something I've done is unbearable. But I can't help wondering if staying together is only prolonging the pain instead of somehow healing it."

"Do you want to be with men?"

"Ruth, don't."

"Do you?" She insisted. "'Because if you want to be with men, that's not going to work with me, clearly!"

"I've always been a good husband to you. I've always cared for you. I've given you everything you needed, including sex."

"That's not the point!"

"Well, maybe it should be."

"So, you want to be with men." Ruth pushed.

"I don't know," Sam said quietly.

This was a defeat and a win for Ruth. For weeks, she had been pressing Sam to be honest about his real inclinations. Now she had it—the truth. He was genuinely leaning towards being with men or at least unsure that he *didn't* want to be with them, and that was quite the leap away from where things *had* been, the certainty that his future lay with her and her only. Suddenly, Ruth felt panicked again, that Sam would choose some man over her, would leave her and their marriage and their kids and she would be alone without her best friend in the world, without the person who knew her better than anyone else ever would. Testing him, Ruth pushed again. "Then we should end this."

"If that's what you want," Sam nodded.

Ruth wanted to scream. "No, that's not what I want. I don't want any of this. But, if you want to be with men, then that's what has to be."

"It never mattered before you found out," Sam said.

"So, you're saying if you could have just continued to lie to me everything would have been okay?" Ruth scoffed.

"Fine. Tell me what to do 'cause it won't go away—the feelings. They're not overwhelming, but every few months they creep in. They claw at my insides until I give in to them. Then I'm fine. I'm okay for weeks, for months. I've gone years before. But they always, *always* come back. And I've prayed, Ruth. I've prayed like you wouldn't believe. And I've told myself each time I've given in that that would be the last time, that that would be it—I would never touch another man like that again! But it never works. Never!"

Ruth stared at Sam and the embarrassing honesty she had forced out of him, that belittled what was left of his ever-shrinking stature. Inexplicably, she opened her arms to him. "Come here," she said.

Sam looked at her uncertain and cautious, scared of her.

"Come here," she said again.

Tear-stained and limping in spirit, Sam moved over to Ruth, and for the first time in weeks, they embraced. It felt good to momentarily bridge the immense chasm between them. Sam pawed at Ruth with all his strength, willing her to mesh into him, become him, understand the depth of his love for her. Then Sam's scent overwhelmed Ruth, and she was wet. She gripped him, pulling him towards her, grinding her pelvis against his. They both kissed each other on the face and the neck, but when he tried to kiss her on the lips, she looked down instead and unbuckled his slacks. He was growing hard. HARD. This was what confused her. She forced herself not to think of the incongruity. Instead, she shoved his hand down her shorts so he could feel how much she wanted him, and she grabbed hold of his warm, throbbing manhood, which felt so good, so much like some phantom appendage of her own, so like the way things used to be. Then she let him jerk her panties to the side, and she let him slip into her, there under the heavens and the very eyes of God himself.

The Queen

Ruth was eleven years old when Trudy's health began to fail in a noticeable way. It wasn't that she was suddenly sick all the time, so much as it was that walking home from church and work seemed to take Trudy longer, and those rides she had refused years before, when Ruth still had her milk teeth, were now accepted. As they sat to watch movies and baseball, Trudy fell asleep faster and napped more extensively. She would forget small things like locking the front door in the morning or turning off the oven in the evening. It was perfect, in a way, how Ruth was now more capable just as Trudy was faltering. Their roles of caretaker and case had begun the switch. Not that Trudy was genuinely incapacitated by any stretch, but without a doubt, in less than a season, Ruth had quietly begun to pick up the feeble crumbs Trudy accidentally and unknowingly started to leave in her wake.

What was most jarring to Ruth was Trudy's lack of desire to converse. For years she and her grandmother had spoken at length about so many details of their lives together that when Trudy began to retreat into deeper, more sustained silences, Ruth worried about Trudy in a profound way, and she also started to worry about herself. *What would become of her if Trudy passed on? Who would she tell? Where would she live?* When Ruth pressed Trudy on what might be expected if her health failed, Trudy would laugh Ruth off, and tell her she wasn't leaving this world anytime soon unless God himself came down to earth and dragged her to heaven. Lordy, no! She would live to see Ruth married and have kids of her own, maybe even see Ruth's kids have kids. The idyllic dioramas of their future that were constructed for Ruth from

Trudy's imagination were wondrous, but unfortunately more and more implausible as Trudy seemed to shrink back from this life into some past one. Ruth wondered if perhaps it was a life where she and Dexter were still rebel lovers, dancing in the dark of his '60s apartment to jazz songs crooned out from the speakers of an old radio. Sometimes, Ruth would hear Trudy talking as though Dexter was there with her. It was little things she heard Trudy share with the ghost of him, pestering like only a doting wife could. It was beautiful in a way, the mental deterioration of age bringing back a friend who could help ease Trudy on into the next stage of existence after this one. Still, Ruth worried and planned for the worst case scenario despite Trudy's insistence that she was fine. Ruth thought about who she would call in case of an emergency, how she would pay bills, remain in the house, and just . . . stay alive.

Even with all of Ruth's imagined strategies ready to go, there were honestly few options when it came to taking care of herself or Trudy if some darkness were to befall them. So, church and Ruth's relationship with God became everything. More and more she found herself praying, and more and more she turned to the Bible for heavenly guidance on matters of the earth. Her favorite stories were those of the Old Testament heroines like Queen Esther who schemed with her uncle Mordechai to marry King Achashverosh in order to save the Jewish people—Esther's people—from extermination. Or there was Miriam, the older sister of Moses, who saved him and God's chosen people by her quick thinking after Moses was discovered floating in the reeds by the princess of Egypt. Even after reading the story numerous times, Ruth still felt goose pimples when she read about the sly Israelite Yael who seduced a captain of the Canaanite forces and drove a rod through his head in order to bring a quick end to the slaying of the Israeli army. On and on accounts were written of women chosen by God to do spectacular things—to save His people. In ways, Rahab the Prostitute, who helped Joshua capture the city of Jericho, and Mary of Nazareth, who bore baby Jesus, became Ruth's maternal life guides, inspiring her to think on her feet, to prepare for the worst, to be wise even in the most testing moments.

Ruth's real mother, Florence, had appeared throughout her childhood now and then like a rainbow full of color and promise only to dim and disappear before one could pin her down to a fixed position. Because of this fragile yet charged quality with which Florence existed in her life, Ruth had never taken Florence very seriously as her parent or even as a person. It was never known when Florence would waft through the door of Ruth and Trudy's craftsman, and it was never known when she would drift back out. By the time Ruth was twelve, she had only spent a couple weeks with her mother over the course of her entire life, and in truth, those times seemed more like mirages than actual memories.

For her part, Trudy never demeaned Florence while she was visiting or after she went AWOL once again, nor did she try to sway Florence from her transient ways. Trudy could not, for the life of her, figure out why Florence turned out the way she had. Instead of fighting against this enigma with no discernible prize for winning, Trudy simply accepted Florence as she was—a study in an unanchored life. Florence was the ultimate hippy who, so far as Trudy knew, made her way through existence without a possession to her name. Perhaps the way Trudy looked at her daughter was the healthiest way in which she *could* see her; it was the way in which, if Ruth ever came to need Florence or Florence needed Ruth, they could approach one another without a lifetime of grievances that would keep them at arm's length. At least this is what Ruth came to realize when, on a Sunday afternoon in the spring of '93, Ruth discovered Trudy unconscious on the floor of the craftsman's kitchen.

The scene Ruth happened upon was inevitable, the oozing fracture in Trudy's forehead, the blood splattered against the green cabinets and pooled on the yellow tiled floor like red pigment from a dropped paint can, the cut crystal casserole dish Trudy had been drying to put away smashed and scattered around her body like diamonds, the queer pose of Trudy's arms and legs, her spine curled back as she lay sprawled out like a dead bird, her white silk slip showing under her mint-green dress. It was a scene Ruth had become so accustomed to preparing for in her imagination, when she saw the real thing, she was almost non-plussed. It had finally happened, she thought. Trudy was gone. Ruth was now alone in the world.

First things first, Ruth lowered her grandmother's dress over the exposed slip. Then she shook Trudy ever so slightly. "Grandma? Grandma?" There was no answer except the foreboding way the dead weight of Trudy's body responded to Ruth's touch. Yes, this was the moment Ruth had been visualizing so that she could handle it with wisdom and confidence like one of her Biblical heroines, so she could save herself from an uncertain and potentially dreadful future.

Ruth went to the phone, dialed 9-1-1, and waited for the operator to answer. When he did, Ruth calmly explained what had happened, but for a moment the operator didn't believe what Ruth told him. She was too calm, he said. Was she sure what she had described truly occurred? That's when Ruth lost it. "YES!" She balled into the phone. "She's dead! She's dead! Please come help me!" Ruth cried out. Instantly, the operator changed his patronizing tone and assured Ruth an ambulance was on its way. When he asked if she was alone, she told him a lie. Her mother was gone to the grocery store and would be home soon. And this was the story she stuck to when the EMTs arrived at the house to take Trudy's body away. Ruth would wait for her mother to come home. That's what her mother had told her to do. The EMTs, a muscled guy in his twenties and an overweight man in his forties, weren't sure they should leave a twelve-year-old girl all by herself, but Ruth was insistent. Not interested in arguing with a child, the EMTs agreed to leave Ruth be, but they assured her the police would drop in soon for a statement, and Ruth's mother would need to be home or the cops would take Ruth into protective custody. Ruth assured the men she would relay the message to her mother, and the EMTs left.

Suddenly, the house was quiet and terrifying. The shadowless light of foggy dusk stared through the windows ominously, and every creak of the wood floor or rattle of glass in the front window was foreboding. Ruth first went to the kitchen to wipe up the blood and glass. It's what her grandmother would have told her needed to be done before anything else. "Always keep things tidy" was a Trudy maxim. Ruth tried not to think about the reality of the crimson she squeezed out of the dishcloth each time she rinsed it in the sink after mopping the floor. And she tried not to cry as she swept up the tiny fractured pieces of the cut crystal dish that had scattered everywhere. When the kitchen was finally back in order, and all signs of the tragedy scrubbed away, Ruth went into her grandmother's room. The bed was made, and the contents on top of the dresser were organized the way Trudy liked them.

Trudy's room still smelled of her, and a lump swelled in Ruth's throat. She would breakdown now. She would curl up on her grandmother's bed and cry until the police came and took her away to some home for kids with no parents. No. NO! Ruth stopped herself from getting emotional. She swallowed back the ball blocking her windpipe.

It felt like trespassing to open Trudy's dresser. Still, it was necessary. In the top drawer Ruth knew she would find Trudy's address book. It was something Trudy kept up with precision, a leather-bound diary of names, birthdays, addresses, and telephone numbers the size of a long novel. Like a history of Trudy's life, it was a scribbling of signposts towards everyone Trudy held close at one point or another.

As Ruth cracked open the ancient ledger, she could quickly deduce which acquaintances had stayed in one place and which ones had been transient by the fade of the ink in which their information had been scrawled with Trudy's beautiful looped penmanship, marked out, and then rewritten.

Ruth fingered through the pages carefully. She was looking for one name in particular—that of her mother, Florence Kuhn. In her mind, Ruth had practiced the conversation she would have with Florence. She would tell the truth that Trudy had passed away, but Ruth would assure Florence everything was okay; Ruth had it all under control. Still, Ruth would suggest that Florence come back to DC and help arrange the funeral. Being only twelve, Ruth obviously couldn't take care of the matter herself. However, she would convince Florence the ordeal wouldn't be a burden, and when the funeral was over, Florence could go back to wherever she had come from, and Ruth would continue to take care of herself and live in her and Trudy's home alone. It was a plan whose success hinged on Florence consenting to each of Ruth's proposals without much thought, something Ruth believed with the right words could potentially be achieved. After all, Florence had left home when she was very young and had taken care of herself just fine. Why couldn't Ruth do the same now? She would need Florence to come back for the funeral though. She would need her to assure the police she was Ruth's full-time guardian. Florence would only need to play along, and then, she could leave just like she always had without another thought or care for anything, least of all Ruth.

When Ruth reached the tab for "K," she slowly flipped through the next pages distinctly aware she might not find her mother's name at all. Just like Florence had never possessed much by way of material things, she wasn't sure Florence had ever possessed an actual address or a telephone number with which she could be reached. Then Ruth found it, the Florence Kuhn page—or at least that's what it seemed to be—two pages, in fact. There was address after address, telephone number after telephone number, dates of duration of stay, names of various contacts at each address. It was much like Trudy's dead body, the thing Ruth knew she would find—a total and complete mess. Luckily, as with all the other contacts in Trudy's address book, old addresses had been struck out, and the new addresses were updated in fresh ink. The final three possible locations for Ruth's mother looked as though they had been scrawled out in the last year or two: Roanoke, North Carolina; Truth or Consequences, New Mexico; or Coronado, California. Along with each address there was a contact name, and with two of the addresses there were also telephone numbers. What had been sadness choking Ruth's throat now became a throttling of nerves.

Night had fallen completely at some point, but there was something about the deep dark of the house with no lights on that comforted Ruth, that made her feel secure like she was camouflaged from anything that could harm her as she left Trudy's room, made her way to the kitchen, and pulled up a chair next to the phone. For a moment she sat there, her mind blank—too many emotions to find just one to lean into. Then she picked up the receiver and dialed the number listed next to what seemed to be her mother's most recent known place of residence. As Ruth took a breath and tried to focus, instead of a ring on the other end of the line, she was met with an alarm blaring into her ear and the words of a pre-recorded operator, "The number you have dialed is no longer in service." Ruth quickly silenced the stomach-churning sounds coming from the phone and dialed the number once more. Maybe she had dialed incorrectly. Once again, however, there was the repeating electric alarm and the irritatingly calm voice of the operator, "The number you have dialed is no longer in service." This time Ruth was a bit slower to hang up, thinking maybe somehow a miracle would occur and someone would break through the distressing signal to say, "Hello." But, of course, that didn't happen.

Ruth sucked in a deep breath and dialed the number listed above the previous one. It appeared to be an older number, but it was all she had. And this time, it rang through. She had no idea who would pick up on the other end, but it was ringing, and that—at least for a moment— gave her hope.

A harried man's voice answered, "Dan's Bar."

"Uh, my name is Ruth Kuhn. I'm calling from D.C.—" but Ruth was cut short by the man who sounded irritated.

"Uh, I think you've got the wrong number young lady."

"PLEASE!" Ruth calmed herself. "Please, I'm looking for my mom. Her name is Florence Kuhn. This is the only number I got." A tear dripped down Ruth's cheek, but she tried her best to ignore the desperation threatening to upend her.

There was a long beat on the other end of the line.

"Hello?" Ruth asked, voice quaking.

The man sighed a heavy, resigned sigh. "Yeah, I'm here."

"My grandma passed away today, and I need to find my mom. She would . . . She needs to know," Ruth explained.

Another silence and Ruth wondered if she was making any sense at all.

"I haven't seen your mom in a year or so darlin'," the man said, his voice losing the irritated tone and wrapping Ruth in the comfort of someone who seemed to care about her plight, maybe someone who had experienced her plight himself on some level.

"Would you know anyone who might have an idea where she might be," Ruth asked.

"How old are you, darlin'?"

Now it was Ruth's turn to pause, considering her answer and the possible outcomes of it. She decided maybe telling the truth to the stranger on the other end of the line might engender some sympathy and perhaps more eagerness to help her. "I'm twelve," Ruth managed to get out.

"You all by yourself?"

Once again, Ruth considered her answer. What would Queen Esther say? "Yeah," Ruth finally ventured.

"Lord help you," the man said. "Look, I can't promise you anything, little lady. Your mom . . . she's . . . she's hard to track down even when she's right in front of you."

Ruth nodded but didn't say anything.

"I know a couple guys who were friends of hers. Maybe . . . Maybe they might know something. Is there a number where I can reach you back?"

Ruth thought about giving the man her number and couldn't see how it would hurt anything. So, she relayed it to him.

"I'm sorry for your loss," he offered.

"Thank you," Ruth said.

"You take care of yourself, little lady. You call a neighbor or something to come look after you."

"Okay," Ruth lied.

"Okay," the man agreed.

After a beat, the line went dead. Ruth sat with the earpiece cradled against her chest not wanting to give up, not wanting to let go of the only other person in the world who knew her desperate secret and who seemed sympathetic to it. She considered the man's advice about calling a neighbor. She thought about the members of the church who she and Trudy considered friends, but she ruled out contacting any of them. They might only follow the orders of the law and turn her over to child services, and that, she could not allow to happen. She'd heard the stories of Oliver Twist and Orphan Annie. She knew what happened to kids in "the system" as Trudy called it. Trudy and Ruth had talked at length about those "poor kids" in their neighborhood whose parents were "addicts" and "alcoholics" and "ne'erdowells," who were put in "the system" to protect them. But the system didn't protect them, Trudy assured Ruth. The system was bad.

Suddenly, the earpiece sounded the alarm that the phone was off-the-hook, and needed to be placed back in its cradle. So, Ruth put it back. She was exhausted. She laid down on the cold tile floor. She wanted to pray. In her head, she knew she needed to pray, to ask God to help her fix things, but it was as though she couldn't form the words—she was too tired. And before she even realized it, she was asleep.

Crank

Despite having sex with Sam, Ruth knew when it was over, nothing was better between them. Instead, they simply held one another in silence, knowing the moment they began talking, their words would almost certainly devolve into criticism and conflict—the only way they communicated these days. As quickly as the spell had seemed cast over them—that had inclined them to get naked and have intercourse—they were back in reality, shamefully pulling on their clothes, the distance between them once more making them the awkward strangers they had recently become.

As they walked back to the house, the sky waxed silver and a summer breeze whispered past their salty bodies, Ruth wondered if a storm would blow in, a tornado perhaps? Maybe God would smite them for their hedonism. Maybe he should obliterate them like Sodom and Gomorrah. In times past, she would have asked Sam his thoughts on the weather, and she would have probably agreed with whatever he postulated. They used to agree about everything. Instead, she saw the cabin in the distance and dreaded the thought of going back to it and the farmhouse and Naomi and Joe and even her own children.

"We need to take a look at that rental tomorrow," Ruth told Sam. "You got his card, right—the realtor?"

Sam nodded. "Yeah." He produced the card from his suit coat pocket as if to prove so.

"I can't stay on this farm much longer," Ruth shuttered.

The next morning, after dropping off Rachel to help Mike with his bees, Sam and Ruth arrived at Delmer Green's Realty Office which was tucked into a small storefront just off Conway's town square. The brass bell over the front door jangled on cue as they entered the rather unimpressive space that smelled like burnt hair to find a middle-aged woman, who was no stranger to makeup, sitting behind a desk talking on the phone.

"Oh, they're here. I'll call you back," the woman whispered before hanging up and turning to Sam and Ruth. "Mornin'," she said brightly.

"Mr. Green here?" Sam questioned.

"Delmer said to tell you he'd be right along," the lady assured them.

"You have a restroom?" Sam asked.

"Right at the back there." The lady pointed towards the dark end of the office with one of her extra-long nails, an impressive pink talon that matched her earrings and bracelets.

Sam headed for the restroom, and Ruth took a seat on an old, maroon chair next to a potted plant with rusted tips.

"I'm Susan," the receptionist said.

"Ruth."

Susan blushed just slightly. "I know who y'all are. I've seen you on TV a few times. I always liked you. You seem like good people."

Ruth looked down at her hands. This was why the immoral acts Sam had indulged in held such shame for her; people had admired Sam, admired her too—at least they used to. Ruth forced a smile. "Well, we appreciate that."

"Look, I know it ain't my place to say nothin'," Susan lowered her voice and leaned forward conspiratorially, "but I know how it is."

Ruth cautiously peered up at Susan unsure what she might possibly be getting at.

Susan lowered her voice even more. "Crank will make you do all kinds of crazy things."

Ruth attempted to hide her shock at Susan's overtness.

"You do it even one time, good chance you'll be addicted the rest of your life. I seen it happen to plenty of folks. Done it myself, to be honest. Lost my kids and my husband before the whole ordeal was through. That was about five years ago."

Ruth didn't know what to say, the honesty of Susan's statement brought to the surface one of the most disturbing details of Sam's affair with Red that Ruth still couldn't fully comprehend—the crystal meth it was revealed Sam and Red had consumed at each of their encounters. *Crystal meth!* There it was in every single one of the accounts of Sam's great fall. Even while she could somehow get her mind around the fact he had slept with another man, it seemed impossible Sam would have consumed illicit drugs. The closest Ruth had ever come to partaking in any illegal substance was drawing a toke from one of her mother's joints, but it had burned her lungs so badly, she never entertained the thought of going anywhere near illegal drugs again. And she hadn't. For his part, Sam didn't deny snorting the crystal meth, but he had brushed it off as just another unsavory element of the original sin he had committed.

Susan picked up a small, heart-shaped frame from her desk and turned it to Ruth with a lovesick smile. "Sadie and Lula are my baby's names. I miss 'em. Doubt they'd even know who I am nowadays." The photo was of two young girls, who looked to be around five and six, dressed in matching blue skirts, white turtle necks, and red sweaters, enthusiastically embracing.

"You haven't stayed in touch?" Ruth asked.

"My ex told me to keep my distance. He said I'd just confuse 'em. He's probably right. They were so young when everything happened. They'd probably just accuse me of messin' up their lives if I showed back up, now," Susan said, placing the framed photo back on her desk with a defeated sadness in her eyes that Ruth understood.

Ruth sighed, "They'll probably accuse you of messing up their lives no matter what you do. Trust me." Then Ruth added a bit of hope, something a month ago she would have said to a suffering congregant without a second thought. "Children are a blessing from the Lord. Psalms one-hundred-twenty-seven, verse three. Can't imagine anything would keep me from mine."

Susan looked at Ruth with a beaming smile. "Yep. You always seemed like good people on TV. Bet you still are. It's just that crank. It'll make you do crazy things."

Interrupting the moment, Delmer walked in the door of the office just as Sam was returning from the bathroom. "Sorry, I'm late. Y'all ready to get to it?"

The residence of the former Fort Wood family that sat half a mile down Hassick Road on the outskirts of Conway was about what Ruth expected it to be, a two-story house that looked like just another one of the vinyl-sided, faux bricked, cheap suburban homes popping up everywhere nowadays.

"It needs a bit of clean up," Delmer said, motioning to the overgrown, two-acre lawn as Sam and Ruth stepped out of their Escalade and joined him at the front door.

The inside of the house matched the outside. Everything was new but also cheap. It was spacious. Each of the kids could have their own room, and there was a master with a soaking tub that looked out over the back yard and the forest beyond.

"The river is just down the hill there," Delmer said as they entered the open concept kitchen. "Perfect for fishing and swimming if you like that sorta thing."

"The kids would love it." Ruth smiled, even as she ran her fingers over the granite counter top noticing how poorly the seams of two different pieces of granite had been joined. She had become well versed at noticing the details of things. It was in the details you could tell if something was quality or not, especially in buildings. Where the joints didn't quite perfectly kiss, the walls weren't straight and clean, or the grout and tile wasn't smooth and level on the surfaces, one could only imagine how poorly constructed the pieces out of sight might be.

Delmer moved over to a single French door that led to a large deck. "I know I probably sound crazy to ya'll, but what I can't figure out is why anyone *wouldn't* want to live around here? I mean, the only traffic you have is the McGuire's cows crossin' the road in the mornin', and every night instead of city lights, you got fireflies dancin' in your back yard." Delmer sighed. "Anyway, the cabinets are all solid oak, not veneer, and that granite is from a quarry up near Sulfur Springs."

Ruth couldn't help but admire Delmer's body leaned against the back door. She wondered what it would be like to kiss a man with a mustache. "Doesn't it get a little too quiet?" She asked.

Delmer looked at Ruth, grinned. "Ah, sometimes it does. For sure. But no place is perfect." Then he nodded to where Sam stood, looking into the darkened fridge. "The appliances are all top of the line stainless steel. It's a great deal for this area, at least if this is the size of place you're lookin' for."

Sam closed the door on the fridge. "No, you're right. It's great."

Ruth moved over to the cheap stainless steel sink. "I can't imagine what our other house would rent for around here," she mused.

"Big?" Delmer asked.

Ruth didn't answer. She was suddenly irked that she was even looking for another home.

"You sell it?" Delmer ventured.

Ruth looked pointedly at Sam. "It belonged to the church."

There was suddenly an uncomfortable silence. Delmer sucked in a deep breath. "Why don't we check out the back porch. It's got a view of the river." Delmer opened the French door and headed out of the house into the humid morning.

Ruth was about to follow him when Sam gently laid his hand on her's. "You could . . ." But Ruth snatched her hand away from his, and Sam didn't go on.

"What?" Ruth asked.

Sam averted his eyes. "It's just . . . Well, our situation . . . I know you can't . . . I just . . . I can see that you like him . . . Delmer . . . And, I . . ."

Ruth cut her eyes at Sam hoping he wasn't trying to imply something as ridiculous as the idea that since he'd had his fun, she could have hers. "What?" She hissed.

"If you want him . . ." Sam finally managed, "I would understand."

There it was. Ruth was incensed that Sam had placed her into the same debased category as him—someone to whom sex mattered more than her commitment to her marriage. Then simultaneously she was thrilled. She *did* deserve to do whatever she wanted. She deserved to make him mad with jealousy, to make him suffer the way she had. Not that she would ever do what he had done, even with permission. Sure, she liked the way Delmer Green looked in his jeans and his flannel shirts, and she had even let herself imagine him in small ways she never would have allowed weeks ago, but to follow through on those desires, that was unconscionable.

Suddenly, there were tears in Ruth's eyes as she looked at Sam who stared weakly at the ceramic floor tiles in this pathetic excuse of a house. Then without stating what she was doing, Ruth walked out the front door, loaded up in the Cadillac, and drove away.

She didn't turn on the radio. She didn't care if she could find her way back to the Christianson farm. She just wanted to be alone, to drive, to feel like she was doing something. Forward momentum. But forward to what? While tears over the last few weeks had run down her cheeks in concern for her kids and her marriage and in fear for the black hole she seemed to be swallowed up in, now the tears fell just for her—like when Trudy had passed away, and she had found herself all alone in that little craftsman in DC with no hope. She pitied herself then, and she pitied herself now. She deserved better than this. She had done everything right. She had been a good girl, and she had grown into an even better woman. *Why? Why was this happening to her?*

Ruth knew she was playing the victim and playing the victim never got anyone anywhere as her mother Florence taught her quite thoroughly. But at the moment it felt good to wallow in it, and that's what she wanted to do. Forget making decisions. Forget the right thing. She wanted to sleep, to disappear, to let someone else be in charge. Then just like when Trudy died, Ruth stopped herself from feeling pity for her circumstances. She had to make a plan, and she had to stick with that plan, and all would be well again. *But what should that plan be? Should she leave Sam and demand custody of the kids? Where would she go? What would she do for money? Sure, they had saved a bit, but they had put so much of their cash back into the church and their ministry, believing it would return to them later ten-and-twenty-fold. She would need a lawyer. Did she need a lawyer in Missouri or one in South Carolina or both? Should she tell Sam what she was planning or spring it on him as so much had been sprung on her?*

With the fierce crunch of gravel against asphalt and rubber, Ruth pulled the Cadillac onto the shoulder of the road and threw open the door. She vomited all over the blue-black tar of the highway, and even after the watery bits had emptied from her stomach, she was still dry heaving, clinging to the door of the Escalade for balance. When the wave of sickness had finally passed, Ruth wiped her mouth with the back of her hand and made sure there was nothing on her pants or shoes before, once again, she climbed into the driver's seat. But this time, she leaned her head back against the headrest, closing her eyes.

"Dear Lord God, I'm so lost. I literally don't know what to do. I'm scared, and I'm confused." Then, she stopped. Start by saying what you are grateful for, Ruth thought. This was something she had learned from her Sunday school teacher, Peggy Pengrasse.

"Don't get down on your knees and start telling God everything you want Him to do for you. He's supposed to be your friend. You're supposed to have a relationship. What would happen if every time you saw your friends, you immediately started begging them for things? Well, God doesn't want to just hear your wants," Ruth could hear Miss Pengrasse say. "And God also doesn't want you talking all the time. Sometimes, He wants for you to sit and listen to Him."

Ruth took a breath and tried to start over. "Jesus, I'm so thankful for my kids. I'm so grateful they are healthy and strong. I'm grateful that we have a roof over our heads, and I'm so happy that . . . " Once again, Ruth stopped.

The silence in the car was deafening, the soundproofing of the vehicle superbly holding back the reality of the world outside. Ruth imagined the quiet rating of the Cadillac being a question on one of the surveys car companies sent out three months after your purchase. How would you rate the soundproofing of your vehicle: (1) is poor, (5) is excellent.

She hit a button and lowered all the windows on the Cadillac allowing the thick, ripe summer air to infiltrate the otherwise sterile environment. Along with the rush of heat came the sound of the trees rustling in the breeze, a woodpecker drilling away somewhere in the distance, the usual cicadas vibrating their timbals, and crickets stridulating as though their lives depended on it. *Was this God's voice?* Ruth wondered. *Was this Him speaking to her through this symphony of nature in HD surround sound? It certainly wasn't the voice in her head which she attributed to Him. But what was that voice really—the one muffled and lodged deep in the back of her mind? Maybe that was just her voice, and she had simply learned to disassociate herself so perfectly from it over the years, she now took it unquestionably and erroneously as the musing of some higher power.*

Instantly Ruth felt guilty. *What was she saying? God wasn't real? His voice was merely her inner voice? NO! God was real! He was most certainly real! She knew beyond a shadow of a doubt that He was. She was simply exhausted. That's all this damning line of questions was, an attack from Satan on her moment of weakness to make her distrust what was eternally true!* There had been a constant war since the beginning of time between God and the Devil for the souls of man, and while she had always been one of the strongest warriors in the battle for heaven's glory, Ruth knew Satan's goal was to trip you up, to make you weak, to make you question, to cause you to lose faith. Then he had you. *Satan was a trickster*, Ruth reminded herself. Then, another thought struck her, something she had never conceived of before. It was an awful thought she wanted gone as soon as it appeared in her mind. It was the idea that maybe after all these years her atheist mother was right. *Maybe there was no great holy war raging amongst the spirits unseen. Maybe there was no heaven or hell. Maybe there was no Satan. Maybe there was no . . . God.*

"No," Ruth said out loud, as if to stop the tsunami of hysteria in her mind. For good measure, she pushed the ignition button on the Cadillac, threw it into gear, and jerked it back out onto the open road. At first, she drove with the windows down. It was nice, letting the balmy wind whip at her hair. She felt like a rebel. She felt alive. Then, once more, it hit her. This reckless abandon was something her mother would have preferred. So, Ruth rolled up the windows, sealing herself shut from the life outside her perfect leather and fiberglass bubble, and she drove down the stretch of road before her in silence.

The Family Thing

It had been two days since Trudy's passing when someone rapped hard on the front door of the craftsman. Ruth was in the middle of brushing her teeth when she heard the noise she had been awaiting shatter the stillness of the otherwise deathly silent house. She carefully, quietly spat out the toothpaste in her mouth and moved over to the doorway of the bathroom, listening intently into the hall for the sound to be repeated. Sure enough, it soon was. Ruth waited for the jangle of keys or a voice to announce who was trying to get in, but neither came. Just another hard series of knocks—knuckles against wood—sharp and eager. Then . . . nothing.

Ruth rinsed off her toothbrush and put it back in its holder next to the sink, cleaned off the counter with a hand towel, and tiptoed back to Trudy's room where she slipped into the cubby she had created for herself under Trudy's bed—a dark protected place where an intruder couldn't easily find her. Ruth punched her pillow up into a ball for her head and scraped together the quilt around her to keep her warm. Then she reached into the darkness until she found the thick, weighted presence of Trudy's Bible lying on the floor. Scarred black cover with onion-thin, cream-colored pages, Trudy's Bible had been handed down from Dexter's forbearers, and when he died, Trudy had become its custodian. The words "HOLY BIBLE," which had once been gloriously emblazoned with gold leaf on the cover, could now hardly be made out, and the edges of the onion thin pages, which were once bright red like the blood of Christ, were now salmon-pink faded by time. Inside, different colors of ink and various styles of handwriting had meticulously recorded the names and dates of birth of all of Dexter's extended family going back as far as their crossing to America from Germany. And on the proceeding pages were the names of Trudy's family, though their ancestry dated back only two generations.

Ruth nuzzled the Bible close and thought about how it would keep her safe. "Put on the full armor of God," Ruth remembered hearing in one of her Sunday school classes. "Jesus is the way, the truth, and the light," was another mnemonic that gave Ruth comfort. God was watching out for her. "God knows the names of every sparrow that falls from the sky."

It was hours later when Ruth woke up with a start. Instead of knocking this time, she heard glass shattering on the tile floor in the kitchen, hushed voices, and then someone opened the back door and was inside. Whoever had broken in wasn't particularly stealthy or perhaps wasn't trying to be quiet. Ruth imagined the trespassers were a couple of the poor homeless folks she and Trudy would occasionally pass on their way to church whom Trudy taught her to look at with "compassionate caution." Trudy warned when they would see one of the vagabonds curled up on the sidewalk that perhaps they were simply sleeping off a rough night, but it was also possible they were dangerous because they were on drugs.

Ruth attempted to silence her breathing as she listened to the footfalls in the kitchen, but in doing so, she could hear her heartbeat pounding in her head so loudly she felt like it was reverberating off the walls of the house like a hammer. There was no way she wouldn't be discovered.

From what Ruth could tell, there were two intruders. One was a woman, and one was a man. They talked as they made their way through the house room by room seemingly taking stock of the place before making any move to steal something. When they reached Ruth's bedroom, she heard them going through her drawers and looking in her closet. She imagined her room: mint-green walls, white lace bedspread, cream and gold dresser against one wall with a pink jewelry box sitting on top that, when opened, played "Baby Mine" for a tiny twirling ballet dancer inside. Ruth heard it, "Baby Mine." Ruth's mind raced through all the keepsakes she had hidden inside her jewelry box and grew angry imagining whomever the intruders were taking even a single item. Almost as soon as the song had started, the box had been closed again. Then, Ruth heard a word that sounded familiar but completely foreign at the same time, "Ruth?" Ruth tried to decipher the word being called out. She heard it again, "Ruth?"

Ruth knew the word—her name—and she knew the voice of the woman who was calling it. But, instead of moving out from under the bed to go to her long lost mother, Ruth laid there on the floor under the bed in shock. She was saved. Florence had come. She would not be an orphan. She would not have to live alone. But these thoughts of deliverance were halted when Florence entered Trudy's bedroom with the other person—the man—and sat down on the bed right over Ruth's head.

"Who knows what's happened to her." Ruth heard Florence say, irritated.

"What do you want to do?" the man asked.

There was no response, but Ruth could hear her mother lie back on the bed just inches above her. There was the sound of cloth and leather against skin as the man took off his clothes. There was more squeaking of the bed as Ruth's mother and the man laid down together. At first they were quiet, and Ruth wondered if she should say something, alert them to her presence. Before she could gather her resolve, she heard her mother moan and a little laugh from the man. Soon the bed was squeaking again as it seemed her mother and the man were trying to find a more comfortable position in which to rest. But the squeaking grew louder and louder and more and more intense. And suddenly, Ruth heard her mother whimper so emphatically, it sent nightmarish images shooting up Ruth's spine to her mind of her mother being hurt by the man. Ruth imagined blood dripping over the sides of the bed as the bed began to rock and the man could be heard whispering, "Fuck, yeah! You like that, you fucking bitch?"

Ruth didn't know what to do, but she couldn't let her mother die! She would have to think quick to save her mother's life. Before Ruth could come up with a plan, she heard her mother wailing louder and louder as though the life were being choked out of her, and that was it! Ruth charged out from beneath the bed, her face flushed in anger, tears streaming from her eyes. "Stop it! Stop killing her!" Ruth screamed.

But across from Ruth, there was no grisly murder scene. Instead, there were two naked people, her mother and a blonde-haired, blue-eyed man on top of her, both pale with shock at Ruth's sudden appearance. For a moment they all stared at each other. Then Ruth turned and ran, disappearing into her room, slamming the door behind her.

Inside her room, Ruth curled up against the far wall and cried to herself. *What was going on? Everything was backward. Nothing made sense.* She kept seeing her mother and the man there on Trudy's bed, her mother's bare breasts, his round backside, and the hair—the wiry hair—that lead down below where they were joined together.

There was a knock on Ruth's bedroom door. "Ruth? Baby?" Ruth didn't answer. Florence appeared in nothing but what looked like a man's flannel shirt. Florence approached Ruth with what Ruth could only think of as "compassionate caution." "Ruth, it's your momma," Florence said. She sat down on the floor across from Ruth. "You remember me, right?"

The man appeared in the doorframe of the room next: no shirt, no underwear, buttoning up the last button on his jeans, concern on his face. He had a mustache, Ruth realized.

"That's Kenny," Florence said.

"Hey." Kenny nodded and made a little wave.

Ruth looked at Florence. "What were you doing in there?"

Florence sighed, smiled a slight smile. "You know what sex is?"

Ruth shook her head.

Florence sucked in a deep breath, rolled her eyes. She looked at Kenny begging him to help get her out of this uncomfortable moment. He just grinned. Florence sighed again, looked back at Ruth. "Sometimes, sex helps people feel better." Then, she asked, "You hungry?"

Ruth nodded.

Florence stood up. "Great. Let's go get somethin' to eat."

In a padded blue booth at an almost empty White Castle, Ruth sat devouring one of three mini-burgers Florence and Kenny had bought for her while they both drank sodas and stared at her with eyes fearful of what her existence meant to their own.

"I'm glad you called Dan when you did. Can't believe he took the time to track me down." Florence lit a cigarette. "How did you have his number?"

"Grandma had it," Ruth said.

"Well, I'm glad you had the sense to call him and tell him what was going on—real smart of you. We're gonna take care of your grandma's remains and do a proper burial and all that. Don't know where I'm gonna get the money, but we'll figure it out. I'm sure Trudy had something stashed away."

Ruth said nothing.

"You got a little ketchup on your chin there, kid," Kenny said and wiped at his own chin to demonstrate the spot Ruth needed to swab.

Ruth wiped the spot, and sure enough, a smear of ketchup was left on her napkin. She liked Kenny. While Florence always seemed like she was trying to be effortlessly cool and relaxed, Kenny was. He was clearly younger than Florence too, though Ruth couldn't tell by how many years. He had a way with Florence that managed her like a lion tamer in the circus manages an unpredictable beast, getting her to do things, even things she didn't like, with relative ease and not much more than a little growl here or there.

"We're gonna move into the house and try and do the whole family thing long as we can," Florence sighed. "But, don't go expecting me to take care of you the way Trudy did. I ain't no momma, and I never wanted to be. I'm sure you know that."

"Hey now," Kenny scolded gently.

"I'm just sayin'. I'm already stressed out enough as it is. I don't want everybody placing expectations on me about how I need to act and behave. I don't cook. I don't clean. I don't coddle."

"Then what do you do?" Ruth asked innocently.

"I'm a thinker. I need time to come up with ideas and thoughts. People like me, we're here to show the world how things ought to be."

"How should they be?" Ruth asked.

"Well, the government should get out of everybody's fucking business for one thing. And second, people need to free themselves of the shackles of traditional roles like being moms and dads and husbands and wives and little girls."

Ruth took Florence in dubiously, and she wondered if Florence was genuinely sold on the bill of goods she was offering. "I'd like to go to church tomorrow morning," Ruth said.

"Church? No! Absolutely not. The church is worse than everybody else combined!" Florence huffed.

"I have friends there. I like it there," Ruth said.

"The church has never done a thing for anybody other than fill their heads with garbage, assuring perfectly good people their very nature is evil, and they won't be happy unless they abandon everything that makes them human in order to follow some absurd moral code made up by white men thousands of years ago to keep the world repressed, all the while adding to their coffers."

"What are coffers?" Ruth asked.

Kenny interjected, "Babe, if she likes church, what's a little Sunday school gonna hurt?"

"That's how it starts, innocent enough, with a little Sunday school. And before you know it, you're hooked. You're giving them everything you make and living your life for some ridiculous patriarchal rules that will supposedly get you into heaven."

"But what's wrong with heaven?" Ruth asked sincerely.

"Heaven is made up, baby! Do you really think there's a place lined with streets of gold and mansions for everyone? That's crazy talk. If there is a heaven, and I assure you there is not, it would be so far out of our realm of understanding you wouldn't even be able to describe it, kinda like God. You know there are like five thousand different religions in the world. Five thousand! And every single one of those religions thinks their God is the one! Mohamed, Jehovah, Christ, Shiva, Buddha. You name it. Don't be ridiculous, Ruth. I know your grandma loved the church, but now that I'm here to take care of you, church is out of the question."

Ruth was devastated by her mother's edict, but Ruth thought maybe she should allow Florence to settle in. This was whole new territory for all of them, and maybe after a while, Florence would see that the church Ruth loved was not her enemy or out to destroy Ruth's humanity or anybody else's as Florence had proclaimed. Ruth resolved that she would still pray and read her Bible, but she would do so secretly in order not to rock the boat. She needed Florence to look after her otherwise she'd be an orphan. And that, she suspected, would be worse than any hell the Bible proposed. Besides, on their way home from White Castle that very day, Kenny suggested they find Ruth a kitten, a friend she could have to replace her acquaintances at church. Despite initial hesitance from Florence, they eventually found a pet store where Ruth was allowed to pick out the kitten of her choice and bring her home to be part of the "whole family thing" as Florence resentfully put it.

Custard was the name Ruth came up with for her blonde-haired tabby who purred astonishingly loud when Ruth pet her. Even Florence quickly grew fond of Custard, whose sweet blue eyes were trusting and bright. Custard would have to be housebroken, Florence said. And that feline tutorial was one hundred percent Ruth's responsibility. Kenny assured a nervous Ruth there was nothing to worry about; he would help her train Custard. And when they arrived home, after Kenny had patched up the broken window pane in the backdoor with a piece of plywood, he showed Ruth how to put litter in the small, yellow tub they had purchased. Then they found a place out of the way to hide the box so it wouldn't annoy Florence, who was sure even the slightest whiff of cat piss would make her sick. Almost as soon as they set Custard in the litter box to sniff around, Custard relieved herself, and Ruth couldn't be more excited. Custard was trained!

"Was it really that easy?" she asked Kenny.

"Maybe, kid," he answered back. He cautioned Ruth there might be a few accidents here or there, but he figured Custard was a pretty smart cat, and she would figure out the way things were supposed to be fairly quick.

That night, Ruth went to sleep in her room after what seemed like an eternity hiding out under Trudy's bed, and despite the passing of Trudy tugging at the back of her heart, Ruth couldn't help but feel better than she had expected with Custard snuggled up next to her and Florence one room away. The next day was Sunday and Ruth was sad she would miss church, but she also prayed maybe over time Florence would soften towards the prospect of her attendance. And as she drifted to sleep, Ruth imagined Florence and Kenny eventually walking to church with her just like she and Trudy used to do, all of them holding hands and attending service just like so many of the other families.

Later that night, Ruth awoke to the sound of angry voices rising from behind the closed door to Trudy's room. This was a confusing sound to Ruth who had never heard such violence vocalized. It froze her in place as she tried to decipher what was being yelled. Custard was alert too and purring loudly, either to comfort herself or to soothe the terror Ruth was suddenly experiencing, a terror Ruth had never known growing up with Trudy, a terror in which she suddenly wondered if maybe she would have been safer had Florence and Kenny never found her.

Uncle Willie

In the decades before Wheels Antique Emporium filled the large, domed building off highway M outside of Conway, it had been home to Wheels Roller Rink. Back then, it was the hotspot on Friday and Saturday nights. Even then, it wasn't just a roller skating rink. There was also pool, burgers, chili-cheese fries, and arcades enough to keep visitors busy for hours. Ruth and Sam had never darkened the doors of Wheels Roller Rink, though it was still a hangout back when Sam first brought Ruth home to meet Naomi and Joe. Ruth had asked to pop in a few times over the years whenever they would pass by on their way from the farm into the little town of Conway, but Sam always rankled at the suggestion. Finally, Ruth queried him as to why dropping by for a soda seemed like such an off-color proposition. Sam reluctantly told Ruth how, when he was young, Joe had decried the roller rink as a Pleasure Island where anything and everything indecent was sure to go down, especially amongst youngsters. Indeed, Wheels had experienced its share of unsavory moments, like when a young woman had accused five local men of drugging her there one night and taking her out to an abandoned barn where she was raped. There were the two nights Wheels had been robbed at gunpoint, though luckily no one had been hurt and the robbers only managed to get away with a couple hundred bucks. More than debauchery, Wheels had been known as the place to throw a birthday party, a wedding reception, or the Conway high school prom. Then the owner passed away, and his niece turned the roller rink into an antique mall.

Whereas in years before the pristine parking lot was filled with shiny hotrods, nowadays it had been reduced to weedy pavement and ill-patched potholes that hardly welcomed visitors. There was only a Mazda up on blocks and a dusty Chevy truck sitting outside when Ruth came upon Wheels minutes after having her mini-breakdown on the side of the road. Being as she was all by herself and in need of a pause from reality, instead of passing by per usual, this time she parked the Escalade and made her way to the entrance. She couldn't be sure the place was open, but when she tried the faded red doors with rusty, steamboat windows, they gave way with little more than a metallic groan.

A few cheap fluorescents had replaced the disco lights and mirror ball in the ceiling and gave the place a sickly green hue. Luckily the air conditioning seemed to be running just fine, so Wheels made for the soothing retreat Ruth needed. No one appeared to be working the front counter where cubbies sat filled with pairs of dusty skates, and the roller rink floor that had surely once gleamed bright was now littered with booths filled with junk.

Ruth slowly perused each grimy cubicle wondering what the chances were she would find some "Antiques Roadshow" treasure that looked like scrap but was actually worth money. She wasn't an expert by any stretch. But she had prevailed upon the antique stores in Charleston with enough frequency many of the owners knew her name, as well as Sam's. That was one thing they had enjoyed when they began dating again after the kids were old enough to be left with a sitter—antiquing. But it wasn't the silly knickknacks they looked for: they loved finding big pieces of furniture—wood, metal, glass, paintings, vases, chandeliers —items of weight that held stories. They liked to hear about the history of an ornate mirror or the provenance of a particular tapestry. Some-times the pieces they found were fakes, reproductions of another time that mimicked the masters. In the good antique stores, you could always smell a fake by the price, and the legitimate dealers would be sure to let you know when you were looking at a piece that had no meaningful legacy other than to have been forged at some point to appease someone who couldn't afford the original. Or perhaps those who first bought the counterfeits were idiots, Ruth thought. Then again, who was she to call anyone an idiot for not knowing the difference between the genuine article and a fraud? Look at her marriage.

Ruth picked up a set of old, aluminum measuring spoons, dinted and worn, not worth a penny now, but she wondered who had once owned them, what had been measured out, what had been made? She imagined sugar cookies cut in Christmas tree shapes, angel food cake spongy and sickly sweet, and pumpkin pie. In the next booth she found a silver tea service and turned over the teapot to look at the manufacturer. It was merely a Sears and Roebuck rip-off of a revolutionary era style, barely an antique, and hardly a steal for the rather significant price labeled in blue ink on a neon-green sticker stuck to the bottom of it. A few more booths down there was a display of paintings by a local artist. His name was Kyle Martin, according to the business cards also set out in the display. The paintings were terrible, unfortunate imitations of the famous PBS painter Bob Ross's wet-on-wet oil technique. Maybe the images themselves wouldn't have been so awful, but the colors were off, primary and bright like velvet paintings from decades past. Suddenly Ruth laughed out loud and then instantly covered her mouth, embarrassed. No one should be judged for trying, and maybe Kyle Martin was color blind.

As she meandered through the next few booths, Ruth wondered if she had been laughed at behind her back by the antique dealers she and Sam visited? So many of them had been flamboyant enough, it was easy to suspect they were homosexual. Had they known when they met Sam about his proclivities? The thought stung the depths of her stomach. Was that why Sam enjoyed antiquing with her because he was gay? Gay—she hated that word. No one in Christian circles used that word. Gay meant happy, and homosexuals weren't happy. They were deviants, sinners, perverts of God's natural plan. No, you must call them homosexuals if you had to refer to them at all.

Ruth came upon a booth decorated with white Christmas lights and lots of baby items including a crib. Clearly, someone was trying to offload their children's hand-me-downs. She picked up a stuffed cat pillow and thought of her yellow tabby, Custard. She shivered at the memory, and quickly returned the pillow to its place before heading for the back of the rink where she smelled the sappy scent of raw wood and heard the buzzing of heavy machinery.

What she found at the rear of the building was an overweight figure with a sandpaper face who could have been a man except for the large breasts that heaved at her flannel shirt and overalls. When Ruth came upon her, the woman was bent over a lathe turning an ornate spire.

When she saw Ruth watching her, the woman straightened up as much as she could and scowled. "What do you want?"

Ruth smiled, "I was just looking."

"Well, I don't like people staring at me," the woman stated curtly.

"Sorry." Ruth noticed a half dozen different rocking chairs nearby in different states of finish. Now these were a find, clearly handcrafted and stunningly beautiful. "Are these yours?" Ruth asked, making her way over to them.

"Yeah." The woman took the piece of wood she had just turned over to a rocking chair that was in the first stages of assembly.

"They're beautiful," Ruth said, admiring the fine grain of the chairs with an appreciation she hadn't given to a piece of furniture in years.

"They're four hundred a piece, and don't try to jew me down. If you don't want to spend four hundred bucks on a rocking chair, then go elsewheres."

Ruth was taken aback by the woman's language and attitude, but she tried to be kind. "Only four hundred?"

"They're maple wood. Lifetime guaranteed."

"I'm Ruth . . . Christianson." Ruth hesitated to say her last name. But she figured there was little chance the hermetic woman had seen the news or knew anything about her or Sam or the scandal.

"Aileen Cotton. I own this place."

"You're the niece," Ruth said, "of the man who built the roller rink."

"Only livin' relative," Aileen said. "That's what happens when you're a fag."

Ruth felt the wind knocked out of her. "Excuse me?"

"When you're a fag you can't breed. So all your belongings they pass to the next of kin, which in Uncle Willie's case meant me."

Ruth turned to go.

"Your husband's a fag too, right?" Aileen asked. "Reckon Uncle Willie is the one who turned him. He'd give all the boys blowies in the back. Paid 'em five bucks a pop is what the rumor was."

Ruth stood frozen in place; her mind spinning.

"That's how he died, you know. Killed by one of them boys one night. Hit over the head with the left side of a pair of roller skates." Aileen laughed.

Ruth grabbed the partition of a nearby booth to steady herself.

"You alright?" Aileen asked.

Ruth didn't remember how she managed to make her way to the Escalade, but somehow she had exited the roller rink and found herself in the bright light of day walking to the Cadillac. As she reached it, she gripped the handle of the driver's side door with both hands and squeezed it tight. There was a ringing in her ears as though a bomb had just gone off next to her, but even through the ringing, she could still hear Aileen's laugh and words. *Reckon Uncle Willie is the one who turned him.*

"Stop!" Ruth yelled out, "Stop!"

Silence.

Ruth looked back at the roller rink turned antiques emporium. *Was nothing what it seemed anymore? Was everything a nightmare? Why couldn't she just go back to not knowing? Ignorance is bliss*, she thought, *absolute, delicious bliss!* Ruth opened the car door and stepped up into the Escalade, scrambling to turn it on. She flicked the air conditioning vents so that she was blasted with the oxygen they exhaled even if it was hot and dusty. *Breathe*, she thought, *just breathe.* She wanted to get out of the parking lot. She wanted to get away from all of it. She knew she needed to compose herself before driving. That was when accidents happened, when people drove while they were emotional. Suddenly, Aileen came wobbling on her stumpy legs out the front doors of Wheels, waving her hands at Ruth to catch her before she made her escape, and Ruth panicked. Instead of rolling down her window to hear whatever it was Aileen had to say, Ruth threw the Cadillac into reverse and peeled out of the parking lot. She peered into her rearview mirror to see if she had simply imagined Aileen coming towards her. Aileen was no longer there.

Ruth didn't know where to go or what to do, her mind a blank. For mile after mile she drove—semi-consciously. Then as awareness of her surroundings returned, Ruth remembered she was supposed to pick up Rachel at Mike and Connie's at noon, which was now twenty minutes ago and fifteen miles in the opposite direction. With a groan of resignation, Ruth made a U-turn and headed back in the direction she'd just come. Minutes later, when Ruth passed the antique mall again, she couldn't help but interrogate herself. *Was it all a dream, the stop she had made? Maybe it was. Maybe everything was! Wouldn't it be fantastic if she was merely lost in a very vivid nightmare, a reverie she could wake up from, and all that had gone wrong in her life was instantly right again?*

By the time Ruth arrived at Mike and Connie's homestead, which overlooked a particularly beautiful stretch of the Piney River, Ruth sensed that Mike was flustered at having been left to babysit her teenage daughter for longer than they had agreed, and Rachel seemed relieved that Ruth had finally come to pick her up as well. Ruth conjured some excuse about her and Sam's house hunting getting the best of their time, and that perhaps she was being too picky. Mike regretted to inform Ruth that Connie had still not returned from Champaign but had sent her best.

In the car on their way back to Joe and Naomi's farm, Rachel scratched at the corner of the label on the fresh jar of honey Mike had given her along with twenty bucks for her help. "So, you and dad found us a place to live?" she asked.

Ruth shook her head. "Not yet."

"I thought you liked the house you looked at? That's what you told Mike."

"I left early."

"Why'd you leave early?" Rachel asked.

"Would you not pick at that label?" Ruth said.

Rachel looked out the window.

Ruth instantly felt bad for barking at her daughter, tried to smooth things over. "Did you have fun with Mike? I can't believe you didn't get stung."

"Me either," Rachel said shortly.

"How was it?"

"It was hot and sticky."

"Did you enjoy yourself at least?"

"I don't know," Rachel said.

Ruth tried to remember what a typical conversation between her and Rachel would have sounded like two months ago. "Have you heard from any of your friends?" she asked.

Rachel hesitated before answering as if she was embarrassed to admit the truth. "Tisha. She still has my sweater."

"Oh. How's Tish?"

"Better than me," Rachel said.

Ruth was annoyed at Rachel for being so angry, but she ached for Rachel too. "I'm sorry you're having to go through all of this, sweetie."

"You've already said that like a hundred times."

"Well, I am," Ruth ceded. "How do you think your brothers are holding up?"

Rachel didn't say anything.

"You think your brothers are doing all right?" Ruth asked again.

Once more Rachel didn't say anything, and Ruth looked at her angrily only to notice a tear had dripped down Rachel's cheek. Ruth softened, hated herself, wanted to stop the car, wanted to drive them both back to Charleston immediately. Then she made a mistake. As soon as it was out, she knew she never should have said it, never should have put the responsibility on Rachel's shoulder even for an instant. But Ruth wasn't thinking things through. She was as confused as anyone.

So, the words slipped out unchecked by her usual maternal vigilance. "What do you want me to do?" Ruth asked.

Rachel was silent.

Immediately, Ruth backtracked, "I'm sorry. That's not your responsibility. I didn't mean to—"

Rachel interrupted her, "I think you should leave him. I would. He lied to you. He cheated on you. He did drugs, Mom."

"It's not that simple."

"He's gay. That's pretty simple."

"Your father is not gay."

"When you're a guy who sleeps with guys, you're gay!" Rachel rolled her eyes.

"He's your dad. He's my husband. He made some mistakes."

"Well, I don't know how you can just pretend everything is normal? I certainly can't."

"You think I'm pretending it's normal what happened?" Ruth scoffed.

"I don't know, Mom," Rachel sighed, "you certainly seem to want us kids to act that way, as well as Grandma and Grandpa and basically everybody else."

"I don't want anyone pretending. I just . . ." Ruth knew, on a certain level, Rachel was right. She did want everyone to pretend, to not judge, to act like things were normal until she—Ruth Christianson—could figure out what to do. "Do you think your brothers are okay?" Ruth asked again.

"No."

"Have they said anything to you?"

"No, Mom. Tim isn't speaking, in case you forgot. And all JD talks about is how Conway's football team sucks, and he's not even going to try out 'cause he refuses to play with a team that's never been to state."

Ruth cringed at the notion JD would give up playing football. It was everything to him. He wasn't even in high school yet, and up until a few weeks ago, he was already obsessing about how he was going to get a scholarship to play for Clemson and then be drafted in the first round for the Panthers. "Well, JD's got a couple weeks of summer left to reconsider that."

"So, we're staying in Conway?" Rachel asked.

"Why do you think we're looking at houses?"

"I don't know. I thought . . . I don't know."

"There's no easy answer for any of this, Rachel. Your dad and I are doing the best we can."

"What about God?" Rachel asked. "What is He saying? Aren't we supposed to be listening to Him and doing what He tells us?"

"I don't know what God is saying, right now."

Rachel groaned. "Yeah. Surprise. Surprise."

"What's that mean?"

"What do you think it means?" Rachel asked.

JD and Tim were sitting on the back porch of the farmhouse unhappily shucking corn when Ruth and Rachel pulled up to the welcoming barks of Holly and Potato. Before Ruth was out of the car, Naomi was exiting the backdoor of the farmhouse and wiping her hands on her apron. She had something on her mind, and she was headed Ruth's way in earnest. Rachel quickly trotted off, avoiding her grandma's rabid course. Ruth shifted her sunglasses up onto the top of her head.

"Everything all right?" Ruth asked.

"The boys are over there shucking corn," Naomi said.

"I can see that. You need help?"

"Timothy is still not talking, and JD said he's running away, and he's taking Timothy with him."

More? Ruth thought. *How much more could the universe throw at her before she literally lost her mind?* "Well, if he told you he was leaving, clearly he couldn't have been that serious about it," Ruth said.

"Oh, he was plenty serious. That boy has all kinds of rebellion in his eyes."

"He's *that* age, Naomi. They all have rebellion in their eyes at *that* age."

"Well, I'm watching them, and you should too."

"Anything else?" Ruth sighed weakly.

"Dinner is at five sharp," Naomi hissed, and she turned to go.

"You don't have to feed us, you know."

Naomi swiveled on her heels. "And what—you're going cook for them?"

"How do you think they've eaten all their lives?"

"Well, pardon me for wondering, but . . ." Naomi trailed off, not completing her thought.

"What?" Ruth demanded.

"Well . . . clearly you've failed in your spousal duties. How am I to know how negligent you've been in your maternal ones?"

Ruth shook her head. There it was, the thing Naomi had wanted to say for days. *The snake!* Ruth thought. She seethed, "I've been a *good* mother and a *good* wife."

"Had he been fulfilled at home, he wouldn't have strayed," Naomi stated matter-of-factly.

"I thought we were happy. Trust me, I thought we were happy! What was I supposed to do, grow a penis?"

Naomi's eyes widened in shock. Taking in a righteous breath, she snapped back at Ruth, "Don't be vile."

"No. After everything that's happened. How dare I say something—anything out of line!" Ruth rolled her eyes.

"Now I see where your children get it, the heresy," Naomi smirked.

"I have been every bit the woman of God I promised Sam I would be when we married, even to the point of leaving my house and my life to come back with him to this godforsaken place and you godforsaken people!" Ruth shot back.

Across the yard, Ruth knew the boys were staring at her. Even if they couldn't hear her every word, they could see the angst playing out between her and Naomi.

Naomi had pulled what she wanted from Ruth—mutiny. "When you're ready to act like an adult, we'll talk," she glowered.

"You ever think I'm not the one responsible? You ever think it was you and your self-righteous husband? Maybe I should be the one judging you the way you do me," Ruth continued.

Oh, this was more than Naomi could have hoped for this; this was real ammunition she could use later whenever she needed it. Ruth could feel Naomi barely holding back a smile. "I pray for my family every night," Naomi offered evenly. "I pray for Joe and Sam and the grand-kids, but I'll be saying an extra prayer for you, Ruth," Naomi said with a menacing tone that gave away her knowledge that this statement was the closer. Who could possibly say no to being prayed for? And what could possibly be said after a statement like that? Ruth had used the very same phrase herself to get out of situations in which she knew she was on the losing end of an argument. "I'll pray for you," or "I'll pray about that." She'd even done it with Sam. That phrase—everyone knew it was a cop-out in which no matter what confrontation you found yourself in, no matter how wrong you might be, you could leave your opponent feeling as though they were the one who had erred, they were guilty of something, they were less than you.

With her holier-than-thou checkmate played, Naomi turned and walked back to the farmhouse like the last living martyr of the faith. The boys sat motionless, uncertain as to how they should react. Ruth gave them a small wave and a half-hearted smile. It was all the assurance she had left. Then, she headed for the cabin where, as soon as she closed the door, she slunk down to the floor sobbing.

They hurt—the tears flowing out of her—like they were being squeezed from her by a vice. It was relentless, the pain of feeling like her life had been an absolute waste, and she wondered if the agony of it could kill her: the pressure on her lungs, the stab in her belly, the pounding in her head. As she curled up in a ball, Ruth flashed back to the only other time in her life when she had felt this wretched, and to this day she wasn't sure how she had survived.

Gay Pride

It was evidence of the remarkable resiliency of youth that within weeks of Florence and Kenny's arrival, Ruth's world felt upright despite having changed in all kinds of ways. The most significant difference was that while her life with Trudy had been measured and tranquil, the energy that *now* surrounded Ruth was frantic and unrestrained. Not long after their first night together, Ruth began to grow accustomed to the spontaneous outbursts that erupted between Florence and Kenny in which abominable words were shouted, doors were slammed, and objects were broken. While at first these explosions had frightened her, after a while she became fascinated by them. Why did Florence blow up because Kenny used the butter knife to spread his jam? Why did Kenny become so enraged when Florence reminded him to take out the trash? Both Florence and Kenny would assure a wide-eyed Ruth their brawls meant nothing, that she was safe, that it was okay for adults to express themselves raucously. One of them would inevitably find her after a particularly ferocious spat and "talk shit" to her about the other. That's what they called it, "talking shit." And though they both claimed that wasn't what they were doing, Ruth began to realize much of Florence and Kenny's actions and words ran diametrically opposed to everything they said they believed in—peace, love, unity, etc.

Soon the house lost the clean and tidy luster that had been a staple of Trudy's presence in it. Ruth tried to hold back the tide of clutter and dust and dirt, but eventually she gave up. Florence assured Ruth that earth was good for you, that she would die faster from exposure to the chemicals in the glass cleaner and dust spray and toilet bowl powder

Trudy kept under the kitchen sink than she would a little dirt. When Ruth complained about the smell that would arise from a sink of dirty dishes or a bathtub slick with grime, Florence would laugh and tell her to open the doors and let a little fresh air inside. When the neighbors complained about the length of the grass in the front yard, instead of mowing it, Kenny flipped them off and told them to mind their own f'ing business. It was a free country he said, and he could grow his grass as long as he damn well pleased. Ruth saw the worried looks formerly friendly neighbors now gave her as she played with Custard on the stoop, and more than once, she heard them muttering about "hooligans" and "drugs."

A few women from Foundry Methodist dropped by to check in on Ruth after she had repeatedly failed to turn up at Sunday school, and Florence failed to hold a proper funeral service for Trudy. Ruth watched from the window of her room as Florence smiled at the ladies, disappeared back inside the house, then returned with a blue and gold urn she said was filled with Trudy's ashes. Florence told the ladies if they wanted to have a funeral for a pot of grey dust they could, but she didn't personally see a reason for it. Once you died, you died. There was no heaven. There was no hell. There was just this life. And when your life was over, that was it. Sure it was sad, and we missed people, but personally, Florence said, she couldn't bear to hear anyone talk about how they would see Trudy again in the afterlife. What did this life matter if all we were living for was the one after? The three women stared at the urn and then Florence, who was dressed in a pair of ripped shorts, a tank top, and no bra despite the fact it was cold enough there had been snow flurries only hours before. At length, one of them asked if they could see Ruth. Ruth knew this woman. Her name was Mrs. Tracy and she always brought Nilla Wafers and Kool-Aid to share with the children's church class. Florence told the women she wasn't comfortable with religion if they couldn't already tell, and she didn't want them filling her daughter's innocent, little head with nonsense. Once more, the women weren't quite sure how to respond to Florence, but then, no one ever really was. Florence was brash and confrontational, spoiling for a fight. She would stand her ground no matter what was being dished at her, even if it was coming from three very well-meaning church ladies. In this case, the women simply offered Florence their condolences, asked her to please pass along a hello to Ruth. Then, they quickly walked away.

After her stint at Foundry Methodist Preschool, Ruth had begun attending Meyer Elementary. From kindergarten to sixth grade her life at Meyer had been mostly uneventful. She never missed class, she studied hard, and she made good grades. However, after Trudy's passing, Florence frequently talked about pulling Ruth from public school and homeschooling her. Ruth wasn't sure how she felt about this proposition. Florence assured Ruth that she would learn more spending time with Florence than she would a whole lifetime at some governmental brainwashing institution or hanging out with other indoctrinated lackeys. Kenny was initially on Ruth's side of the matter, telling Florence to let things be, but Florence never met an itch she didn't like to scratch. So, it was not uncommon for her to pull Ruth out of school to make protest signs and attend political demonstrations.

The first march they all attended was only weeks after Florence and Kenny's arrival. It was a rally for lesbian, gay, and bi equal rights and liberation. Ruth had no idea what lesbians and gays were, and she didn't ask, fearful that Florence would harass her about her ignorance. All Ruth knew was that Florence bought poster boards, markers, and glitter to make large signs they would hold as they protested. In truth the glitter was "lifted," Ruth heard Florence confide to Kenny with a laugh. The signs said, "Equality for All" and "Cure Hate" and "Fuck Don't Ask, Don't Tell!"

"Wear something colorful. The more color, the better," Florence said as she raised her tie-dyed shirt above her breasts and put black tape over her nipples.

Ruth dawned her favorite green shorts, a light-pink tank top, and a red strawberry necklace Trudy had given her one year for Christmas.

Ruth had been to the National Mall on field trips to see the Lincoln Memorial and the Washington National Monument with various school classes over the years. She and Trudy visited too, walking along the vast stretches of the sumptuous grass past the National Museum and the National Gallery of Art. They ate homemade sandwiches on a bench across from the reflecting pool. This part of DC, felt like a magical place to Ruth, a place where all was right with the world, and nothing bad could happen to you. Amongst the stately neoclassical buildings and the watchful eye of the nation's Capitol, Ruth felt at peace. She could also sense that Trudy was put at ease here as well.

"On those steps right over there," Trudy pointed to the steps of the Lincoln Memorial, "Dr. Martin Luther King Junior delivered his most famous speech, 'I Have a Dream.'" Trudy smiled and closed her eyes as if remembering the day. "Your granddaddy brought me with him to watch it. And I brought your momma. She was only three years old. But what a speech. Black folks stretched clear down the mall listening to it. Back then people like your grandma, we weren't very well liked." Trudy said.

Ruth knew that Grandpa Dexter had died covering protests after the death of Dr. King, and she wondered as she grew older if that was the reason Florence became so obsessed with marching and protesting, to somehow connect with the father she lost when she was only eight.

When Ruth, Florence, and Kenny arrived at the National Mall for the lesbian, gay, and bi political rally, Ruth could barely believe her eyes. Everywhere she looked—people! Most didn't look any different than any other person she had seen, and for the life of her, she couldn't figure out what *was* different about them or *why* they were all marching. Then, she saw it—two men kissing in front of a rainbow flag while reporters with cameras snapped photos of the moment.

"Isn't it beautiful?" Florence exclaimed when she noticed Ruth gawking.

"Those are both boys," Ruth said quietly.

"Those are both *humans*," Florence corrected. "And they love one another just like anyone else, and they should be treated equally just like anyone else."

As Ruth processed what she had seen, she followed Florence and Kenny deeper into the crowd where she began to witness more men holding hands with other men and women holding hands with other women. Some seemed happy. Some seemed angry. Some wore colorful outfits like her and Florence. Some wore barely anything at all. The energy was enthralling, and if it hadn't been for the recognizable landmarks like the rooftop of the Smithsonian Building shining brightly under the warm spring sunshine, Ruth would have believed she had been teleported to another planet entirely.

They made their way towards one end of the mall where a large black stage had been erected with video monitors on each side. Currently, there was no one standing behind the microphone, but she could hear a man's voice exclaiming loudly from the speakers in a prerecorded message: "America stands at the crossroads of a national conscience!"

When Kenny realized Ruth had no view of the spectacle, he lifted her onto his shoulders above the crowd. The sight took Ruth's breath away. What she had imagined being hundreds of people now seemed to be thousands, millions even, blanketing the field on which they stood all the way from the Capitol to the Lincoln Memorial, bordered on her left and right by the famous cherry trees that were in the middle of their taffy pink bloom. The protestors held signs with pink triangles on them and the words "Fight back!" and "Act Up!" On stage, the message from President Bill Clinton ended, and a man appeared and introduced a woman whose arrival whipped the crowd into a frenzy. Even Florence and Kenny were whooping and clapping.

"You know who that is, kid?" Kenny asked Ruth excitedly.

Ruth shook her head. "Who?"

"That's Madonna, man!" Kenny said, and he cupped his mouth to let out another whoop.

Ruth had no idea who Madonna was, but just like everyone else, Madonna seemed fervent in her appeal for lesbian and gay rights. Ruth had begun to piece together lesbian and gay rights were being demanded of the government in order to protect people of the same sex who loved each other.

Honestly, it had never occurred to Ruth that boys could like boys or girls could like girls the way Trudy and Dexter or Florence and Kenny liked each other, and it seemed odd to Ruth that if you were a boy who liked other boys it would be a problem in the first place. Why should it be?

People in military uniforms took to the stage next, dozens of them all cleaned and polished and impressive. They had been discharged from their posts for being homosexuals, they said. Suddenly, the crowd began to shout a chant that echoed like a rapturous song along the length of the mall, "We're here. We're queer. We're not going away!"

If it hadn't been for Florence making out with another woman, perhaps the day would have been one of the most euphoric days of Ruth's life. And if Ruth hadn't understood that Florence was never happy unless she was the center of attention, she wouldn't have been able to comprehend her mother's actions, especially in front of Kenny who was the only other person Ruth had seen Florence kiss. But Ruth knew Florence needed to get a rise out of someone somewhere or she wasn't content. While at first, Kenny laughed off Florence's make out session with the purple-haired woman in black leather boots, when Florence grabbed the woman's hand and encouraged her to accompany them for the rest of the afternoon, Ruth could sense a chilling off of Kenny's usually up-beat demeanor. When Florence insisted the woman come home with them after the march, Kenny said no. That's when it happened, just like always—a perfect day shredded to unrecognizable bits.

Florence laughed off Kenny's command for her to leave her "new friend" behind, but when he insisted, Florence called him a "homo-phobe" and a "misogynist." For her part, the friend, whose name was Sprite, refused to help matters by disappearing. Instead, she clung to Florence like a lost puppy, holding her hand, whispering things in her ear when Kenny would try to make a point about *not* ruining the day by turning it into something that it wasn't.

"If you hate homos so much, why were you marching with them?" Florence taunted.

"You want me to go make out with some dude?" Kenny asked.

"You can if you want to. I think it would be good for you," Florence shot back.

"No, you don't. You say that, but the moment I did, you'd lose your shit." He rolled his eyes.

"Why do you have to be such a traditionalist?" Florence asked. "You know how much I hate that."

"We've had a nice day. Can we just go back to the house and enjoy the rest of it without your friend there tagging along?" Kenny begged.

"First of all, it's my house. And secondly, most guys enjoy watching two women together. Are you sure there's not something you want to tell me?" Florence jeered.

"Fine. You want to go back without me? *Fine!*" Kenny let go of Ruth's hand and stopped in the middle of the sidewalk three blocks away from the National Mall.

"Do whatever you want. It's a free country!" Florence said, and she pulled Sprite even closer to her as they continued walking down the street.

Ruth was left in the middle unsure of what to do, follow Florence or stay with Kenny. "Come on, Ruth! Jesus Christ!" Florence snapped.

Ruth put her head down and quickly followed her mother. Were they really leaving Kenny behind? Ruth ventured to take a sneak back to where he was standing, but he had already turned and was walking in the opposite direction.

When they arrived at the house, Florence and Sprite opened beers and sat on the couch to whisper and giggle and make out more. Ruth went to her room with Custard under her arm and closed the door. Recently, instead of sleeping on top of her bed, Ruth had taken to sleeping under it like she had slept under Trudy's bed in the days following Trudy's passing. For whatever reason, the muffled dark was a comfort to Ruth. There, she could hold Custard tight and read her Bible via flashlight without fear Florence might see her and scold her for her "weak-minded hive mentality." Today Ruth knew just the story in the Bible she wanted to read. It was in the book of 1st Kings. It was a harrowing tale about two women who came to King Solomon with the strangest problem Ruth could ever imagine.

King Solomon was a king who asked for wisdom when God had offered him anything his heart desired. As such, not only had Solomon received wisdom, but he had been given riches beyond compare. Well, when he was approached by these two ladies who had both recently given birth, he put that wisdom to good use. The problem was that one mother said her living baby was stolen by the other mother whose baby had died, and they needed the king to settle their dispute over who the living baby truly belonged to. King Solomon heard them out. Then, he proclaimed that the living baby should be cut in two and each mother would receive half of it. Well, the mother to whom the baby truly belonged begged for the king to spare the baby's life while the other mother was fine with halving it. Through their actions, King Solomon instantly knew who the real mother was—the mother who wanted to spare the baby's life. Every time Ruth read the story, it thrilled her. Wisdom, she thought. That's what she wanted, just like King Solomon.

Ruth heard Florence and Sprite in Trudy's bedroom emitting the noises grown-ups made when they were naked together and "making love." Ruth cringed at these sounds, felt guilty for hearing them. Florence assured Ruth there was nothing to be nervous about in seeing her or Kenny naked. She said shame was the worst thing a human could feel. Ruth wondered though, hearing her mother and the purple-haired girl now, if that was entirely true. She kept seeing Kenny's face, pale and dejected, as he tried to reason with Florence about taking Sprite home with them.

When Ruth woke up hours later, in the muted grey of the early morning, it was to the sound of Kenny and Florence yelling at one another. This was the most chilling fight she had ever heard them engage in. Their words were more than the usual nagging complaints of vexed lovers. They were terrifyingly aggressive. Kenny didn't sound like himself at all, his verbiage slurred and vile almost beyond recognition. And behind Florence's seemingly cocky comebacks there was the hint of fearful supplication.

Ruth worried for Florence's safety. Then she wondered if she should plan an escape for herself. Suddenly, she needed to use the bathroom, and she opened her door enough to hear what was being said, to gauge where Florence and Kenny were in relation to the toilet. Could she make it to the restroom without them seeing her? Should she try? The sliver of an opening in the door was just enough room for Custard to slip between Ruth's legs and run down the hall towards the kitchen. Ruth knew this was a terrible development. When moments later she heard Kenny viciously yell at Custard for jumping up on the counter for a drink from the kitchen faucet, she froze. There was the sound of Custard screaming violently and Florence yelling horrified. Then the ratchet cry Custard emitted ended with the crushing thud of fur and bone against the wall. And all was quiet.

A patter of urine hit the floor. Ruth couldn't stop the flow until a full puddle of mortification lay beneath her. Ruth closed the door and clenched her eyes. *Jesus. Jesus. Jesus. Help me*, she thought. *Please, let Custard be okay. Let everything be good again. Please, help Mommy and Kenny stop fighting. Please, Jesus. Please!* Ruth side-stepped the puddle of wet and instantly removed her nightgown to soak up what was on the floor. Then she removed her underpants and wiped off her legs. She took the wet bundle and put it in a pink unicorn trash can she'd found at a garage sale with Trudy three years earlier. Naked, she wrapped herself in a blanket and crawled under the bed. *Jesus, you can take care of this*, she said in her mind. *Yea though I walk through the valley of the shadow of death, I will fear no evil*, she prayed. *I will fear no evil. I will fear no evil. I will fear no evil. You are with me.* Ruth truly believed Jesus was there. He would look out for her, even if no one else would. He would be her daddy and her momma and her best friend. No matter where she was, He would never leave her. She could feel His arms embracing her, holding her tight, telling her everything would be okay.

You are strong like Esther. You are wise like Solomon. You are unique and special in all the world. And I love you. I am your Father God, and I know the plans I have for you, plans to prosper you and not to harm you, plans to give you hope and a future.

Ruth nestled deeper into her blanket and whispered, "Jesus, I love you more than anything."

And I love you back.

"Jesus, please don't let Custard be hurt."

I'll keep watch over Custard.

Ruth began crying, "I love her so much."

Cast all your cares on me, Ruth, for I care for you.

Whatever had occurred in the ghostly minutes before daybreak, Ruth never quite learned, but it was the worst moment in her young life. For years after the trauma, she would regret the moment she opened the door to her room. She would blame herself for Custard's untimely demise even though she would never forget the sobs as Kenny apologized over and over while Florence called the cops and demanded he leave. By the time the cops arrived, Kenny and his blue Camaro were gone, and when Ruth left her room the next morning to take in what she imagined to be the horrific scene in the kitchen, she found instead the counters, sink, and floors gleaming in a way she hadn't witnessed since before Trudy passed.

Acrimonious Oppression

Ruth woke up, cheek pressed against the cool Linoleum of the cabin floor. She had fallen asleep right in front of the door. No, she had passed out. All she could remember is crying uncontrollably, and then nothing.

She picked herself up, head swooning from the quick move to her feet and the sharp glint of the sun streaming through the windows into her eyes. *What time was it?* The clock on the kitchen wall read almost five. She moved to the bathroom to take in her current state and splashed her face with water. *Nearly five and no one had come upon her resting body?* Ruth supposed she should be grateful for this, but she was somehow disappointed. *Did she matter to anyone? Had she ever?*

Ruth wondered where Sam was, checked her phone. No messages. She looked out the window into the yard. The thought struck Ruth that something awful might have occurred, that there might have been a car accident. No. She was being silly. Then she wondered if Delmer would hurt Sam, even kill him like Uncle Willie had been murdered. What if they were driving down some back country highway and Sam tried to make a pass at Delmer, touch Delmer's leg? Maybe it would have started with a little harmless flirtation; Sam could be so charming. But what if Sam took it a step further, and Delmer let him. Maybe Delmer would even pretend to like it, turn down a deserted gravel road, park deep under the camouflage of the trees, and . . .

Ruth stopped herself. She needed to pull it together, and make her way to the main house for dinner before Naomi threw a fit. Considering the tension that had boiled up between them, the last thing she needed was Naomi concocting even more ammunition to use against her.

When she entered the back door of the farmhouse, Joe was washing his hands in the mudroom.

"Hey, Joe." Ruth smiled.

"Where's your husband?" Joe asked, grabbing a raggedy dish towel off a hook and drying his hands.

"I don't know," Ruth said. "I thought he was already over here."

Joe stepped into the kitchen where Naomi was spooning hot mashed potatoes into a large bowl. "Your son ain't here," Joe told Naomi as he passed by, heading for the dining room.

Naomi looked at Ruth who had followed Joe. "Where is he?" Naomi asked accusatorially.

Ruth tried a smile once more. "I don't know."

The kids were already seated at the dining table when Ruth deposited herself next to an empty chair where Sam should have been. Joe was at the head of the table unfolding the cloth napkin that had been neatly placed next to his plate. Stretched out before them was an endless spread of sustenance: iced tea, fresh corn, fried tomatoes, warm rolls, gravy, and chicken-fried steak. It looked like a Norman Rockwell painting from the Corning Ware plates, Corelle drinking glasses, and heirloom silver, to the faded floral tablecloth and linen napkins. Yet, despite the romantic visuals, there was no felicity in this rural Americana banquet. In fact, there was an acrimonious oppression that permeated the air with an unseen brutality that gagged Ruth's senses like a decaying carcass. She wanted to scream. She wanted to rip the cloth off the table, sending all Naomi's hard work flying. She wanted it to land all over Joe. She wanted to ruin their perfect holier-than-thou performance of Christianity, of America, of life. *How dare either of them judge her? How dare they consider her or her family less than? Who were they? Why did they think they were so special?* No sooner had Ruth thought this question than she had the answer to it. They were better than her because they believed they were, and she believed it too.

Ruth reached for her glass of water and surveyed the table. Was anyone aware of the meltdown she was experiencing internally or had she managed to conceal it?

Naomi appeared with the potatoes. Slices of American cheese food had been laid over the mound of grey mush and melted in the microwave. "Be careful. They're hot," Naomi said, as she set the potatoes within reach of Joe. Then she took her seat, bowed her head, and clasped her hands; it was time to pray.

"Our dearest Father in heaven, thank You for the food we're about to eat," Joe began, his eyes clenched and head bowed, a mirror image of his wife at the other end of the table. "We are not worthy to ask anything of You, for we are worthless sinners indebted to Your Son and the blood that He shed for our salvation. Yet, we beg You to care for us this day, to bless this food to our bodies, and help nourish it to our bones . . ."

Ruth's children sat with their heads bowed. She wanted to assure them Joe didn't know what he was saying, that they were more, *so much more* than "worthless sinners." Yet, she herself had said the same exact thing in her own prayers throughout the years.

"And we pray this day for those who have gone astray from the righteousness of Your word, that You will punish them for their wicked ways so that they might find the light, once more, and be returned to the straight and narrow path that leads to heaven," Joe continued. "In Your name, we pray. Amen."

Everyone repeated, "Amen."

Joe grabbed a serving spoon with one of his meaty paws, pierced the fake cheese food that had been melted over the mashed potatoes, and dug out a heaping spoonful of the tacky pulp to slap onto his plate. Ruth stared at the hole Joe left in the dish, and she was disgusted. For the first time in her life Ruth saw everything on the table as bloated and overdone. Gone were the days when Ruth relished the heirloom quality of the fruits and vegetables grown in Naomi's garden. And she wondered if she had ever truly delighted in the bleached white flour, pure granulated sugar, and dyed yellow margarine that Naomi used to cook up everything in her kitchen "from scratch." But Ruth's revulsion extended beyond the food, the table, the antique dining room. *How had she put up with these people and this place for so long? How had she smiled and played the understanding daughter-in-law? And for what? Who were these people anyway? Who was she?*

Outside a truck crunched down the driveway, and the dogs began bellowing their welcoming tune. Ruth didn't look back over her shoulder towards the living room window. She didn't need to. It was Sam, riding shotgun in Delmer's truck. It had to be. She wondered if he would go to the cabin before realizing the whole family was in the main house gathered around the dinner table or if he would know to come here first. There was the soft shut of a truck door and the familiar sound of the vehicle performing a three-point turn on the gravel before driving away. Then there was the sound of Sam's feet on the front porch.

Naomi and Joe continued to pile their plates with food as though the incoming presence of Sam was of little consequence to them, but Ruth and the kids exchanged looks. Did they feel it too, the oppression, the dark storm that seemed to be blotting out the crystal bright sunset slicing through the windows? Before she was ready for it, Sam appeared in the dining room and sat down at the table next to her.

"Hey, everybody," he said quietly.

No one responded to Sam's greeting. So, he simply began digging through the serving dishes on the table filling in his empty plate. He knew his tardiness was a strike against him. Then again, everything about him was currently an assault on someone somewhere in the room. Ruth would almost feel sorry for him if it hadn't been for their conversation earlier that morning during which he had laid siege to her moral compass. Ruth imagined what Naomi would think of that—Sam offering to let her bed another man in exchange for the affair he'd had with a male prostitute. Ruth almost smiled at the thought and might have even laughed out loud if Naomi hadn't broken the silence.

"JD, you didn't get a corn cob. After all that time we spent shucking today," she tsked.

"I already told you I don't like corn. Why would I put it on my plate?"

"Corn is good for you," Naomi countered matter-of-factly.

"If you make him eat it, he'll throw it up. That's what always happens," Rachel explained.

Naomi set down her fork and looked appalled at Rachel. "That is not polite dinner table language."

"It's true, grandma," JD assured Naomi.

"Well, you're going to eat some corn. And you're going to keep it down," Naomi said, shaking her head and picking up her fork again as if the conversation was over.

JD looked at Sam and Ruth wide-eyed. Did he really have to eat corn? It was true he would throw it up. It was something he had done since he started consuming baby food. One minute he was all smiles, but give him something he didn't like the texture of and next thing you knew, everything in his stomach would do a one-eighty. Ruth admitted to other mothers that it made no sense to her; JD could hack mud and blood and snakes and spiders, he could play basketball or football or soccer for hours, but force him to eat corn or carrots, or, God forbid, peas, and one would quickly discover JD's Achilles heel.

"Naomi, if you want us to continue to have dinner with you as a family, you need to respect that no one in my family will have food forced down their throat," Ruth said evenly.

"Don't be silly. You gotta force kids to eat. Isn't that right, Samuel? He wouldn't have eaten half of what was on his plate when he was little if I hadn't made him," Naomi laughed. Then she picked up the plate of corn, selected a cob, and set it on JD's plate like an exclamation point that meant the last word in the matter had been stated.

Sam said nothing, and in her mind, Ruth seethed at him for it—for not standing up for their son. Then again, Ruth knew all the stories about Naomi and Joe and their weird obsession with Sam's diet throughout his childhood. When Sam had refused to eat macaroni and cheese as a kid, Joe had told him to put ketchup on it to make it taste better. When he did, and he still couldn't down it, they told him he couldn't leave the dinner table until he'd eaten every last piece, especially now that he'd wasted ketchup on it too. For three hours he sat there until Naomi finally sent him to bed hungry and threw the macaroni, cheese, and ketchup down the drain angrily. Another time Sam had been forced to eat Salisbury steak against his most sincere pleas against it, and when he'd thrown it up, Naomi forced him to eat his own vomit. Not all of it, of course, because after he began gagging on the first bite of his own bile, Joe ripped him out of his chair by the arm and whipped him with a belt until he was screaming. He was eight at the time. It was weird fixations they had too. Sam was told he could by no means stir his ice cream and turn it into soup. On the flip side, if Naomi made a pie, he couldn't have a slice unless he ate it a la mode, which Sam detested because it watered everything down.

Now, Ruth sat there looking at her own son with a corn cob on his plate that he didn't want. If he hadn't yet hit the low point of his young life, tonight was it. She slowly scooted her chair back from the dinner table, dabbed her mouth, and placed her napkin right on top of the food she had barely touched. "Well, I've lost my appetite. If any of you kids want to come back to the cabin, I'll open some ice cream," Ruth said as she stood to her feet. She walked to the back door and stepped out of the house. She could only imagine the look on Naomi's face—the horror. Ruth smirked at the thought. Then she heard it—raised voices.

"Where do you think you're going?" Naomi asked, and Ruth knew Naomi was snapping at the kids.

"Let them go," Sam said.

"No, I will not," Naomi said. "I deserve better than this!"

Ruth could see Naomi through the dining room window, staring daggers at Sam. Ruth could also see her children half out of their chairs, caught in the middle of the tug-of-war between Sam and his mother.

"Let them go," Sam reiterated.

"And just who do you think you are to tell me what to do in my own house?" Naomi scoffed. "Perhaps you should take your family and find somewhere else to stay."

Sam slammed his fist on the table and screamed, "We've got nowhere else to go! I put everything—EVERYTHING—we had into starting up that church, and they gave me nothing. Not a penny when we left. Trust me when I tell you we don't want to be here anymore than you want us here, but like I said, we don't have a choice."

Naomi raised her napkin to her mouth in exaggerated shock` at Sam's outburst, but Joe continued to eat seemingly unfazed.

"I'm sorry," Sam continued more softly. "I am. From the bottom of my heart, I apologize for what's happened, for hurting my wife and my kids and you! But can we please try and be civil? If not to me, then to them? Is it too much to ask that we walk in a little forgiveness? Is it too much for me to ask that we try and get along? I . . . I . . . I made a mistake. One single mistake is all—"

Suddenly, Joe roared to life, tossing his plate into the air as he stood to his feet and pointed at Sam. "YOU MADE MUCH MORE THAN A MISTAKE!"

Even where she stood in the yard, Ruth jumped.

Inside, spittle hung from Joe's clinched mouth as he gritted his teeth, his eyes bulging out. "Do not ask me to forgive you! If you were a rapist, if you were a murderer—maybe. But this . . ."

Sam stared back at Joe evenly, "You and Mom sheltered me from the world my entire life, and then you pushed me out into it and expected me to survive. Well, I'm sorry if I haven't lived up to your expectations, but I've done the best I could."

"Having another man's cock up your anus is the best you could do?" Joe laughed viciously. "I'm not sure I'd even want to be alive if I was you."

The way in which Joe glared at Sam with such unflinching disgust was something Ruth had rarely seen one human do to another. For his part, Sam never flinched, never swallowed back fear, matched Joe's stare eye for eye. "Is that what you really believe?" Sam asked.

Joe turned and walked out of the room. Sam looked at Naomi for some consolation, some assurance that his being alive was better than him being dead. She simply stared straight ahead, refusing to meet his gaze. After a beat, he stood and walked to the back door.

The kids filed out of the house behind Sam, and Ruth stood there in the yard like a stupefied welcoming party of one. When Sam's eyes met

Ruth's, he opened his mouth to say something, but nothing came out. Instead, tears simply began streaming down his face. And what eyes he had, though the beautiful blues were vacant in a way Ruth had never seen before. For the first time in weeks Ruth realized she was angry at someone who was perhaps only guilty of desperately trying to be the second coming of Christ to his family, his friends, his congregation, to strangers on the street, to the world. Maybe he had only failed to be the God everyone made him out to be, including her. Tears slipped down Ruth's cheeks now too, and she went to him, gave him her hand, and he held it as they walked to the cabin, their kids moving solemnly in their wake.

Liberty

Florence and Ruth never discussed what transpired with Kenny or Custard, even years later when Ruth was older and learned to stand up to Florence's particular brand of madness. As threatened, Florence tried to pull Ruth out of high school when she was fifteen so they could spend more time protesting the injustices of the Republic, but Ruth assured Florence she would report her to the authorities if she so much as attempted to keep Ruth from going to school even once. It was their first true standoff, and Ruth was surprised by how quickly Florence backed down. The woman she feared, the woman who couldn't be tamed—maybe she wasn't such a wild cat after all, maybe she was nothing more than a wounded sparrow.

Not long after refusing to quit school, Ruth announced she was returning to church as well. Although now she was going to attend the nondenominational house of worship one of her friends from Johnson High attended. Trinity Fellowship had a youth group that met on Sunday and Wednesday nights with free soda and games and a youth pastor named JJ who had taken all the stories from the Bible and given them new life and relevance for her as a young adult. The story of Cain and Abel was suddenly filled with adolescent angst. Jesus's mother became more than a virgin saint; she was a teen mom, the same age as Ruth, whose future depended on the love of her boyfriend to save her from certain death if she were found pregnant before their marriage. Teenage Jesus was more than just the Son of God, he was a rebel *with* a cause.

Florence mocked Ruth for her religious devotion, and she would often be drunk or stoned when Ruth returned from service. But after realizing Ruth could not be swayed from her increasingly dogmatic beliefs, Florence began asking questions about the nights Ruth spent at Trinity, and she enjoyed the stories of the various characters in Ruth's youth group, which Ruth would recount for her.

Despite seeming angry at everyone around for just about anything and everything, Ruth was the one person Florence somehow mostly accepted for who she was. Ruth loved her mother back in a certain unconditional way too. It wasn't the love she had felt for Trudy or God, but it was an intense sort of caring that seemed appropriate and good enough for them both.

Occasionally, Florence would go off about how life used to be before settling down in DC, and she would promise she was going to run back into the wild and disappear for good. But she knew Ruth would never accompany her if she left, so the threats were nothing more than grand wishes tethered to the truth of what had become her reality. And though she was encouraged to "win hearts and minds for Jesus," after a while, Ruth ceased trying to turn Florence into a believer. It wasn't that she didn't want her mother to go to heaven or have a personal relationship with Jesus Christ. It was that Ruth hoped in being a living example of Christ's light and love, eventually Florence would want to follow His path of her own volition. Vice versa, Florence felt that in being a living example of strident atheism, Ruth would eventually side with *her* reality.

It was to Pastor JJ that Ruth confided her only true ambition. The admission was made after youth group one Wednesday night. During a pre-class icebreaker game, Ruth had been embarrassed to talk about her plans post-high school, and later, when he could pull her aside, Pastor JJ asked ever so gently if there was a reason Ruth had been hesitant to share? Thoroughly flustered by Pastor JJ's attention, Ruth acknowledged her desire to be a Sunday school teacher like the ones who had influenced her growing up, but Ruth said she didn't know if being a Sunday school teacher was an actual job. Pastor JJ told Ruth getting paid to teach at a smaller church might not be possible because those types of churches had less tithe coming in and so many of the opportunities in youth and children's ministries went to anyone with the time to volunteer and a little bit of talent. But, he said, if she attended college at some place like Liberty University—his alma mater —there was a real possibility she could end up at one of the various megachurches sprouting up across the country, places that would pay good money for an actual theologian to hold a position as a leader of a children's ministry.

When Ruth received her acceptance letter from Liberty in the spring of '99, she was surprised. She also wondered if Florence would forbid her to go because it was a "conservative" school. Instead, when Ruth gathered up the nerve to share with Florence her news, Florence did something Ruth never expected. She sat Ruth down, took her hands, and said there was something she wanted to make sure Ruth understood before she accepted Liberty's offer. Ruth had never seen Florence so measured. Florence told Ruth, the problem wasn't that Ruth was going to a Christian college. The problem, Florence said, was that Jerry Falwell, who founded Liberty, was known to have marched against Martin Luther King Jr. and fought racial desegregation of public schools in the '60s. Lynchburg Christian Academy, as it had been known back in '67, was founded as a segregation academy—meaning that it was established to be a school for whites only. When the IRS threatened to revoke the school's tax-exempt status in '74 if Blacks weren't admitted, Falwell used the ultimatum to rally evangelicals and convince the "moral majority" of America that the government was out to destroy their "Christian" heritage. What he was rallying for was, of course, radical racism. Though he was eventually forced to follow the rule of law and open the school to other races, Florence asked Ruth if—having had a grandmother who was Black—she could attend such a place knowing the foundation on which it had been built? Ruth was surprised to hear Florence's account of Liberty University's founding, but Ruth was also in a bind. Liberty was the only college she had applied to attend.

"It's not segregated now though, right?" Ruth stated as if this cleared the school and her conscious of all possible wrongdoing.

Florence nodded quietly.

"So, they don't feel that way anymore," Ruth offered positively.

"But now there are other things," Florence sighed.

"Like what?"

"They're against gays and lesbians and feminists, and well, pretty much any actual intellectual agenda."

"I really want to go there. It's supposed to be a good college if you want to work in a church, and I really think I would be great teaching Sunday school."

Florence released Ruth's hands and stood to her feet.

Ruth had never seen Florence so pale and dispassionate. "Mom, it'll be okay," Ruth assured her.

Florence said nothing and headed for the kitchen.

Ruth rushed after her. "Mom, please don't be upset about this."

Florence stared at the floor of the kitchen. "I can't imagine how hard it must have been for you when Trudy passed away. I wish I had known her better, but I've always dealt terribly with the people I love most."

Ruth looked at the floor too and could almost see Trudy lying there dead, though tthe memory had faded into little more than dusty cobwebs in the corner of her mind. "You aren't terrible," Ruth offered.

"All I ever wanted was to be the change I wanted to see in the world, you know—make the world a better place like my dad did. Clearly I've failed at that." Florence moved over to the sink and turned on the faucet to wash the dirty dishes that had piled up.

Ruth said, "I want to make the world a better place too."

Though the campus was only three and a half hours to DC by car and four by train, Liberty felt like another planet to Ruth, a heavenly body all its own, an evangelical utopia in which Biblically based morality was assertively enforced. At breakfast, lunch, and dinner, everyone bowed their heads and prayed. There were no TVs. Gospel was the only music played. No one cursed. Crosses and ichthuses dotted the landscape on necklaces, buildings, T-shirts, backpacks, and bumper stickers. No hugging the opposite sex for more than three seconds. No sexual relationships outside the bonds of heterosexual marriage. No drugs. No alcohol. At first, Ruth couldn't believe it—the way people referenced Jesus in every conversation in which they engaged. For years she had looked at the world through the lens of her relationship with God, and now she was surrounded by thousands of people her age who did the exact same thing.

Her roommate was a chubby, blonde-haired girl named Cassie McKenna from Arkansas who talked with a syrupy drawl and loved to tan until her skin was the darkest bronze Ruth had ever seen. Cassie was studying to be a Christian counselor because she loved chatting with people and helping them work out their problems.

"It's all in the family," she dripped.

Cassie's father was a pastor of a big ol' Baptist church back in Little Rock, and her mother worked as his secretary. For as worldly as Florence had encouraged Ruth to be, Ruth found that Cassie was infinitely more knowledgeable of all things secular. She knew the lyrics to all the most popular songs, and she had seen all the most popular movies. Cassie assured Ruth that knowing about profane things meant you were better prepared for Satan and the infinite traps he had set up for you. In fact, that's why she read certain magazines like *Cosmo* and *Vogue* and could answer just about any question there was when it came to sex.

"I feel terrible for those sweet girls in their gunny sack dresses and their long hair who've been so sheltered their entire lives they have no idea what's waiting for them when they get here and experience a little bit of independence for the first time. They're the ones who are the first to get abortions, I'll tell you what." Cassie sighed. "And once you have an abortion, well, I just don't think there's any place in heaven for you after that."

Indeed, despite certain brethren arguing that no sin was greater or less than any other, it seemed abortion was hands down the greatest trespass a Christian could make around campus. And despite Florence instilling in Ruth that a woman's body was her own, and she should be free to make any decision about her body without a guilty conscience, Ruth couldn't help but feel swayed by the arguments on the other side. After all, Jeremiah 1:5 said, *Before I formed you in the womb, I knew you. Before you were born, I set you apart.* Indeed, if everything from the smallest pebble of sand to the largest galaxy in the universe was known by God, why shouldn't He know every egg that was fertilized and every cell that began to split and form a life? Besides, if you didn't engage in sexual activity until after you were bound by the holy bonds of matrimony, abortion wasn't an issue anyway. Abortion was only for deviants who were looking for an easy escape from the consequences of their extramarital sins.

The other trespass that seemed to be gaining distinction amongst young evangelicals was one that Florence had also warned Ruth about—homosexuality. All over America, the gays were demanding more rights, like the right to marry and the right to adopt. The Bible made clear numerous times in the Old and New Testaments that homosexuality was an abomination. Two men or two women should not lie together in any sexual way unless they desired to spend eternity in hell. 1 Corinthians 6:9-11, *Do you not know that the unrighteous will not inherit the kingdom of God? Do not be deceived: neither the sexually immoral, nor idolaters, nor adulterers, nor men who practice homosexuality, nor thieves, nor the greedy, nor drunkards, nor revilers, nor swindlers will inherit the kingdom of God.*

Cassie said she was pretty sure her hairdresser back in Arkansas was gay, but he had never admitted it. She suspected if he had, she would have had to find someone else to tame her "white girl fro." Cassie's pastor father literally hated gays, and she wasn't too fond of them either. "A lot of them have AIDS, and they like to transmit it to others just out of spite," Cassie smirked. "But, it's God's punishment for fudge packing. He didn't create Adam and Steve. He created Adam and Eve."

The problem was, there were scripture verses that railed against everything from makeup to football to eating shrimp, and for reasons of social convenience, Christians collectively decided to overlook them. Why were Christians drawing the line at abortion and homosexuality? Ruth decided it was better not to argue the point and instead pretend she agreed. Who was it really hurting anyway to say two men shouldn't be allowed to marry or a woman shouldn't be allowed an abortion?

When she wasn't working at the school bookstore or studying for class, Ruth joined a Bible study group, Life Savers, that met on Thursday nights at a pizza place in downtown Lynchburg called Tino's. The well-worn eatery was a regular haunt for Liberty students, and the owner was an evangelical woman who welcomed the kids and their Bibles. There were spontaneous praise and worship services that broke out some nights in which everyone from the cooks to the clientele would burst forth in song. Other times, prayer circles would form with wailing and talking in tongues. It was almost expected that, with their appetite, a person should bring their Bible, and along with their pizza, they would get a heaping dish of the Holy Ghost.

There were fifteen members of the Life Saver's group, and they all arrived at Tino's with a hunger not just for food but the desire to pepper one another with questions about God and religion, forcing each other to come up with answers to any quandary or roadblock a potential convert might have that would keep that sinner from falling to their knees and asking Jesus Christ for salvation. In the fervor of the company she kept, Ruth never once stopped to ask herself about the task she and the rest of the Life Savers had set themselves to, because she had come to believe nothing else mattered than living a life for Christ, saving others, and eventually dying and going to Heaven to be with the Almighty. And really, what was the alternative? Well, it was eternal damnation. "Imagine your worst nightmare," Ruth would tell a potential convert. "That's hell," she would say. "That's where you will go when you die if you don't accept Jesus into your life."

It was at Tino's that Ruth first met Sam Christianson. She had seen him on campus, once at the bookstore rummaging through CDs, and the second time in chapel praying with a group of friends. Sam was attractive—shaggy brown hair, angular face, lithe body, clean-cut clothes—but he also possessed a self-assuredness that demanded attention. Their first conversation occurred in line at Tino's. Sam asked Ruth if she needed a menu? She told him she had her heart set on a pepperoni calzone; it was the one treat she afforded herself each week. He smiled at Ruth's economy and the way she seemed to relish her upcoming order. He said if some cheese-stuffed dough was *that* good, maybe he'd have to try one himself. When it came time, he ordered two—paying for Ruth's calzone *and* her soda. Ruth found Sam to be as charming in actuality as she had imagined him to be inside the fantasy she had framed around him in her mind. When Sam asked Ruth if she wanted to sit together, all she had ever imagined about herself and the opposite sex seemed to expand so rapidly inside her, she almost fell to the floor.

"Are you alright?" Sam asked sincerely when Ruth was forced to balance against the wall.

"I have a Bible study," Ruth said, and she pointed to a group of tables that had been pieced together by a few of the Life Savers already present in the corner of the room.

"Is it a private club—this Bible study?" Sam asked.

"Oh, no. If you want to hang out with us you can. But just know we're pretty serious about what we do."

"And what's that?"

"Leading people to Jesus." Ruth smiled.

Sam shrugged. "Cool. Well, I love meeting new people, and I love Jesus. I'm pretty sure I can handle it."

"Well, then," Ruth said, and she smiled way too large, "I'll introduce you."

Ruth kicked herself internally for being a total geek as she guided Sam towards one of the end tables. "Hey everyone, this is Sam. He's a Liberty student, and I told him he could join us."

The half of the group that was present offered "welcomes" as Ruth and Sam found seats.

"How did you know I went to Liberty," Sam whispered to Ruth?

Ruth's cheeks flashed crimson. "I guess, I just figured you went there. Doesn't everyone around here?" Then she touched Sam's arm lightly and shook her head. "That's not true. I . . . I've noticed you there before. I work at the bookstore, and I've seen you in chapel."

The sad eyes with which Ruth seemed to offer this honesty forced a smile to spread across Sam's face. "Thank you for inviting me to sit down with you," he assured her.

For a moment, Ruth and Sam's gazes coddled one another, and she felt as though she could see into Sam's soul. She imagined that it was beautiful there in the depths of him—perhaps the most untroubled place in the universe.

After a vigorous study group in which Ruth felt herself talking more passionately than usual, and with an energy she cringed at even as it was happening, Sam walked her to where her bicycle was chained to a bike rack near the square. "I could give you a ride back to the dorms if you want," Sam offered. "I have a truck."

Ruth imagined stepping up into Sam's truck—whatever kind it was —and listening to soft music while he drove her over to South Tower with the windows down and the night air on her face. She wondered if he would try to hold her hand and if she should let him.

"I'm okay." Ruth smiled.

Sam nodded, "I like your friends. They're full of the Spirit."

"It's all very new for me—this place. The way I grew up wasn't like it is here. And God . . . Well, if it were up to my mom, He wouldn't exist at all," Ruth said.

"My dad's a pastor, so this is all pretty familiar territory to me, but it's different too. Back where I'm from things are super strict. You either believe the doctrine or well . . ." Sam trailed off. "I like how here we can discuss the Bible and God and perhaps even challenge the traditional interpretations of the scriptures. Like, maybe there are better ways to illuminate the Word than some explanation that's outdated. I mean, God is perfect. But man, well . . . We make mistakes all the time."

"So, you think the Bible is a living document—subject to change?"

"No. I think the Bible is God's word—subject to man's interpretation. And I'm not ready to accept that certain explanations are the hard and fast rule on the greatest book ever to be written, especially if they came from fifty to a hundred years before science and education taught us better."

"Be careful saying that, especially around here," Ruth teased.

"Anyone who disagrees is the one who needs to be careful. The church as we know it and religious dogmatists will be left in the dust if they don't evolve their thinking. You watch. The world is moving quickly, and we need to keep up with what's coming, or twenty years from now there will be an evangelical crisis brought on by Christians themselves, and it will do more damage to the faith than they could ever imagine."

Ruth absorbed Sam's sincerity, and once more she felt a deep affinity for him, for his passion. Sam had it—that thing certain people had that made them stand out in a crowd, that made them seem to shine a little brighter than others. You could trust him. You could believe his word. He was one of those people who really *could* save the world, she imagined. He had the faith of a mustard seed. Just give him the opportunity and he would move mountains.

"I guess when it all comes down, God is love, and what the world needs is love," Ruth said. Then she felt self-conscious and moved to quickly decode the padlock on her bike.

For a moment Sam didn't say anything. When Ruth looked back up at him, he was staring at her with a cocked smile and glazed eyes as if he was high on the words she had spoken, as if they were a fragrance wafting through the night his olfactory senses had caught hold of and which had, for a moment, inebriated him.

"What?" She asked nervously. She had never had a boy look at her the way Sam was looking at her.

"My plan is to start a big ol' church—you know, one of those places with three services every Sunday and valet parking and a Starbucks. How about you?" Sam asked.

"Uh, me? Oh, I'm hoping I can be a part of a children's ministry somewhere, you know, help little kids, bring them up in the way they should go."

Sam smiled at her with that cocked smile again. "You'll make an incredible children's church leader."

Ruth couldn't help wondering if Sam was joking, but she quickly realized he was being one hundred percent genuine, and with that recognition, she felt an intoxicating confidence shoot through her veins she had never felt before. "I want to go on a drive in your truck with you. I really *would* like that, but just . . . not tonight. I have a curfew, and well, I barely know you. And—"

"Tomorrow then?" Sam interrupted.

"You want to see me tomorrow?" Ruth asked with uncertainty.

"I want to see you every day you're free," Sam stated confidently.

"You don't mean that," Ruth blushed.

"Just try me," he said. Sam stared at Ruth with such conviction, suddenly there was a flash flood of feelings, of facts, of fantasy, of foreboding between them that neither of them could possibly withstand. And though it was there, right in front of her, it seemed impossible to Ruth that on this unexceptional sidewalk in front of this unexceptional pizza joint in this unexceptional city, two seemingly inconsequential people were awash in something cosmically uncontrollable and tremendously remarkable, that only weeks, days, hours, moments before neither of them had planned for, and now would never forget no matter how long they lived. It was like the salvation she had led so many towards. It was life. It was love. It was God.

Blackwater Creek

Sam was created as a result of winter's cold passions, at least that's what Ruth always imagined, being as he was born on November 18th, 1980, nine months after the deep freeze of a Missouri February. Sam was an uncomplicated child, according to Naomi, and it was an effortless birth from what Ruth understood. Even with as easy as Sam was for a first, he would end up being the only child Naomi and Joe would bear. This was odd for Ruth to imagine, being as the Christianson's were so devout and the Bible commanded man to go forth and replenish the earth. But while the poetic details of Sam's grandparents' lives and love stories were laid out for her, most of what made Naomi and Joe tick remained a mystery.

It was only by accident Ruth learned the controversial way in which Naomi and Joe met and why Joe decided to marry Naomi so quickly. Ruth had been standing in line at the post office waiting to buy a post-card during her first visit to Conway, back when no one knew her face or name. Conversationally, but without mentioning how exactly she was aware of it, Ruth had brought up the beauty of the Christiansons' farm to the postmaster, a prune-faced woman named Cheryl. Well, next thing Ruth knew the whole anti-Semitic affair between Joe, Naomi's parents, and Naomi herself had been spilled. Later, when Ruth gathered the nerve to ask Sam if it was true, reluctantly, he had verified the gossip and then some. After their Christian wedding, Naomi disowned her family and their Jewish faith. And her family decided not to fight her defiance. Instead, they silently slipped out of her life, selling their two grocery stores and moving up north to be nearer to Naomi's aunt.

Beyond Naomi's parents, Joe angered many locals with his militant ideas of what was and what was not considered decent and moral for their community and Christians in general. Still, if anyone were to ask Joe, he would say that he left it up to others whether they wanted to listen to God speaking through him or turn away from the Almighty's voice. "After all, Jesus never demanded his disciples harpoon men, all he asked was that they fish for them," Joe would smirk.

Despite the black hole that Joe and Naomi managed to maintain about most of their own history, many parts of Sam's existence had been memorialized in grainy photos adhered to the pages of various picture albums and held captive in dime store frames around the Christiansons' farmhouse. Sam's life was the Kodachrome dream Ruth had always wanted for herself—a family life, a Christian life, an American life. In the photographs she saw, the Christiansons' world was better than Ruth's. It was purer, she remembered thinking. Sam was captured watching attentively at the age of three as his mother read him the Nativity story next to the family's fresh cut Christmas tree. Sam could be seen smiling from ear to ear at the age of five in camouflage next to a wild turkey he and Joe had shot for Thanksgiving dinner. In another photo, Sam stood enraptured by a chocolate cake with a toy fire engine and a lit-up number seven setting atop it. The first time Ruth and Sam visited the Christianson's farm, Ruth giggled at every likeness of the love of her life, and she delighted in nestling in between Naomi and Sam on the divan as they reveled in their shared past and argued hilariously over certain details of particular memories they recalled differently.

Now, Ruth couldn't help but wonder how many of the stories Sam had told her about his past were faithful representations of what occurred and how many were contrived to create the persona he wanted others to believe about him? She wondered if Naomi and Joe were in on the deception or if they had indeed been beguiled all these years, as well? The obvious questions spiraled through Ruth's mind like: Did Sam *really* have crushes in high school on the two girls he claimed to have liked, Adina and Magdalena—sisters—whose parents were immigrants from Romania, and was his first kiss really behind the town barber-shop with a girl named Angela who was later caught having sex with the football coach? It was bone chilling for Ruth to grasp how it was entirely possible she knew very little about the man with whom she had spent half of her life.

Maybe it was *her* fault. Despite the layers of her own past that she had unspooled for Sam in rich detail, Ruth realized he had somehow managed to leave vast amounts of his story to her imagination. He asserted that he liked to live in the present, and this claim had always seemed refreshing and healthy, and in fact, Ruth had even tried to live that way herself. But now, Ruth racked her mind for pieces of Sam's story that she could count on, that would somehow make him whole to her once more. His favorite teacher in high school was Mrs. Brooks who taught biology, and his best friend was a linebacker named Corky who had died while serving in Afghanistan. She had seen photos of these people, Sam smiling next to them at various life events through-out high school. They *had* to be real. His stories about them *must've* been true. She knew Sam used to relish going for a dip at one particu-lar swimming hole below the house on hot summer afternoons, and whenever he could, he would slip away to sit in the hay barn and watch the sunset with his beagle, Minnie. The remembrances he had shared were vivid enough if she closed her eyes, she was there too, tasting the sweet summer water or watching barn motes turn to flecks of gold. She knew that Joe had whipped Sam furiously when he was young if he got out of line, and Naomi had taught him to vacuum, wash dishes, and fold laundry like an army sergeant. Sam wasn't allowed to watch TV, listen to secular music, or read comic books that weren't Christian. His curfew, up until he left for Liberty, was ten o' clock every night of the week. Ruth knew Sam. She *knew* him! No, what she knew about the nineteen years Sam had lived before she met him, she could recount in less than nineteen minutes. That was not knowing someone.

Perhaps it was borderline insane that after their meet-cute at Tino's, the most crucial question Ruth thought to ask Sam the next time she saw him was when he had invited Jesus into his heart to be his Lord and Savior? But this was *the* question. Forget everything else. The only thing that mattered was the moment when you understood you were a sinner and the only way to get into heaven and live forever with God was to give your life to Christ. God was the key that would unlock the pearly gates. His blood was the thing that could wash you clean of all the immorality you might have deliberately or even inadvertently committed as a mere human. Once you knew another human's "born again" status, you knew everything you needed to know about them, right?

It was a familiar tale amongst Protestants. Every Sunday, no matter what the sermon preached, as church service ended, an altar call would be made. Everyone in the congregation would be asked to stand and bow their heads. The pianist would begin playing a somber hymn like "Just as I Am." The preacher would ask if there were any congregants who might need prayer for healing or some other distress, especially some situation that might have to do with the homily given. After praying for anyone who raised their hand, the preacher would then ask if there was anyone in the congregation who would like to receive Jesus as their Savior, to know for sure that if they died that day they would go to heaven. It was always an exciting moment to wonder if a hand would be raised. Many Sundays no one lifted so much as a finger, but on occasion hearts across the sanctuary would stir when the preacher said something like, "Yes, I see you in the back with your hand raised." Then he would say if that person who had raised their hand truly wanted to be a follower of Christ, they had to make their faith known to everyone. He would ask them to come forward and pray the sinner's prayer with him. It was always hard not to look and see who it was that walked to the front. But everyone was urged to keep their eyes closed and pray along for the sinner who was now coming into the fold. Of course, once the prayer was prayed the suspense was lifted as everyone opened their eyes to see who was standing at the front with the pastor. For many young people it was only a matter of time, only a matter of hearing altar call after altar call, Sunday after Sunday, year after year, before they realized if they had never prayed the sinner's prayer, it was something they needed to do in order to attain the spiritual breadth of the folks around them. Sometimes salvation happened there in church. Sometimes it happened quietly back at home with a parent.

For Sam, salvation occurred when he was six, after he fell from a stack of logs while playing outside one Sunday afternoon and broke his arm. It was all very dramatic, Sam's scream from the ground, his arm twisted into an unnatural shape, the race to the county hospital, the cast, the throbbing pain. When they got back to the house after the whole ordeal, Sam told Joe and Naomi he wanted to ask Jesus into his heart because he was afraid if he died, he wouldn't go to heaven. Instead of assuring Sam he wouldn't pass away from breaking an arm, Joe told Sam he'd made a significant and life-altering decision, and right then and there, before putting him to bed, Joe led Sam in the words he should say, words which he fervently believed would save his soul.

Sam told Ruth the story of his conversion when he picked her up— just as he'd promised he would—for a ride in his truck the day after they met at Tino's. She was leaving her shift at the bookstore when she discovered Sam sitting against the wall outside, his nose stuck in required reading about the history of the Protestant faith. He was killing time waiting for her, he said, and he asked if she could still be convinced to take a spin with him? Without answering, Ruth motioned for him to follow her far enough away from the bookstore no one could hear them speak. Then she said, yes.

Ruth wanted to take a ride with Sam more than anything. She could barely sleep the night before thinking about seeing him again, wondering if she would, imagining when it would happen, what he might say and what she might say back. Various scenarios had spiraled through her mind, but glorious or tragic, the reality was they needed to be careful; she didn't want either of them losing points for breaking the Liberty Way code of conduct when it came to fraternization. Sam agreed, and with a conspiratorial wink, he promised to pick Ruth up a couple buildings away five minutes later.

Sam said he was taking Ruth to the Blackwater Creek nature

preserve when she nervously climbed into his old, silver Ford. They would stop and get Starbucks on the way he smiled—his treat.

Ruth had heard of Blackwater Creek from other people at school. It was a good-sized nature preserve with various hiking trails that wound their way through forests and fields and even across an old suspension bridge. The bridge had become a bit of a local landmark made even more iconic by all the wedding and senior photos taken there. Even Ruth's roommate, Cassie, had been to the bridge a few times, though Cassie's account was that it was absolutely nothing special and wasn't worth the spit to shine your shoes. Still, to most people, it was a special place, and word was that if a guy took you there, it was because he had only one thing on his mind—romance. Ruth wondered if this was indeed why Sam was taking her there now? She certainly hoped it was.

Despite having an achy fatigue in her bones from lack of rest and work all day at the bookstore, the cool breeze blowing through the windows of Sam's truck made Ruth feel a sense of vivid aliveness. She sneaked indirect peeks at Sam, his muscled arms when he shifted gears, his strong thighs when he let off the clutch. What a man! What a glorious, beautiful man! And he was all hers . . . at least for the afternoon.

With a grandé mocha in her hand and a ventí black coffee in his, Sam and Ruth arrived at the preserve in the aqua blue light of a setting October sun. All around the formerly green grass had become straw, and the leaves of the trees were turning shades of persimmon.

"Look. Right there," Sam whispered. He gently touched Ruth's arm and pointed. There was a young doe frozen in a thicket of cedars fifty yards away staring at them. Then with a flick of her white tail, she bounded away.

Sam laughed, "If I'd had my gun, she'd a been a goner."

"You would have shot her?" Ruth frowned.

"Of course," Sam said, "for meat. That's all we eat back in Missouri." And in one simple move, Sam's hand went down to Ruth's, and he clasped it just as naturally as if this was something they'd always done—held hands.

With his warm, rough palm balled up next to hers, a current of heat shot through Ruth's body. She was holding hands with a guy, a guy who she liked, a guy who made her feel like no guy had ever made her feel before, and she relished it—all of it. Was it possible for someone to be perfect, for his voice to be perfect and his brows to be perfect and his skin to be perfect and his laugh to be perfect? Even the old, stained hoodie he had thrown on over his collared shirt was just . . . perfect.

They reached the bridge without much effort, and Ruth was pleasantly surprised to find no one else around.

"If you could travel anywhere, where would it be?" Sam asked, as he and Ruth stepped onto the old wooden planks.

"You mean like on a mission trip?"

"No. I just mean, like, if you could go anywhere in the world where would you like to go?"

Ruth tried her best to absorb the weightless gravity of each step as they moved towards the middle of the bridge. "I'd like to see the redwoods in Big Sur, California. My mom told me stories about them from when she was out there, and I've seen pictures of cars driving right through the middle of them. They're so big. They're amazing. Apparently, there's even a little gift shop in one of them somewhere—like a little hobbit store."

"Redwoods, huh?"

"I think it'd be neat to see something that's been here for two thousand years. I mean, most of those trees were literally around when Jesus was walking the earth."

"That *is* wild."

They stopped in the middle of the bridge and looked over the edge watching the cold, black water rippling almost silently underneath them.

"How about you?" Ruth asked.

"Antarctica."

"Antarctica?" Ruth laughed.

"What?"

"Don't you think that would be a little cold?"

"I wanna go someplace people have never been, you know? Or at least, very few people. I wanna breathe air no one else has ever breathed before."

Ruth took Sam in appreciatively. "I'd go with you to Antarctica."

Now it was Sam's turn to appreciate Ruth. "Would you?" he asked.

"We could go save some penguins." Ruth smiled.

"Now you're making fun of me." He rolled his eyes and moved to the other side of the bridge.

Immediately, Ruth was scared she'd offended her perfect guy, and she turned to him and wrapped her arms around him assuring him via her touch she had no intention of hurting him. It was the most natural thing to grasp his body, just like holding his hand. He stood there and let her hold him from behind. He enfolded her hands in his around his stomach.

"You know, in Antarctica there's no sound because there's no life—at least not deep in the heart of the continent. It's just rock and ice. No birds. No animals. No cars or airplanes. I can't imagine that kind of silence, but sometimes I think I would love it. I wonder what it would be like to hear nothing, to be the only living thing for hundreds of thousands of miles?"

Ruth leaned her head against Sam's back. "It might be a little scary."

"Yeah, maybe. But if it was just you with no one else around . . . It might also be amazing. Sometimes, I think that if I were the only person left on earth, I'd be okay with that. Is that weird?"

Ruth closed her eyes. "No. I've literally thought the same thing."

Somewhere nearby a songbird decided to herald the early evening with an aria. It was peaceful, this place, this moment—the gentle rustle of the gossamer leaves, the purl of the creek below, and that bird.

Sam turned around and embraced Ruth, looking into her eyes. "Is this how it's supposed to go?"

"What?" Ruth asked.

"This. You and me. Here." Sam said. "I've never done this before. I've never met anyone I . . ." Sam didn't finish his thought.

Ruth smiled. She could see the gears in Sam's mind working overtime, his thoughts spinning and whirling like the mechanisms of a clock.

"Me either." Ruth shrugged.

"Can I kiss you?" Sam asked.

Ruth attempted to suck in a breath without drawing attention to her nervousness, and she nodded the smallest nod with what seemed like all the strength in her body. Suddenly, it was happening. Sam was leaning towards her with his lips pursed and eyes closed. Ruth closed her eyes too. Like some small miracle their mouths touched perfectly and gently and meshed like tectonic plates suddenly creating a whole new continent, a whole new world in which they were now together and would be for the rest of their lives.

When they parted lips, Sam stared at Ruth, and she stared back at him. Now everything was spinning and whirling inside her too. *Don't overthink things*, she could her Florence say to her.

Sam was the one to finally break the silence. "You're beautiful," he sighed.

"Thank you," was all Ruth could think to reply.

"I want to see you."

"You're seeing me right now." Ruth smiled.

"No. I mean, every day, all the time," Sam said, eyes dreary with the dopamine rushing through his blood.

Ruth laid her head on his chest. It was the first time she had ever put her head on a man's chest, and it felt like the answer to every problem in the world. It felt like all that was good and right and wonderful lay just behind Sam's breast bone. It reminded her of Jesus and how He had comforted her so many times when she was growing up. But this—this was tangible. This was . . . she stopped herself, pulled away from Sam. "You're my first kiss," Ruth said to Sam quietly.

Within weeks everyone knew Ruth and Sam were an item. Despite trying to keep their relationship as quiet as possible, Cassie was the one who let the proverbial cat out of the bag. She was trying to cover her own back after her and Ruth's RA had confronted Cassie with three opened pregnancy test boxes found in their dorm trash. According to Cassie, Ruth was dating Sam Christianson, and they had been spending a lot of time together "off campus." Ruth was sure she would be kicked out of school, and she wondered if she should submit to a gynecological exam that would prove she and Sam had done nothing more than kiss. Luckily, receipts for the purchase of the tests were discovered linking the boxes back to Cassie, who then proceeded to swear she bought them for a friend whom she was trying to talk out of getting an abortion.

The fact that Ruth and Sam's relationship was now public was terrific at the same time that it was terrifying. Tremendous, because from the moment Ruth and Sam kissed, she had wanted to shout about it from the rooftops. Terrible, because now they were officially under a microscope of puritanical surveillance. In truth, it was all very chaste and proper between them. If things got too hot Sam would stop what they were doing, and they would pray together and ask Jesus to keep them on the path of righteousness. Sam also made sure at least half of their time spent together was doing something for the Lord, either by way of ministering with the Life Saver's, which he had now officially joined, or by way of volunteering through the school at a local homeless shelter or food bank. Ruth admired Sam's ability to keep their sexual desires in check. But even Sam admitted to Ruth that he was hardly immune to what they both wanted physically. That's why within three months of meeting they were talking marriage, and within six months they were engaged.

Heath Macintyre

No one had said a word in the last four hours, at least not one Ruth had heard. Rachel and the boys disappeared to the small upstairs bedroom of the cabin with their ice cream, and Ruth imagined them all sleeping, Tim nuzzled in his big sister's arms while JD curled up on one of the bunk beds.

Ruth herself had laid down on the orange velvet couch in the cabin living room, and Sam asked if he could lie next to her. It was a hard request for Sam to make, and it wasn't any easier for Ruth to answer. But who was she to say no to a man who had lost everything, whose eyes begged for a scrap of kindness?

Sam had let Ruth hold him in the past when he was sick or when he was particularly exhausted. It wasn't often that she was the big spoon, but when she was, Ruth found herself surprised anew at the size of him, his broad back and shoulders, his thick chest and taut stomach. He felt good in her arms. He smelled good, her face pressed up against the back of his neck. In this case, it was also nauseating. Yet, like the sex they had indulged in days before, it was exactly what they both needed, and in the deliberate bliss of their davenport embrace, they had both quickly fallen asleep.

Later, when Ruth woke up, she counted the minutes until she could gather the nerve to pull her arm out from under Sam's head and awaken him once more to the hostile world in which they both existed. When they first married, Ruth hated when Sam fell asleep before her. His unconscious body next to hers scared her. This is what it would be like if he were to die or become a vegetable, she thought, his body would be there, but he—Sam—would be elsewhere, lost and unavailable. Imagining a world in which Sam couldn't look at her, couldn't speak to her, couldn't touch her, terrified Ruth. Back then, she would remind herself that eventually they would be reunited in heaven for all eternity no matter what might happen to either of them or their kids. But now, imagining this scenario didn't make her feel better. It made her feel panicked. *What happened if she and Sam split up and she never found another husband? Would she be able to marry in heaven? Was that a thing? Or would she be single for all eternity? And what about Sam? If he was truly gay and there was no separating himself from his feelings of same-sex attraction, would he be allowed past the pearly gates? After all, as had been made perfectly clear to her over and over recently, homosexuality was a damnable transgression. But what would heaven be without Sam? Would it be . . . heaven?*

Ruth knew the answer she might give someone else struggling to reconcile the vast gulf between the dream of heaven and the realities of earth would be that in heaven a soul would be so overcome by the glory of God's presence, nothing else would matter. The afterlife was an eternal existence of praise and worship and exultation at finally being reunited with one's Father and Maker. But now the concept of dancing merrily into paradise seemed awful to her, especially when she imagined eternity without the others whom she loved. Suddenly, the question was there again, the one that had begun gnawing at her: *What if it was all just a fairytale? What if God, religion, faith—it was all just a ruse to get people through their otherwise tragic lives? What if . . .?* But Ruth wouldn't let her mind finish the thought. Instead, she pulled her arm out from under Sam and struggled beneath his weight to sit up. She needed to breathe. She craved oxygen to clear her head. She was losing it again. Immediately upon her movement, Sam awoke and adjusted to give Ruth space. But she couldn't wait for him to finish moving out of the way, so she shoved his legs away with her own and curl up at the other end of the couch untouched, sweat suddenly breaking out on her forehead.

"Ruth, what's wrong?" Sam asked nervously.

"Tell me about the roller skating rink," she said shakily.

"What?" he replied.

"I want to know about Uncle Willie and the roller skating rink," Ruth repeated.

Sam sat himself up now too, though he did so carefully, his eyes still puffy from sleep. "I don't understand."

"Did you have sex with Uncle Willie?" Ruth asked.

Sam ran his hand through his hair. "How do you know about Uncle Willie?"

"Is that why we never went to the roller rink when we visited here, because you felt guilty, because you knew what went on there?" Ruth whispered.

"Stop. Just . . . stop for a second." Sam looked at Ruth pale-faced and uncertain. "Where is this coming from?"

Ruth peered at Sam who now seemed as distressed as she was. They were so much alike. They'd been that way when they met at Tino's and over the years they had become even more so. They both even liked dick apparently, Ruth thought. A wicked smile suddenly spread across her face at the thought of this sickening coincidence.

"Ruth, you're acting crazy."

Ruth laid her head against the cool, old velvet of the couch. It smelled soured and moldy and wonderful. "I just want to understand," she said. "A month ago, I thought I knew you. I believed I knew everything about you. I thought we were the same. I thought we shared the world. Suddenly there's all this truth that's sprung up like weeds in the garden of our life choking out everything, and I'm lost amongst the tangles of it, Sam. It's like so much of who I am no longer matters. It's like it was all a lie. So I'm lost. I'm lost, and I'm struggling, and I just want to know. I just want to see everything clearly again. I'm begging you, please. Tell me who Uncle Willie was. Was he your first? Was it good? Was it better than me? Do you think about him now? Do you imagine him when you and I are together?"

"You sound like an insecure school girl, Ruth. You sound like one of Rachel's friends."

"Oh, I'm much worse off than that!" Ruth spit at him.

Sam watched Ruth for a moment, measuring his response. "The truth is, I don't know the truth."

"Fuck you."

"Ruth!" Sam's eyes widened in genuine shock.

But Ruth wasn't having any of it. "FUCK YOU!" she shouted. Instantly, she felt immense guilt. This was her mother coming out of her. This was the way Florence sounded when she was angry and upset, and Ruth had never let herself be like that before, had sworn to herself she never would.

Sam tried to reason with Ruth quietly. "I don't know the truth because all of my life, even as . . . things . . . were happening I would tell myself they weren't. I lived how I wanted life to be, while what . . . was . . . didn't exist any further than the time and place in which those . . . things . . . occurred." Now it was Sam's turn to curl up at his end of the couch defensively.

"For Chrissakes, Sam! I just want to know when you were with a man for the first time! It's there somewhere in your head. Somewhere you know when you first touched another man. Access it! Tell me! Tell me before I lose my mind!" Ruth knew the kids could hear her if they were awake, and after screaming the way she had, they most certainly were. She imagined their little eyes wide at the sound of her hysterical voice and Sam's muffled excuses, and she was ashamed of herself. She knew exactly what it was to feel the way they were feeling, the uncertainty of being a child with parents out of control. But part of her wanted them to hear her, wanted them to understand the pain of their father's betrayal. She wanted them to be as disgusted by him as she was so that when she left him, they would come with her and years later not blame her for the way things had turned out. She wanted them to comprehend just as she now wanted to comprehend. Ruth thought of her mother, Florence, once more. *Was this why Florence let Ruth hear her anger so often? Was Florence in so much pain over the death of her beloved father she couldn't bear it alone? Did she simply want to be understood by the only person in the world she cared about after him?*

Ruth's thoughts were interrupted by Sam's steady and somber voice.

"I remember baling hay with my dad one summer. I don't remember how old I was, but I was young—like ten or eleven, maybe twelve." It was the deadness in Sam's tone that grabbed Ruth's attention, like he had somehow suddenly become a robot spitting out data and not the charismatic man she had always known, like he was giving her some piece of him that he truly had never processed before now, didn't know how to process.

"Back then it was all small, square bales, not these massive round bales everyone makes now. Anyway, Dad always hired high school guys to come help load 'em up on a trailer so he could store 'em in the barn to feed the cows over winter. From as soon as I could touch the gas pedal on the farm truck, I would drive while they tossed those bales onto the flatbed trailer being pulled behind me." Sam looked out the dark window and squinted as if he could see it—the sunlit memory flickering before him.

"There was this one guy, Heath. The others gave him a hard time 'cause two bales in and he'd have his shirt off—showin' off his muscles. Say what you wanted about him, Heath was a hard worker. *And* funny. He always had a quip that got the other guys laughing even though I never understood half of what they said, partly because I guess I was too young to understand and partly because I was up there in the cab of the truck watching in the rear view mirror nervous as heck I was gonna do something wrong and kill somebody. I think everyone always thought Heath took off his shirt 'cause he wanted to tease whatever girls might happen to drive by, but the thing is, we lived half a mile down a dirt road. No girl was ever gonna see him out there half naked under the sun." Sam raised his eyebrows and sucked in a deep breath as though struggling with what he was about to share next.

"Every so often, they would take a break for water and to use the bathroom—the guys. Every time—*every time*—Heath went to pee, he pulled up next to the tire at the back of the truck and unzipped his pants facing the front where I could see him in the rearview mirror relieving himself half on the grass, half on the tire—all of him. One day he noticed me watching, but instead of zipping up or saying something, he just stared at me with his . . . dick held in his hand. After he looked to make sure no one saw, he began pulling on himself, making himself hard. I don't know why. I don't know if he was joking around with me or wanted to embarrass me or what. But when he did that I, of course, looked away." Sam shook his head embarrassed as if remembering himself and his childhood timidity. "He didn't stop. When I looked back, he was still there gently making himself harder and harder. Suddenly, I got hard too, and it felt so good. It felt so right. It felt like the first thing that had ever made sense in my whole life."

Even though Ruth had demanded it, even though Sam was now telling her the thing she had wanted to know, something clearly dug up from deep inside him, it was Ruth who suddenly didn't know how to process.

Sam looked at Ruth, his eyes wet with pain. "I wanted him," Sam said. "Heath Macintyre. I wanted him like I had never wanted anything in the world. After that day, I would lay in bed at night and touch myself imagining what he smelled like, what he tasted like. I'd imagine kissing him and holding him. And I wanted him to touch me. I wanted him to see me hard like I had seen him. I wanted it like food, like . . . air." Sam looked around as if checking to make sure no one else had heard him. Then he continued almost conspiratorially. "I made plans the next summer. I was going to approach him. When he went to pee, I was going to step out of the truck and do the same, show him myself, see how close I could get to him, to his body, to his . . ." Sam shook his head regretfully. "But by the next summer Heath had married his high school girlfriend, and he was working on her dad's farm somewhere out by Fayetteville."

Sam clenched his eyes. "I was devastated. I was . . . a wreck. I'd imagine seeing him out somewhere or even finding him somehow—little thirteen-year-old me—and . . . I don't know, telling him I loved him." Sam smiled at this clearly ridiculous thought. Then he went on. "It wasn't just Heath, though. It started to become everyone—every man I'd see. I was drawn to them. I wondered about them, even my own dad. I would sneak peeks at him when he wasn't aware. I would fantasize about him, masturbate thinking about him. And I hated myself for it. I would cry myself to sleep sometimes; I was so angry over this thing that I was.

"I wondered if at some point my dad realized what was going on with me, 'cause suddenly, a couple years after the incident with Heath, he started railing against homosexuals particularly hard, you know? He was screaming about them in practically every sermon he preached, yelling about 'Ellen Degenerate' and gay rights and how they were all an abomination, how they were all worse than murderers and rapists and . . . I don't know. Maybe it was all a coincidence. But regardless, it shook me.

"For every thought I had about a guy, I'd force myself to think about a girl. Every time I masturbated, I'd promise myself it was the last time. And when I finally did jerk off, I'd force myself to fantasize about some girl or other until I'd get a blister I was trying so hard to cum while thinking the thoughts I was supposed to think—that any other guy my age would think. Of course, to cum I'd finally think about Heath or some other guy, and well, immediately . . ." Sam raised his eyebrows guiltily.

Ruth nodded but wasn't satisfied. She looked at Sam directly. "But when? When did you first touch another man?"

Sam swallowed back his nervousness and pain, and he snorted back the mucus accumulating in his nose. "It wasn't Uncle Willie. I never had anything to do with him. I was too afraid. He was too visible. There was too much gossip about him. He was too . . . *gay*."

"Then who?" Ruth asked.

"There were a few guys. It always started as horseplay, you know. Getting into a wrestling match and someone would get hard. Or having a sleepover, someone would start talking about girls, and I . . . I'd suggest we jerk off thinking about 'em."

Sam looked steadily at Ruth before continuing. "Ruth, I . . . I never actually touched a guy until I . . . I was at college."

Ruth felt her stomach drop, and she wondered if maybe she didn't want to hear this. She couldn't help herself though. The curiosity was just too strong. "Who was it? Where was it?"

"That park I took you to, you know the one with the bridge."

"*Our* bridge? Where we had our first kiss?" Ruth spat at Sam incredulously.

"I had heard guys went there to cruise. It was word around campus, you know. Some guys had said we should go hold a prayer meeting there, lead the deviants who hung out there to God."

Ruth began shaking her head, but she didn't stop him. Sam stared at his hands and continued, "The first guy I touched was this older man with a grey beard and mustache. He looked like a trucker or a farmer or . . . I don't know. He was sitting up on this rock back up in the woods when I walked by. It was there, that thing that exists between two men who want each other. The fear and longing in his eyes was the same fear and longing in mine. Well, when he casually reached down and adjusted himself, I knew I could have him. When he got up and walked deeper into the woods behind a thicket of cedars, I thought I was going to pass out following him, my heart was beating so fast and my mind was spinning so quickly. When I found him, he was stroking himself, and after a moment I did the same. Then he moved over closer to me. He smelled like he'd been working in a feed store all day, and he had flecks of something like sawdust in his hair. It was male. It was intoxicating. And when he touched me, that was it." Sam squeezed his eyes shut.

"Was that before or after we met?" Ruth asked quietly.

"After."

"How long after?"

"Does it matter?"

Ruth was quiet.

Sam sighed, ran his hand through his hair again. "It was a month or two after."

"How many times?"

"You mean how many times at school or since you and I met?" Sam asked wearily.

Ruth stood to her feet and moved over to the couch on the other side of the room. "I can't believe I'm having this conversation. *I can't believe I'm having this conversation!*"

"For the first year—there was only him and one other guy—a guy in my class."

"Why did you ask me to marry you? Why? If you knew?"

"I didn't want it to be like this. I thought it would get better. And I'd go for long periods, for as long as I could. Then, at some point . . ."

Ruth stood up again, "I should have known." She headed for the kitchen.

Sam stood up and followed her. "You know it's not that simple. You and I had sex. We had good sex. You never complained."

"Yeah, well. I've never had sex with anyone else. So, how would I know?" Ruth poured herself a glass of water from the sink.

"I'm sorry."

"NO! No more, 'I'm sorries'!" Ruth downed the water and slammed the glass on the counter. "I don't want ANY MORE APOLOGIES!"

Sam said nothing, his perfect, beautiful face downcast and dogged.

"I've never even kissed another man." Ruth laughed. "You were my first and you've been my only." She shook her head amazed at her admission.

Sam remained quiet.

"When was the first time you had sex with a man? You know, let him enter you? Or was it the other way around?"

Sam whispered. "Is this really going to help, me telling you this stuff?"

"I don't know. But it makes me feel better. It makes me feel like I understand this gaping hole in my life that has terrified me the last few weeks."

"The first guy I had sex with was when I was on that trip to preach in Little Rock—to make some money so we could open that church. He was at the hotel where I spent the night, and I . . . I let him inside me."

"Were you safe? Did you ever think about what you could have given me?" Ruth gripped the counter as she came to terms with this new unsavory truth about herself.

"I've been tested for things . . . many times. You're fine."

"What would have happened if you'd given me something? What if you'd given something to our kids?"

"Ruth, please don't spiral on this."

Ruth turned to Sam and saw before her once more the stranger, the manipulator, the deviant, the worst kind of sinner because Sam's sins were deliberate. Over and over he had indulged. *Maybe he was right. Perhaps she didn't want to know all the times he had been unfaithful. But how could she not want to know?*

Ruth sat down on the picnic table there in the kitchen and began crying softly. Thoughts swam through her mind like ghosts through a fog. This whole situation was inevitable. She was bound to end up unhappy. It was the yin and yang of the universe playing out just like it always did, like her mother had warned her about. This was the torment to her laughter. This was the sadness to her joy. She had basked in the glory of something special with a man and believed that she could get away with it indefinitely. After all, love transcended everything. Love was perfect. God was love.

And there it was again, the question that had begun to overtake even the worst doubts she had about her marriage—the MUCH, MUCH bigger question—the heresy, the thing that she was initially shocked by but that she had now begun to feel was an acquaintance. It was the only thing that was starting to make sense anymore. And this time, instead of swatting it away, she let it linger inside her, let it form something solid out of the confusion in her mind. She let it settle and spread out and breathe. And for the first time, she breathed with it.

Lizard Brains

"Do you ever think about dropping out of school and just doing it?" Sam asked. "We could start our own church. We wouldn't even have to be associated with some formal denomination. Everyone is going non-denominational nowadays anyway."

Ruth and Sam were in Sam's truck on their first road trip to Conway for summer break.

"You make it sound like it's that easy to do—just, start your own church." Ruth laughed and squeezed Sam's hand, which was holding hers across the console.

"Why wait? I mean, what's a college degree really going to do for me? Why not just get out there and learn from experience?"

Ruth turned to Sam and saw that he was serious. "Where would you go? What would you do?"

"Don't you mean, where would *we* go? What would *we* do?" Sam chided sweetly.

Ruth was silent. Even if Sam was earnestly considering skirting his education, she hadn't ever imagined not completing hers.

"Come on. You don't think getting a degree in Children's Ministry is going to create the same opportunity for you just going out and starting your own church would make, do you?"

"Where would we get the money? How would we live?" Ruth asked sincerely.

"Where are you going to get the money once you get out of school? How will you live then? You'll be even further in debt. And unless someone lines up some extraordinary opportunity for you, finding a congregation willing to fork over a salary you can live on while you head up their children's outreach isn't going to be easy. So, why not start now; do it on our own terms?"

"But if we finished college, at least we'd both have degrees."

"Okay. I get it. You're not on board."

"I'm just trying to be realistic."

"Look, I understand. I know it's a bit of a crazy idea, but I figured at least I'd throw it out there. I guess I feel like time is wasting away for us at college," Sam said.

"We're not married. We're not even engaged," Ruth said quietly. She wasn't fishing for a proposal, but Sam had become emboldened as of late when it came to talking about *their* future beyond Liberty. He seemed fearless and confident. Yes, it was exciting to dream about what could be, but the reality would surely be a bit more problematic.

"So, what are you saying, you're not *going* to marry me?" Sam asked.

"Of course, I'll marry you. Do *you* want to marry *me*?"

"Are you *asking* me to marry you?" Sam replied.

Suddenly the truck was quiet, and they both stared out at I-64 as it cut through the forested hill country of Kentucky. For a moment, Ruth considered their situation. They had known each other about six months. Not a cross word had been spoken between them, and everything Sam had said he was going to do, he had done. Every time he told Ruth he would pick her up to take her somewhere, he had been there to do so. Every instance in which he assured her things would be okay, whether it was passing a test or the two of them making it through their second semester without getting kicked out of school for "fraternizing," he'd been right. When Sam pointed out some piece of God's Word, and interpreted it in a new light that others had been skeptical of, Ruth had ultimately always found the wisdom in his point of view. He even seemed to predict small things perfectly, like when he said it would rain the next day and it did. On top of all that, Sam was taking her back to meet his mom and dad, to see where he had grown up, to allow her into a part of his world he had never let another girl into. Sam had proven himself to be a man of his word, a man of action, a man who was almost profoundly prophetic. Why was Ruth suddenly now so concerned with the grand ambitions he had gone out on a limb to share with her? Who was to say that just like everything else he seemed to somehow know, he wasn't right when it came to predicting the correct course of *their* future?

"If you want to drop out of school and start a church, I'll help you," Ruth finally said in a soft voice.

Sam looked at her. "I'll always take care of you. You know that, right? I'm not gonna lead you down some random path and abandon you there."

Ruth smiled at Sam, appreciating the seriousness of the look on his face.

"And yes, we need to get married," he said. "However you want to do it—whenever—I'm ready. I want to marry you."

Ruth was confused. Sam had always been pragmatic, but he was not without his romantic side. "*Are you asking me to marry you?*" she wondered aloud, hoping on some level he wasn't proposing mostly because, amongst other concerns, they were driving down an interstate with 7-Eleven hot dog wrappers and empty Mountain Dew bottles at their feet.

Sam squinted out at the road ahead contemplating his answer. Then, he nodded. "Yes. If you will, I'm asking you to marry me."

"Just like that?" Ruth smiled.

"I guess I should give you a ring or something, huh? Get down on one knee? You want me to pull over?" Sam started to slow down the truck.

"No. No, it's fine. I mean, I'm not trying to force you into anything."

"Ruth, I want to."

"Okay," Ruth smiled.

"So, that's a yes?" Sam asked.

"Yes. That's a yes!" Ruth beamed. Tears welled up in her eyes.

Sam squeezed her hand. "You're not crying on me, are you?"

She looked at him. "I love you," she said. "I love you so much." She leaned across the console to kiss him on the cheek.

"I love you too," Sam said, and he squeezed her hand and gave her a wink.

That was it. There was no engagement ring. There was no getting down on one knee. Sam had proposed in the slow lane on I-64 an hour and a half outside Louisville.

By the time Sam and Ruth arrived at the Christiansons' farm they had mutually agreed there was no need for gold bands or a big wedding. They would save up all their money to start Holy Light Ministries—the name they had decided upon for their church. When they told Naomi and Joe about their plans to drop out of school and start their own congregation, Joe said it was the most decent idea Sam had ever come up with. Ruth learned Joe had been against Sam attending college entirely, and Liberty was simply the compromise they had landed on if he was going to pursue a secondary education. As for getting married, Joe and Naomi were slightly less enthusiastic about that development until they found out Sam and Ruth were forgoing an expensive ceremony in order to save money for their ministry. Sam proclaimed as prophetically as ever, right then and there, Holy Light Ministries would become one of the biggest megachurches in all of America, if not the world.

Naomi suggested Sam and Ruth get married right away in the small country church Joe had built, but Ruth felt they needed to wait until Sam met Florence. It was only right. She had met his parents. Now he needed to meet her mother. Then, with Florence's blessing, they could do it properly—start their life together bound by the bonds of holy, governmental, and parentally sanctioned matrimony.

Florence had squashed all talk about campus life when Ruth returned home for her first Christmas break from Liberty. When Ruth told Florence about Sam, Florence made up excuse after excuse as to why she wouldn't be available to meet Ruth's beloved each time Ruth mentioned him. After their engagement, however, Ruth decided enough was enough, and without telling Florence she was doing so, she brought Sam along with her to DC for a surprise visit three weeks after their trip to Conway.

Ruth hoped for a congenial meeting between Sam and her mother. After all, Sam was great with people. He made instant friends with everyone from gas station attendants and baristas to dog walkers and junkies. Both Sam and Florence were good people, Ruth told herself, and they shared something in common—their love of her.

At first Florence welcomed them into the old craftsman with the charm she still somehow kept at her disposal. But by dinnertime Florence had begun with the little swipes at religion. Then once Ruth and Sam shared the news about dropping out of school, getting married, and starting a church, Florence started asking inappropriate questions about how far they had gone sexually. Despite the assault, Sam was a gentleman smiling and listening and sure-footedly standing his ground, consistently expressing the Protestant principals of morality and virtue as eloquently as ever. This only served to make Florence even more maniacal about voicing her own doctrine of feminism and atheism before letting loose a diatribe on the history of religious oppression. As if that was the final word in the matter, she lit a joint and told the two of them neither of them was in any position to marry—period. They needed to go out and explore the world, sow some oats, figure out who they were. When Florence asked Sam point blank if he knew he even liked women considering he'd never slept with one, Ruth stood up and said they were leaving.

"What?" Florence asked acting surprised by Ruth's reaction. "I don't know a single heterosexual man who went into marriage a virgin. It's just not possible for them. Humans—and especially men—evolved to procreate as soon as they're able. It's hardwired into their lizard brains. If you haven't fucked a woman within a few years of getting your first erection, I'm sorry, but chances are you prefer cock. It's just the way nature is, sweetie."

Ruth shook her head at Florence, eyes fierce with hurt. "Fine. Let's say you're right about everything. Let's say life is just this random sexfest of slightly evolved monkeys who are born to die and there's nothing special about it—it's just all some arbitrary nonsense happening on a planet spinning haphazardly through the cosmos. Then what's the point? Why not kill ourselves and get the pain and suffering over with? 'Cause isn't that all we're going through—pain and suffering with little moments of happiness here and there on our way to death?"

"Exactly!" Florence said, pointing her joint at Ruth as if proud of Ruth's concise assessment of the human struggle.

Ruth wanted to scream, wanted to throw something. She was infuriated at Florence. Before she could figure out what crazy action she might enlist to help her prove her total and complete anger, Sam touched Ruth's shoulder.

"Baby, it's okay," he said.

The tears in Ruth's eyes dripped down her cheeks as she stared completely crushed at Florence who stared defiantly right back. Was this it, Ruth thought to herself—the final straw? Would she ever be able to speak to her mother again?

Ruth and Sam drove the three-hour return trip to Lynchburg in almost complete silence. They cuddled up on the air mattress in the pitiful apartment they had leased together earlier that week on the seedy side of the city. The next day they went to the courthouse with a few friends from the Life Saver's group and signed a certificate of marriage making them lawful husband and wife. It was a bittersweet day Ruth would attempt to make more romantic each time she was asked about it later in life. They wanted something spontaneous, she would say. They just wanted each other, and nothing else mattered. It was love, she would shrug with a twinkle in her eye. For the most part, this was all true—for the most part.

Their wedding night was slightly awkward, neither of them quite sure how to approach the big event—performing the act of sex. But they both swore they were excited to finally be naked with each other, hold each other, touch each other, enter each other, and do so all without the stain of sin in their hearts. They joked, when the marital intercourse ended with Sam masturbating next to Ruth after making her come way too quickly, that not making mind-blowing, marathon love right off the bat wasn't a bad thing. It simply meant they would have to practice more. And that's precisely what they did, when Sam wasn't exhausted from working as a pizza delivery man at night, a roofer by day, and planning for their future church with the rest of his time.

Ruth found a job working at the mall behind a cosmetic's counter at Dillard's, selling small jars of moisturizers, toners, and lotions that in some instances were the same price as one month of her and Sam's rent. When the opportunity presented itself, she would chat with the various women and men who dropped in to purchase the expensive creams and polishes about their lives and their beliefs. This sort of missionary work was something she was reprimanded for doing by her boss, Dana, who assured her that she was all for Ruth testifying to others about Christ's love and salvation—being as Dana herself was a God-fearing Christian —just not on company time. Unlike the bookstore at Liberty where Ruth was constantly busy stocking books and other items, cashing customers out, or guiding students to various aisles of goods, most of Ruth's time at Dillard's was spent simply standing behind a beautifully polished glass counter in her Sunday best, smiling at customers, offering samples, and staring off into space often thinking about her life.

It was in this time between showing up for work in the morning and leaving late in the afternoon she did what Sam said he always did while working, she began to imagine herself ten years in the future. She constructed a vision of what she wanted her life to look like, who she wanted to be, where she wanted to be, how she wanted to be. At first, it was a simple portrait drawn with lines and not much detail. She was going to be a preacher's wife—the wife of a megachurch pastor. She would be charming and loving—a perfect reflection of Christ. She would always smile and carry her Bible and know just how to comfort people like Jesus and Sam were able to do. Then Ruth began to sense there was more she would need to know—things she would have to be prepared for. That's when she began to fill out the portrait of herself in her mind with blocks of color. Ruth and Sam would need to have a big house. Ruth imagined a beautiful estate where they could host prayer breakfasts and dinners, be alone and find peace away from the world—a sanctuary to reconnect with the Spirit. She would need to learn to decorate and cook and understand social etiquettes never taught to her by Florence. So, on her lunch breaks, Ruth began to wander through Dillard's taking in the home furnishing department. On the various dining room tables for sale, she studied the sets of china and pieces of silverware, the placement of napkins, and the ornate centerpieces. She asked questions of the older gentleman, Gus, who floated about the silk settees, leather Chippendales, and Chinese accent lamps to better understand why certain items were more expensive than others. She asked about draperies and espresso makers, toaster ovens and wine glasses.

Ruth studied the latest fashions in the women's department to try and better understand what it was that set apart one pencil skirt or suit coat from another or what made a salmon cashmere sweater more desirable than a blood-orange poly blend. Then she tried to replicate what she was learning when she visited the Goodwill store, fingering through haggard garments for something that didn't look worn and was, in fact, fashion-forward. At the Salvation Army, she sifted through old side tables and yard sale armchairs, purchasing little pieces for her and Sam's apartment, items she realized, because of her growing knowledge, had more value than what they were selling for on the second-hand market. Even when she showed up with a ceramic lamp for the credenza or a silk tie for Sam's Sunday suit, she didn't let on to Sam about her pursuit of an education in things materialistic. Maybe he wouldn't care. Still, she felt as she studied more of what was considered beautiful and au courant that it might help in some way with their future, that it might give them another dimension many Christians didn't possess. She would know the world. She would be *in* the world, but she wouldn't be *of* the world. With certain knowledge, Ruth understood she could be someone presentable to an audience that might otherwise not see her and Sam's lives as something to aspire to, and she wanted others to aspire to be like her and Sam. Why shouldn't they?

Despite being one of the last to join Life Savers, Sam quickly became its leader. It wasn't a position he had vied for, but soon he was giving mini-sermons to the group and setting the schedule for their mission work. Then one Saturday evening, after passing out tracks at the nearby movie theater, the inevitable finally happened—the Life Savers became something more.

The tracks their Bible study group were distributing were pocket-sized comic booklets in which there was a story about a boy, Jimmy, and his girlfriend, Jenny, who were high school sweethearts. Over and over, Jenny begged Jimmy to ask Jesus into his heart, but he was too cool and always told her he would do it later. Well, when Jenny and Jimmy got into a car accident after prom and both died, Jenny went to heaven where she was welcomed to Jesus's perfect open arms and given a mansion in a bejeweled city with streets paved in gold. Meanwhile, Jimmy was taken to hell where he would burn forever in a lake of fire with all the other people of earth who had never given their hearts to Jesus and asked Him to save them. The twist at the end of the comic was that Jimmy wakes up and the car accident was just a bad dream, but he now knows there is no better time than the present to become a Christian and be saved forever from an eternity of damnation. So, he gets on his knees with Jenny and says the "sinner's prayer," which readers could read aloud to save themselves, as well.

Most people smiled and said no thank you to the tracks the group offered. Occasionally the group was heckled. More often than not there would be a Christian or two who would tell the kids to keep up the good work. Once every few weeks there was a homeless kid or a particularly downtrodden housewife or businessman who would engage the kids in conversation and even pray with them. So far, they had "saved" six people total through their hard work. But on the night they passed out the tracks with the illustrated story of Jenny and Jimmy, there hadn't been a bite. Sensing the troupe was sullen after collecting a few of the booklets people had taken and then tossed down to the gutter, Sam suggested instead of attending their usual assembly at the Vines Center the next morning, they all show up at his and Ruth's apartment for a church service he would lead. He promised it would buoy their spirits. Ruth wondered if Sam's reach might have finally extended too far after this suggestion was met with silence. Then everyone began nodding and shrugging that Sunday service at Sam and Ruth's did sound better than attending the Vine Center where the largess of the place often made one feel like an insignificant bystander of a massive religious production instead of an invaluable member of the Christian community. Marta, a thin, black-haired girl with braces and a penchant for old neon T-shirts, beamed that this was exactly how it happened—visions coming to life. When Sam said he didn't understand, she clarified they had all been praying with Sam that he and Ruth would find the perfect opportunity to start Holy Light Ministries, and this was it!

Manuel Cortazar, a Columbian immigrant who had arrived in America a year earlier in order to become ordained through Liberty, was the first to knock on Sam and Ruth's door the next morning. He had brought his acoustic guitar, which he learned to play growing up in the hills outside Medellín.

"This is the day the Lord has made, *amigo*," Manuel said as he hugged Sam tightly.

"Let us rejoice and be glad in it," Sam smiled back.

"I brought my strings in case we need to do some singing." Manuel lifted his guitar as if it was an offering.

"Good call," Sam said, ushering Manuel into the house where Ruth was setting out every last chair she and Sam owned in a circle around the living room.

"Manuel!" Ruth hugged him. "Grab a seat. There's coffee and donuts on the counter too if you want them."

"It's funny. American donuts. They're too sweet for me." Manuel found a seat and began tuning his guitar.

The next to arrive were Sam and Ruth's closest friends, Kenny and Laura, who had recently become engaged and were eager to tie the knot like Sam and Ruth. Laura brought a coffee cake still warm from the oven. They were followed by three more Life Savers who brought two visitors with them. And they were followed by black-haired Marta, who arrived with her roommate, Connie. By the time Manuel began leading them all in their first praise and worship song, the coffee and donuts had been thoroughly consumed, and the apartment was packed with over a dozen children of the Lord.

Sam leaned into Ruth, "If I had known this many people were going to show up, I would have prepared more."

Ruth kissed him on the cheek and whispered in his ear, "You're always prepared, sweetie. That's why people adore you."

Sam's eyes grew wet. "I never thought we'd get here to this moment."

"Yes, you did. You absolutely did."

As Ruth knew it would be, Sam's first sermon was eloquent and inspired with just the right amount of practice and impromptu. He talked about the Lord speaking to the prophet Jeremiah while he was being held by the Court of Guard as Jerusalem was under siege, how God told Jeremiah to simply call to Him and He would answer. And indeed, God *did* answer Jeremiah's call. He told Jeremiah great and mighty things were about to occur concerning the houses of the city and the house of the kings of Judah, but first the evil who had turned their backs on Him during the siege had to be rooted out. Sam likened he and Ruth's own current experience to Jeremiah's. He shared how even in their little apartment on the wrong side of the tracks in Lynchburg, they prayed to God every morning when they woke up and every evening before they went to bed, asking for His guidance, and they believed fervently in their hearts that good things were on the horizon for them. Sam said that over and over God had answered their calls to Him with visions of future blessings and promises that, as long as they continued to follow His commandments and worship Him with unwavering faith, He would continue to honor His promises too, like the one being realized that very day in which Sam's dream of preaching to his own congregation was coming to pass. Making everyone in the room feel as though they were a part of fulfilling God's oath to Sam and Ruth could not have been more effective. The service went on for almost three hours, and in the end, Manuel suggested they take up an offering. If Holy Light Ministries were to succeed, they would each need to give their ten percent weekly to make it happen. And so, without Sam prompting a soul, everyone dug into their pockets as an antique cobalt bowl Ruth had picked up at a flea market was passed around the room.

Later Sam told Ruth if everyone continued to give as they had that day, they would soon be able to afford the rent on a small space to hold proper Sunday services. And even though Ruth had prayed for it, had staked her very life on it, it all seemed too good to be true. Still, there it was—the promise—Sam's promise, God's promise. In truth, it made Ruth feel vindicated. She had set out on her own to live her life for the glory of Christ, and He had rewarded her with a handsome, doting husband, a dedicated group of friends, and a life in which anything suddenly seemed possible.

Zion

It was four o'clock in the morning when the screams came echoing across the yard, and a desperate pounding thudded through the whole of the cabin with surprising force considering the small woman from whom the commotion was issuing forth. Neither Ruth nor Sam had changed out of their clothes from the day. Sam had fallen back to sleep on the couch downstairs, and he was the first to the door. Ruth and the kids descended from upstairs to find Naomi standing across from Sam white with emotion.

"You've got to come help," Naomi said, grabbing at Sam to follow her back to the main house. "Your daddy, he's . . . I think he's having a heart attack."

Ruth looked at the kids. "Go back to bed."

"No way," Rachel said.

Instead of arguing, Ruth simply turned and followed Sam and Naomi who were already halfway across the yard.

"Did you call 9-1-1?" Sam was asking.

"Yes! Yes! The ambulance is on their way. But you've got to do something. He's stopped breathing, and I can't find his pulse."

Naomi let the back door slam behind her, but Ruth opened it and followed the creaking of Naomi and Sam's footsteps up to the second floor where she saw the door open to Naomi and Joe's bedroom and Joe sprawled in white boxers and a wife-beater on their bed unresponsive.

Sam listened for his father's heartbeat. Then he began compressions on Joe's chest and blew into his mouth trying to resuscitate him. Considering the certain kind of hate Joe had for Sam and his obsession with where Sam's mouth had been, for a moment Ruth wondered if Joe would rather die than have his son's lips anywhere near his own. Naomi watched the scene too, her hands clasped, fretting but hopeful. Ruth wondered what she should do—go to Naomi and comfort her, go to her children and reassure them? Instead, Ruth simply stood at the top of the stairs staring as her husband did his best to save his father while the rest of the world around them seemed comatose in the deep sleep of the backcountry night. She realized this was the first time she was seeing Joe that she could *really* look at him. It was the first time she hadn't averted her gaze for fear of his intimidating presence. He was old, she realized, very old . . . and bloated. Joe was still a large man, but next to Sam he suddenly seemed smaller, and in his current condition—wisps of wet hair matted to his gaunt, pale face—he seemed like the Wizard of Oz, suddenly exposed for the powerless figure he was. *Why had she feared Joe all these years?* She wondered if that's what he had wanted—for people to be scared of him?

Ruth saw the crimson glow of the ambulance lights bleeding through the front windows before she heard the siren, and she was surprised by how quickly the medical van had arrived considering the distance from the farm to the local county hospital. How long had Joe been in cardiac arrest before Naomi came to them for help? It wouldn't be surprising to Ruth if Naomi had waited until the last possible moment to ask for Sam's assistance; she was stubborn as Joe and just as determined not to need her son in any way. Ruth wondered if Naomi's stubbornness would be the death of Joe—if maybe it already had been?

The Lester County Hospital on the outskirts of Conway was a source of local pride. Opened back in the '50s, it was originally built as a way station to stabilize trauma patients before sending them on to one of bigger cities like Springfield or St. Louis and to remedy local ills like snake bites, kidney stones, and broken limbs. However, LCH—as the doctors and nurses called it—had expanded its footprint over the last few decades thanks to state and federal grants, and nowadays all kinds of standard and emergency medical procedures were performed on the premises. It was rated one of the top hospitals in the area according to the plaques that hung on the walls over the emergency room reception desk. Despite the technological advances tucked away in the OR and hidden inside small wi-fi connected tablets used by the staff, most of the infirmary smelled like aged disinfectant, chirped with the sound of footsteps on ancient linoleum, and was repainted in the same matte whites, grays, and beiges that had been used since its inception, leaving the institution seemingly stuck in the past.

At this time of morning the place was also hauntingly quiet, like nothing traumatizing could possibly occur here. It was an illusion, Ruth thought to herself, the idea that silence equaled peace. Case in point, steps away from where she and Sam sat with Naomi in the waiting room, behind sterile doors Joe's naked hulking frame was spread eagle on a table being slammed with high voltage paddles attempting to jumpstart his heart and return him to life, to give him a second chance at the only existence he had known, *the only existence any of them had known.*

It had been forty minutes since Naomi banged her gnarled fists on the cabin door, and in all that time, there was no sign from Joe that he was coming back. Ruth wondered if maybe he had done it, finally found the perfection he had lived his whole earthly life for—heaven. And maybe, upon witnessing the resplendence of Zion, Joe had refused to return to this earthly morass. Even as Ruth considered the belief that there was something after all this that was perfect and glorious, especially for someone like Joe, the notion had a resounding clang of untruth to it. As for heaven, now that Ruth stared once more into the reality of its existence, she wondered, *What was perfection without imperfection? What was glory without defeat? What was light without darkness? What was happiness if you couldn't compare it to sorrow?* She knew these questions would be heresy if anyone saw them flickering in her mind, especially the two people sitting next to her in the aseptic waiting room, but Ruth couldn't keep her thoughts from bursting forth any more than she could stop the morning sun from rising outside the hospital windows. *A Savior. A God. Angels. Mansions. Crowns of glory. Streets made of gold. These are the ideals of a ten-year-old child who also believes in unicorns and fairytale endings and needs something to distract herself from the realities of life dawning on her. Eternity. Heaven. Hell. Satan. Demons. Saints. Sinners. These were the ideals of men who use them as lifelines to counter the weight of the terrible reality so many of them had been born into. Perhaps the only way to withstand the horrible present was to assume there was some future splendor awaiting you at death, and nothing in this life mattered. Otherwise, what was the alternative—that this was it? That this life—this wretched, aging, chaotic, ridiculously brief spec of time glued together by the random grouping of carbons we called flesh—is all there was for us?*

Ruth reminded herself that the fact was, she couldn't imagine heaven with her unenlightened human mind. That's what she had told to others who dared not believe in an afterlife with Christ. She had assured them heaven was something so wondrous and fantastic it was undoubtedly outside their realm of understanding, and all a person needed to do was simply have faith. Now, she was wondering, *Why was it heaven that was given the distinction of being outside the realm of someone's understanding? Why couldn't the singular beauty of this life be given the benefit of the doubt? Why couldn't this be enough, this here in front of everyone—what they could taste and touch and smell and hear . . . and love?*

Doors opened at the other end of the waiting room, and a doctor with gray hair and a white coat appeared with a nurse by his side walking towards Ruth, Sam, and Naomi. Ruth wanted to look at Naomi, to see if she could handle the news that, from the grave look on the doctor's face, was undoubtedly coming. Instead, Ruth gazed steadily at the doctor and the nurse.

As they arrived, Sam helped Naomi to her feet. "Is he going to be okay?" Naomi asked hopefully.

The doctor, who smelled like soap and aftershave, scrunched his bushy eyebrows together and gave her a close-mouthed smile of someone who is sorry. "Naomi, I'm afraid Joe has passed."

Even though she knew the news was coming, even though she had already heard it in her head before the doctor said so, Ruth felt the hammer of his words slam into her chest and knock the wind out of her. He was dead. Joe was dead. She stood up not sure what to do, but eager to do something.

Ruth looked at Naomi and Sam who were both clearly in shock, digesting the news.

"We did everything we could," the doctor whispered.

A silent tear dripped down Sam's cheek, and it was Naomi who patted his hand. "He's in heaven now. He's with Jesus. It's okay."

"If you'd like to see the body, we can give you a few moments with him," the doctor offered.

"Yes, well . . ." Naomi looked at Sam. "Do you want to see your daddy?"

Sam looked at Ruth as if asking her opinion. She shook her head inferring that she didn't know what he should do.

"Yeah. Yes. We should probably go, um . . . Why don't we go see him."

The doctor lead Sam and Naomi away, but Ruth didn't follow them, and neither of them seemed to notice or to care.

"Are you okay?" The nurse who had walked in with the doctor had also been left behind. "Can I get you water or some hot tea?" she asked.

Ruth looked at the nurse who had cropped auburn hair and a full pleasant face, and she was struck with the feeling they had met somewhere before. "Do I . . . know you?" Ruth asked.

The nurse smiled. "I didn't think you'd remember me. I'm Kayla Dowling. We spent Christmas together years ago."

"Christmas?" Ruth questioned, surprised.

"You and Sam were visiting his parents, and I had just gone through a divorce. It was all of us, with my parents Bob and Karen, at the farm." Kayla smiled again.

Ruth grabbed her mouth as she recalled Kayla who looked younger now almost fifteen years later. She was the "harlot" that they were "forced" to share Christmas dinner with on account of the fact Kayla's parents were Joe and Naomi's best friends. "Oh, my goodness. Yes. Yes, you're right. Look at you. How are you?"

Kayla sucked in a deep, steady breath. "Better than I was back then. The question is, how are you?" Kayla gently touched Ruth's arm.

Ruth closed her eyes. "I have no idea."

"I'm really sorry about Joe."

Ruth looked at Kayla confused. "You are? Why would you be? He was terrible to you, all of them were. I remember being so embarrassed by how they treated you." Ruth shook her head as if trying to shake the feelings creeping up on her from the past.

"It's okay. I survived. I'm married again with three kids now."

"And what about your parents? It seemed like they'd never get over you filing for divorce."

"Oh, they haven't. But if they want to see their grandkids, they have no choice but to play nice." Kayla lowered her voice. "They'll be devastated when they hear about Joe."

Ruth nodded somberly. Then she asked something out loud that once it was verbalized, she couldn't figure out how it had escaped her unchecked. "So, are you a Christian, now? Back then, I remember you weren't exactly a fan of what anyone at the table believed. You didn't even close your eyes when Joe said the blessing."

"You mean the blessing in which he basically pointed his finger at me and called me a willful sinner on my way to hell?" Kayla smiled.

"Yes, that prayer." Ruth cringed at the memory.

"It's fine." Kayla sucked in another deep breath and gritted her teeth. "No, I'm not a Christian. I'm still a perfectly happy atheist."

"And you're happy?" Ruth asked.

"If you're about to try and convert me in an emergency waiting room at five o' clock in the morning, don't. I've been witnessed to by every reverend, deacon, and church lady in the tri-county area, and I still haven't cracked." Kayla laughed. "You'd be wasting both our time, trust me."

Ruth's face went pale. "No. No, I'm . . ." But Ruth didn't know what excuse to make for her direct and intrusive line of questioning, and so she wilted and stated the truth that before this moment she wasn't even sure she had admitted to herself. "I'm trying to find some answers, actually. I . . . I've been questioning things for a while now. My mom. She was . . . she didn't believe in God or . . . anything like that."

Kayla realized the seriousness of Ruth's tone, and she touched Ruth's arm again with what seemed like all the compassion inside her. "I've seen the news, the stuff that happened with Sam. I'm sorry. I can't imagine . . ."

"I suspect you can." Ruth smiled weakly. "How many of your ribs did your ex break?"

Kayla grimaced. "Yeah, well." Then, she looked Ruth directly in the eyes and smiled. "You will get through it. That I can promise."

Ruth's body suddenly shook, and tears welled up in her eyes as she whispered like a criminal admitting to a crime. "I can't believe I'm questioning my faith."

Kayla broke into an even bigger smile. "Don't worry. Life is a hell of a lot better on the other side of that looking glass, I'll tell you what."

"What is it like?" Ruth asked, wiping away a tear and looking around the empty emergency room as if worrying someone might hear her.

"You know that last day of vacation when you're sitting there with a margarita on a beach somewhere, and you're watching the sunset, and you soak it in just a little bit more than all the days before?"

"I don't drink."

Kayla laughed out loud. Then she caught herself. "I'm sorry. I'm not laughing at you." She tried to explain another way, "What I'm trying to say is, you know those times when you're filled to the brim with gratitude, and you appreciate everything around you *so much?* When you stop believing in the fairytale that is religion . . . Well, the world becomes like that. It's like the last day of summer with your kids before you send them back to school, and you relish their giggling and their smell and their smiles, and you allow yourself to be immensely, *immensely* happy because you know that that moment right then and there is really all you have. It's a gift, living for today as opposed to living for some future grandeur. It's such a wonderful realization. Life is suddenly so potent. It's why I became a nurse. 'Cause so often you're there for someone's last moment. And I believe if it really is their last moment and there's nothing beyond it—well, I want to make that moment . . ."

Kayla smiled and looked off towards the sun rising outside the waiting room window. "I want to make that moment like the sunset on your last day of vacation."

"Aren't you afraid of what happens if you're wrong?" Ruth asked sincerely.

"No," Kayla said definitively. "Once you see the truth, you can't go back. Once you realize how this right here is all you have . . ." She sucked in a deep breath with a satisfied smile. "You don't want to go back."

Charleston

Ruth had measured her adult life in two ways, by watching the growth of her and Sam's children and witnessing the expansion of her and Sam's church. Their first baby, Rachel, was born the year Holy Light Ministries moved into the former pet supply store in the strip mall on the south side of Lynchburg. It was the most prolonged experience of simultaneous excitement and trepidation Ruth had ever known. Despite planning for both Rachel's birth and working on the details of the new church, there were still dozens of unexpected challenges and moments when both Ruth and Sam doubted their capcity to pull off being either parents or pastors. The hardest blow came when Ruth was forced to quit her job at Dillard's because she could no longer stand behind a counter for hours on end. She and Sam lived off Sam's pitiful paychecks for more months than either of them was prepared to do. It was a lot of ramen noodles and watered-down coffee and prayer. When they discovered mold in the strip mall space where they had begun ripping out the carpet and acoustic paneling, and the owner said they would have to pay for remediation, they wondered if they would lose everything. There were nights when neither Sam nor Ruth slept much more than an hour or two and days when they moved exhausted through the world, making the motions of living without feeling like they were actually alive.

It wasn't all terrible. There were triumphs, like the first Sunday service they held at their tiny storefront chapel. Ruth had never seen Sam so nervous as when he got up in front of all their friends and a few guests to preach that day. It was undoubtedly one of the most critical moments of his life—*of both their lives.* Ruth was six-and-a-half months pregnant with Rachel, and she worried the overwhelming intensity of the moment would cause her to go into early labor. Instead, once Sam began preaching, calmness seemed to pervade both her and Rachel's beings. Ruth would never forget the homily. Sam sermonized that every Christian had a divine right to all the blessings under the heavens. They need only name those blessings and claim those blessings, and their Heavenly Father would bestow on them the riches of His kingdom. Later Sam admitted to Ruth that as he was preaching, he was sure the words coming out of his mouth were garbled nonsense, but Ruth assured him his oration was spectacular, and given how many people returned the next Sunday to hear more, clearly she wasn't wrong.

By the time Rachel was born, they were filling their little strip mall church to capacity, and their worries about the loss of Ruth's paycheck were subsiding due to the healthy tithe the offering plates were bringing in. Even so, they barely had money for baby formula, let alone anything else, so Ruth was forced to cut disposable diapers out of her budget, and she spent more than her share of time handwashing dirty, reusable diapers that Rachel seemed to go through every hour on the hour. There were more than a few moments when Ruth was so exhausted by the excrement and the baby cries and the not knowing what to do that she literally wanted to give up, to walk away, to vanish. But in those moments, she would pray for God's strength, and He was always there for her.

Someone had given Ruth a plaque with the story of the "Footprints in the Sand." It was a short tale in which a disciple asked why, if Jesus had walked beside him throughout his existence, there was only one set of footprints in the sand at the hardest moments of his life? Jesus told the disciple during that time He hadn't disappeared. No, during *that* time Jesus was carrying the man. On particularly hard days Ruth would rest in the knowledge that Jesus wasn't carrying just her, but he was also carrying Sam and even little Rachel.

JD was born the year Holy Light Ministries moved into the old movie house in downtown Charleston. It was a big trek, from Virginia to South Carolina, but it was an opportunity Sam felt he couldn't turn down. He had been wanting to expand the reach of the church, and when one of their college friends heard about a decrepit theater in Charleston that they could have for free if they refurbished it, Sam and Ruth decided to do it—to follow what Sam swore was the call of the Lord on their lives to move six hours south. Despite thinking this time it would be easier than the last time they started up a church from scratch, both the new building and the new baby growing inside Ruth brought whole new challenges that, once more, Sam and Ruth would depend on their faith to overcome.

Though it seemed like an easy enough fixer-upper, the old movie house was much further gone than any local inspectors or Sam could have known from looking at its surface. Once the walls were opened, it became clear the kind of repair that would be needed. The electricity wasn't to code. The plumbing wasn't to code. Half of the structure was so severely termite infested; it would have to be completely rebuilt from the ground up. There was asbestos and mold and dry rot and more. What was supposed to have been accomplished with deep cleaning and a couple coats of paint became a money pit that Sam and Ruth saw no way out of. Luckily, with each new seemingly insurmountable obstacle also came some miracle, some Christian brother or sister with an offer of free labor or supplies or just good ol' fashioned cash to help move things along and save Sam and Ruth from being swallowed up by an ever-growing mountain of debt. Sam assured people left and right that God would bless them tenfold for their trouble, and he promised everyone from the city council to the Better Business Bureau to the chamber of commerce that he would have the theater ready for service within six months of his and Ruth's arrival in Charleston. But it was eleven months and a second baby later before the revolving doors fully opened.

Just like in Lynchburg, Sam befriended the local press who had initially been wary of him. They were the first ones invited to see the finished building. He took them on a tour of the back stage with its new lights and salvaged velvet curtain, and then he led them up to the balcony where a local artist was restoring an almost lost mural on the ceiling that depicted the journey of cinema from black and white to color from Charlie Chaplin to *Gone With the Wind* to *Sleeping Beauty*. At their first Sunday service they rolled out a red carpet and handed out popcorn, and people loved it. Within weeks they had a steady congregation, and all the bills that had piled up were slowly but methodically paid off.

Ruth didn't know how she would manage to be a wife, mother, *and* missionary, but with God's grace, no one around Charleston seemed to notice her anxiety. She was adored for her warmth and charm and admired for her poise, all of which was tested endlessly when JD was born. He was a screamer and a fit thrower and seemed to be endlessly hungry. Luckily for Ruth, Rachel didn't allow her new brother's various and impossibly loud emotional outbursts to affect her demure demeanor. Instead, she often simply patted him on the head when he launched into one of his sporadic tirades and looked at him with complete and total understanding. As for Ruth, she told herself to appreciate her first-born son with all her heart. God had specifically given him to her for a reason, and she wanted to learn whatever the lesson was that JD was born to teach her. The rest of the time, Ruth began doing what she had always wanted to do. In the basement of the movie house, she created a children's church. She painted the walls bright pinks and blues and oranges. They covered the concrete floors with rubber matting so while parents were upstairs worshipping, their young ones could run and play and learn about God just like Ruth had done as she was growing up with Trudy.

Unlike living in DC or Lynchburg, which felt like stopovers on her way to wherever she was supposed to end up, Ruth felt at home in Charleston. She relished the coral blushes of the buildings in downtown, the verdure of the trees that lined the cobblestone streets, the salty warmth of the ocean air, the candied drawl of the locals, and the relaxed pace of the city itself. She didn't sense a rustle of anxiousness to move on past Charleston to something grander once she and Sam settled there. Ruth only wanted to stretch out into the space around her, to get to know all its nooks and crannies, to learn all its mysteries like one would seek out the unknown depths of a lover. She was fond of Charleston in ways she never knew a person could regard a city. But in a way it belonged to her as no other place she'd ever lived, because in Charleston she had choices about the details of her life, choices that came from Sam's success as a preacher and her success as a wife and mother. It had taken a few years, but somehow Ruth and her family had gone from simply surviving to thriving. On afternoons when Sam would watch the kids in order to give Ruth a respite, she would walk through the old parts of the city and visit stores with antique gas lamps flickering out front and grand doors at their entrances carved hundreds of years ago, or she would sit in the park under the sprawling limbs of the ancient live oaks and watch the curly Spanish moss that hung amongst the leaves waft with the breeze, and she would whisper prayers of thanks to God for her life.

It seemed almost as soon as they opened the doors to the old movie house, Sam began looking for another piece of property. An expansion was needed because within two years of offering services at the old theater, they started turning away visitors due to the simple fact they reached capacity before service even began. More than once, the fire marshal kindly dropped by to make sure they weren't accidentally violating any city codes. Just like its predecessor (the pet supply storefront in Lynchburg), the movie house church had overcome its unusual heritage and was reborn a sanctuary where believers could share their truth and welcome others into the fold with genuine smiles and agape love. Many members would show up an hour before service to sit quietly in God's presence or mingle with one another over free coffee and donuts in the lobby. The rest would stay an hour or more after service to continue to worship or to catch up on their fellow Christians' lives. When people asked what it was that drew so many to Sam and the church, he would tell them he believed it was the values and morals he preached. People wanted structure, something to anchor them in this increasingly unfamiliar world, and he provided that. He also believed they showed up for the love that seemed to pervade the place—God's love!

The search for a new piece of property on which to expand the church began in earnest around the same time Ruth began feeling the gnaw in her stomach to expand their family once more. She was almost thirty, and with their finances solid, she started to romanticize the idea of having at least one more baby. While Sam scoured Charleston's real estate market for the perfect old factory or warehouse to transform into their next sanctuary, Ruth laid the groundwork to bring a new addition to the Christianson clan. It wasn't easy to get Sam on board at first, but Ruth judiciously held out on approving Sam's expansion plans for the church until he had come aboard her personal expansion plans for their family. As always, with teamwork, they both ultimately accomplished exactly what they wanted.

When Sam was approached about touring an elementary school, he was hesitant. He was all for finding a piece of land where the church could grow, but transforming an entire school campus would be a monumental undertaking. When he and Ruth went to look at the space, however, the endless possibilities were clear. From the cafeteria, which could be used to feed homeless, to the school gym, which could be used for their bourgeoning youth group, to the endless administration offices and green spaces for outdoor socializing, this would be Holy Light Ministry's permanent home—*Sam knew it!* This is where, Sam told Ruth, they would truly begin to reach the *world* with their message of Christ's salvation. Of course, they would have to run everything past the church's board and begin a fundraising campaign to pay not just for the mortgage on the property but the renovation as well.

The church's board of directors was comprised of Sam and Ruth's most trusted friends, people who had proven themselves to be loyal to the ministry throughout the rough and tumble years. Sam was, of course, the president. Todd McAuliffe was vice president. It was Todd who had urged Sam to bring Holy Light to Charleston, and who had given more than his share of time and money to keep Holy Light afloat. Todd and his wife, Donna, were both lawyers. They had also urged Sam to create the board in order to absorb some of the weight on Sam's shoulders concerning the day-to-day operations of the ministry. Kyle Cantrell was the treasurer. Miniver Waithe was the secretary. Kellen James, an ordained minister turned local contractor, was operations manager and one of the three associate pastors. Finally, there was Stephanie Groves, who was the head of marketing. She owned a string of beauty parlors around the Carolinas but spent most of her time making sure Holy Light maintained just the right aesthetics, from the font used to spell out the church's name to the color of the wallpaper in the bathrooms.

The night the board voted unanimously to buy and begin a renovation of the elementary school campus, they also voted on a code of conduct for members of the church and more importantly its leaders. As Sam led Holy Light out onto a limb, once more, they all agreed with the stakes so high, it was best to stay lean and mean and demand clearly and precisely that any person who held a position in the church, from deacon to janitor to board member or pastor, must also uphold certain Christian values and morals or face disciplinary action and even expulsion based on the severity of their transgressions. It was slightly less fierce than the code of conduct Sam and Ruth had lived with at Liberty, and there wasn't a single moment during the vote where Ruth thought any of the tenants of the code would in any way be broken by her or her husband.

As promised, after the successful purchase of the elementary school, Sam got to work with Ruth trying to have another baby, and little Tim was born one year before they moved into the fully and exquisitely renovated Holy Light Ministries campus. With the gestation of both Tim and the church, Ruth found herself enjoying all the machinations of the process much more than she ever had before. She'd been through it enough now to know all the lows and the highs that accompanied such dramatic life changes, and instead of fighting for or against any of the challenges, she simply went with them—everything that came her way. Both developments, the church and Tim, were her dreams made reality.

For the first time in her life, Ruth and Sam were not worried about monthly bills, and it was odd for her to realize that she could go to Dillard's and be one of the women who bought the two-hundred-dollar face creams she had once sold. It was wonderful to load her kids up into her new Suburban and know that there was little chance it might break down on them in the middle of traffic or overheat on some particularly hot, Southern afternoon. With Tim, Ruth went to all her doctor visits and never worried about how they would afford checkups or prenatal vitamins. The process of living was not so much a chore as it was the exercise she had been preparing so long for—an exercise in how to live right, and it was pregnancy that nudged Ruth further towards what would eventually become her very staunch beliefs about the moment at which life began.

With each child she gave birth to, Ruth felt stronger and stronger that a child's life started at conception, and abortion, which could take that life away months after it had begun its journey, was not just an abhorrent error in American judgment, it was a moral defect that would stain all of humanity forever. "Imagine," she would tell attendees at luncheons and women's retreats where she spoke, "maybe the child who was supposed to cure cancer or Alzheimer's or AIDS was aborted. Maybe the child who was supposed to put an end the conflict in the Middle East was murdered in the womb years ago. Imagine all the lost potential because doctors, who are supposed to 'first do no harm' legally kill unborn children every day."

Abortion was the one thing Ruth would admit forced her hand when it came to politics too. If she had to vote between two candidates of different parties, it didn't matter if the candidate *for* abortion rights was, in fact, a better candidate or even a better person, Ruth would vote for the candidate who would stand *against* abortion—who would stand against what she considered to be a war on the unborn—a war in which babies were slaughtered with no recourse. Liberals like her mother argued vehemently they weren't pro-abortion; they were pro women's rights. But Ruth couldn't understand how anyone had the right to murder a growing life inside them no matter how early that life was discovered or under what circumstances that life had come to be. She believed evangelicals were right to make abortion the titular viewpoint on which to mold their religious authority, and unlike homosexuality, teaching evolution in schools, or even climate change, it was a foundational conviction upon which it was downright impossible to cross the aisle, keeping "true" Christians in lockstep with conservative Republicans for better or worse.

It was after Rachel was born that Ruth began working in earnest as a counselor for women with unplanned or unwanted pregnancies, but it was when Holy Light moved to the renovated elementary school campus that Ruth asked Sam to give her space for an unplanned pregnancy center of her own—a space where women could come and be counseled about giving birth to the unique and special treasure that was their unborn baby. The center which Ruth named Holy *Life* Ministries quickly became renown for not only their work helping women through all the stages of pregnancy, but also placing unwanted babies with adoption agencies and Christian couples who wanted, but were unable, to have children on their own. They also became known for speaking out against abortion and against politicians who were "pro-abortion" a term Ruth instructed others to use instead of the seemingly soft-pedaling, liberal term "pro-choice."

Holy Life Ministries was heralded as the template other evangelical churches around the country should use to help put an end to the "infanticide" plaguing America, and Ruth was a firsthand witness the power of their ministry changing women's lives for the better on a day-to-day basis while simultaneously saving the lives of unborn babies too. Ruth spent more than her share of time at hospitals around Charleston, Lamaze breathing through the births of countless children and coaching their mothers either for life with their new child or for moving on after that child was given to another family to raise as their own. It was constant tears: tears of joy, tears of sorrow, tears of hope, tears of loss. And no, it didn't always end with the birth of a child. Some women would change their minds about bringing their baby to term after being counseled. They just couldn't manage to see the life inside them as anything more than a meaningless cluster of cells that happened by accident and which modern technology could help them dispose of quickly. "Before I formed you in the womb, I knew you; before you were born, I set you apart." Ruth would say, reminding people of God's words on the matter. Ruth herself believed full-heartedly God's words *were* the final words on the matter.

Throughout the growth of her children and the church, Florence remained in the back of Ruth's mind a sort of foreboding presence she wasn't quite sure how to deal with. Since the terrible visit when Ruth introduced Sam to her mother, Florence had limited her interactions with Ruth to phone calls once every few months. Then, as the years passed, their calls grew more and more stilted and infrequent despite the fact Ruth had given Florence grandchildren, or perhaps *because of it*. Ruth didn't want her mother getting her twisted logic into her children's heads or confusing their small, impressionable minds. So, Florence and Ruth remained in their corners until at long last it was inevitable, all the tension that had built up between them over the years would have to come out.

Florence saw Ruth speaking at a pro-life rally at the National Mall, and Florence called to invite Ruth over to the old craftsman for tea. Ruth wondered if Florence might have been one of the pro-*choice* protestors that framed the edges of the rally, but she decided not to ask. Knowing that seeing her mother probably wouldn't be the most pleasant experience, especially since her mother knew the reason she was in town, Ruth offered to meet Florence at the hotel where she was staying instead of her childhood home.

When Florence arrived in the lobby of the hotel in a dingy muumuu, her grey hair in tangles, and a pair of oversized prescription sunglasses on her face, Ruth was shocked to realize how old Florence had become in the last ten years. Ruth adjusted her lilac blue Donna Karen jacket, feathered back a few wisps of hair, and wondered what passersby would think about her sitting down with this seemingly fragile bag lady. Then Ruth immediately hated herself for allowing such a thought to cross her mind. She ministered to down and out people all the time. It was only because she *knew* this woman—*her mother*—that she had a feeling of trepidation about being seen with her.

"I guess we can't go to the bar, can we?" Florence said, seemingly annoyed as she brushed past Ruth and moved over to a silk couch near the lobby restrooms, barely looking at Ruth.

Florence carefully lowered herself down onto the settee like another old woman Ruth had once been close to—Florence's own mother, Trudy. Ruth sat down opposite Florence and smiled. "It's good to see you, Mom."

"You've missed the whole point of everything. You always have," Florence stated flatly. She stared off in the opposite direction of her daughter.

Ruth sighed. "We haven't seen each other in forever, and this is how you say hello?"

"In all honesty, I'm ashamed to be seen with you," Florence rebutted, still refusing to look at Ruth.

"*You're* ashamed to be seen with *me*?" Ruth scoffed.

"And I worry for your children."

"Well," Ruth smiled, "at least you're worried about someone other than yourself for once."

"I saw your speech at the Mall."

"Here it comes."

"At least I saw what I could stand of it."

Ruth tried not to roll her eyes. She forced a smile, attempted to restart the conversation. "Mom, how are you doing?"

"What I don't get . . . What I truly don't understand is how you think everyone is supposed to fit into the same damn category as you?"

"I've never said a thing about anyone fitting into the exact same mold I've made for my life," Ruth countered.

Florence laughed. "You preach to the world that your God is a God of infinite possibility, and then you condemn anyone who dares think outside the prison cell all you Christian crazies keep yourselves locked up in."

"Religion isn't a jail, Mom. It's a road map to help you get through life a little easier."

"How has your religion made it easier for gay and lesbians, immigrants and Muslims, or for that matter women? I want to understand what is moral about oppressing others? I want to understand what is moral about saying that everyone has to live their life the same way you do or else?"

"They aren't *my* commandments. They're *God's* command—"

But Florence cut Ruth off. "You sound like the fucking Taliban, and *you are*! Except the way you destroy lives and inflict fear is much more sinister."

"If you're just here to fight, I have better things to do with my time."

Florence finally turned to look at Ruth and pointed a boney finger in her face. "Just tell me one thing . . . Who is God?"

Ruth was a bit taken aback for a moment. Then she shook her head in frustration. "God is God," Ruth said. "He's the alfa and omega, beginning and end."

"Beginning and the end," Florence repeated. "Yes, from *your* beginning until *your* end—you are God. That is true."

Ruth sighed. "That's not what I meant."

Florence continued, "That little voice you hear whisper inside your head, that you insist is some great force speaking to you, that you swear is proof of a higher power's existence—Surprise. Surprise. I've got it. Everyone has it. It's not a God of any sort. It's you yourself. It's your conscience. And it only lasts until you pass. And when you do, that's it."

"So, me and a billion other Christians, we're all insane, and you're the smart one?"

"No, you're all so scared of this life you can't fucking live in it. You've invented a hereafter where all the hurts of this life meet their reckoning, and to prove to yourself that it exists, you've come together and agreed on terms. You've invented an Almighty to oversee these terms, an Almighty that you can conveniently hear if you just listen to that little voice inside you. It's a fantasy that's been passed down from generation to generation all over the world. And it's taken various forms in any of the five thousand different religions that exist. Because the truth is you want to know where you came from and where you're going. And right now—*RIGHT NOW*—doesn't matter 'cause if it did, it might not be enough. And for a lot of people *the now* truly is awful. But I'm here to tell this is all there is, Ruth. If it's the last thing you ever hear me say, I want you to hear me say it loud and clear—heaven is a fantasy, but earth is real, and it's all you've got!"

"I'm sorry you feel that way, Mom, especially because . . ." A tear fell down Ruth's cheek, and she quickly brushed it away. "Your reality has always seemed so awful to me."

"That's exactly my point. You always wanted me to be something I wasn't, something I couldn't be. And the funny thing is, I did what you claim is the right thing. I gave birth to you. But you resent me for it. You resent me for being me. Now you want everyone else to be something you believe they should be when maybe, if you just let people be themselves, you might begin to appreciate their eccentricities . . . you might even be able to love them, not for the things you think make them perfect but for all the things that make them who *they are!*" Now it was Florence's cheeks that became wet. "I love you, Ruth. I always have. I always will. What's funny is that you Christians say, *God* is love. But I wonder if you know what *real* love actually is?"

Florence stood to her feet and waited for a beat as if hoping Ruth would stop her from walking away. When Ruth didn't move, Florence shuffled off across the lobby towards the revolving doors and disappeared.

Ruth took a breath and straightened herself. She looked around to see if anyone had witnessed the encounter she had just had with the woman who brought her into this world. Everyone seemed oblivious, continuing about their business in the opulent marble-clad room. Almost instantly, Ruth felt better. She felt vindicated for all the years she had kept Florence at bay. Florence was a non-believer and worse than that, she was working as a tool of Satan to try and thwart the good work Ruth was doing for Christ.

Ruth remembered walking into her and Sam's elementary school turned megachurch the next Sunday. At capacity, the auditorium could hold five thousand worshippers, and there was an overflow room that could contain another five hundred more. The stage at the front was as big as any Broadway stage with just as many lights and speakers and musical instruments. Ruth drove into church with Sam early on Sunday mornings, and they would walk the pews, row after row, praying for God's blessing on the upcoming service and for his power to manifest itself upon the people who attended. That Sunday, as she walked the pews and prayed, Ruth remembered feeling more empowered than she had ever felt before. Having had the conversation that she did with her mother, she felt as though a weight had been lifted from her life. And now she believed in her heart more soundly than ever that she was on the right side of things. Look at her life. Look at how it had all turned out. Look at her perfect, beautiful kids. Look at her amazing, wonderful husband. Look at their church, their congregation, their outreach to the world. She was changing the lives of people everywhere for the better, leading people the world over to a glorious eternity with their Heavenly Father. What had Florence ever done? There was no comparison between them, and there was no way anyone would believe that her mother knew more *or better* than Ruth.

Just that morning, Ruth had awakened before the sunrise to make breakfast for her kids. It wasn't easy to do so much. She certainly could have given them cereal and called it a day. But she wanted to be more—to be better for them than what Florence had been for her. Ruth made sure their home was clean and their laundry was fresh. She made sure they had new clothes and computers and cell phones. She paid attention to them. She attempted to perk them up when they were sad and encourage them when they were down. Her kids loved her for all she did. Sure, they weren't always cherubs, and she wasn't always a saint, but mostly it was good, the life she had made for them over the years, the life she had made for herself and Sam. Ruth had figured it all out despite her mother. Florence was wrong; things were indeed black and white. There was a right way and a wrong way to be. If anything was clear, *that* was clear.

After a raucous song service, Ruth waited in the wings off stage near a monitor that flashed between close-ups of Kellen, the associate pastor, giving announcements and wide shots of the congregation seated and attentive. The whole production was being directed by their A/V team and beamed out to twenty-seven different countries via satellite, as well as streaming live on YouTube. Ruth was wearing one of her favorite skirt suit ensembles, light lavender with matching pumps, one that gave her a little extra kick in her step. In her hand she clutched her Bible, the same one with the soft, faded oniony pages that she had held onto since she was a little girl. When she was called to the podium, Ruth stepped out on the stage to thunderous applause. Any doubts her mother had planted inside her about the validity of the choices she had made with her life vanished completely. She was Ruth Christianson, perfect wife, mother, and apostle, and she would be sharing a word from God himself with all who were watching. She was His voice. She was His chosen one. He was going to speak to the world through her. She was special. She was perfect.

Get Thee Behind Me

The days that followed Joe's death were muted like the world was underwater, and the hours that passed seemed simultaneously slowed down and sped up like the sun setting on a distant horizon. Despite being a distraction from what had previously been the unwanted attention focused on her life, Ruth knew that somehow the quiet was a false peace and that the horror she'd been fighting was only catching its breath, waiting for the moment to pounce and finish her off for good. She dreaded the instant that Joe was finally in the grave, the mourning was all over, the guests had all left, and the tears had all been shed. There would be hell to pay, Ruth remembered thinking. She hadn't killed Joe, but somehow in Naomi's mind, Ruth would be responsible.

Ruth did her best to comfort the kids, to look them in the eyes and tell them she loved them. She squeezed their shoulders, hugged them, and kissed them on their pink cheeks and mopey foreheads. And when the reality hit that there was no way she could give back the innocence they had lost over the last few weeks, she cried for them when she was alone and no one could hear her.

As for Sam, he was changed. His father's death had aged him in a way that the news of his affair with a male prostitute and losing his church somehow hadn't been able to. Ruth swore gray hairs were sprouting on his head that she had never seen before, and there were lines in his face that didn't previously exist. He helped Naomi with all the preparations for Joe's funeral, and Naomi treated Sam as though, for a brief moment, he was once more the unblemished boy she had raised.

For almost three days Ruth barely saw Sam as he and Naomi

huddled in dimly lit spaces and whispered to one another about what would come next for her, for the farm, for Joe's small congregation. Joe had left no will; he didn't trust lawyers. Naomi would inherit everything as his widow, but that was not much. She would have to make decisions quickly about concerns she never had before like what would happen to the sixty head of beef cows, the hay in the barn, the corn in the fields, and the white-steepled building she had helped Joe erect. Joe had never let anyone help him lead the church. From the accounting to the pastoring, Joe was it. He turned on the lights and turned them back off. He unlocked the doors and locked them back up once more. He'd never even let anyone else preach behind his pulpit.

People dropped by the Christianson farm with all manner of casseroles and perishable goods. Some were good friends. Some were busybodies who wanted to be at the top of the local gossip chain. Naomi received everyone with the graciousness that was expected of a new widow, a battened-up strength that surprised Ruth. In the past Ruth had wondered what would happen to her if she ever lost Sam, and it was only the kids that she believed would force her hollow, lifeless soul to carry on. In Naomi's case, things were different. Sam certainly didn't need Naomi the way Rachel, JD, and Tim needed Ruth. Still, Ruth looked out the window of the cabin the evening before Joe's funeral and saw Naomi weeding her garden as if it was just another day.

An oppressive heatwave hit the morning Joe was buried, and the white carnations that adorned his casket wilted and turned brown before the service was over. The reception that followed was at the farmhouse, and even with the air conditioning running nonstop, there was no escaping the smothering humidity and lung burning late summer temperatures. Even the insects seemed quiet, either out of respect or sheer exhaustion. Ruth did her best to pick up after folks and keep dishes and plates washed and cleaned in order to allow Naomi to sit and appreciate the company of the seventy or more people who had shown up to pay their respects. Of course, Naomi was never one to let anyone else be in charge. So, she was constantly appearing in the kitchen, arms full of cake plates and coffee cups.

"Naomi, please let me take care of cleaning things up. You go be with your guests." Ruth said gently.

"This is my house. I'll do what I want." Naomi pushed past Ruth for the sink where she set the dirty dishes.

"Is there *anything* I can do for you?" Ruth asked.

Naomi said nothing, began scouring the plates, rinsing them, and placing them in the drainer. Ruth rolled her eyes at the stubborn woman and moved over next to her to dry the plates and put them away. For a moment they worked like an assembly line. Wash. Rinse. Dry. Put away. Wash. Rinse. Dry. Put away. Suddenly, Naomi smashed one of the cake plates into the sink basin and shook violently. "Stoppit! Stoppit! You are not wanted here! Don't you get that? Get out! GET OUT! Get out of my house!"

For a moment Ruth froze, and throughout the house visitors became silent. Naomi gripped the edge of the counter, her eyes bugged and staring at the sink where the cake plate lay broken in pieces, the water from the faucet running over its porcelain shards.

Sam appeared from the doorway to the dining room. "Momma, what's wrong?"

Ruth set down the dish towel she was holding and looked at Sam. "I think I'm gonna go check on the kids."

Sam leered at Ruth with an accusing look that irritated her as she headed for the back door, but she tried to remain calm, tried to remind herself that she needed to be the strong one right now.

"I don't want her here," Naomi said flatly. "You can stay. The kids can stay, but her . . . I want her gone."

Ruth stopped just shy of the mudroom and turned to look at Sam to see if he had heard the same words come out of Naomi that she had just heard. He didn't meet Ruth's eyes. He stared at the floor as more and more people were gathering in the dining room behind him to see what all the commotion was about.

"Sam?" Ruth asked, hoping he would look at her, hoping he wouldn't do the impossible and side with his mother in this case.

"Sam?" Ruth raised her voice.

"Just go to the cabin, Ruth," Sam said.

"No. No! I want her gone entirely." Naomi stamped her foot angrily.

"Mom, stop!"

"She's the reason all of this has happened!" Naomi screamed. "She's the reason your father is dead!"

Ruth scoffed at Naomi, "Here it comes. I knew you would do this."

"From the moment she showed up here, I knew she was no good for you," Naomi said. "She's been no good for you as a wife, and she's no good for your kids as a mother."

Ruth cut her eyes at Naomi. "What do you know about anything?"

Naomi pointed a bony finger at Ruth. "It's true. Tim doesn't talk. JD is a bully. And you know why Mike and Connie Murray aren't here today? You know why Mike didn't make it to his best friend's funeral service?"

Ruth was confused. What did Mike and Connie have to do with her kids?

"They weren't here because the daughter you raised—your fifteen-year-old—put the moves on Mike when they were collecting honey from his bees."

"That's ridiculous."

"Your daughter grabbed him by his manhood and told him she wanted him to take her virginity."

Ruth shook her head. "That's a lie."

Naomi smiled. "It's the devil in you. Your momma passed him to you, and you've passed him on to your children as well as my son."

Tears sprung to Ruth's eyes. "Why are you doing this?"

"Connie called and told me what happened. She told both Joe and me. Now, Joe is dead. But I'm not, and I want you to leave here. Get thee behind me, Satan!"

For all the people gathered in the dining room behind Sam, the moment was ghostly silent. Ruth looked from Naomi to Sam. He was clearly in shock by Naomi's revelation. Ruth tried to form words in her mind, something to say back to Naomi, but truthfully all she wanted was to leave the farm just like she'd been asked. She held her hand out to Sam. "Sam, come with me," Ruth said.

Sam didn't move.

"Sam." Ruth's voice quivered, and her hand trembled.

Still nothing.

Suddenly, Naomi began speaking in tongues. "*Ummmnosho-bul-a-ta-ta-ta hemesolufra comteletonta bul-la-la-la ta-ta-ta bul-la-la-la shometake-latelma shometakelamotra-ta-ta hemesolufra ne da-da solufra de na-na-na . . .*"

Naomi slowly ambled towards Ruth like some cultish villain gurgling up the words of a demon lodged deep inside her. All Ruth could think to do was turn and run.

The kids were playing Old Maid at the picnic table in the cabin kitchen when Ruth entered frantic and shaking.

"Mom, what's wrong?" Rachel asked.

"Did you . . ." Ruth started to ask Rachel whether the story Naomi had told her about Mike was true or not. But what did it matter? What if Rachel did get sexual with Mike? It wasn't a moral deficit. It was a natural inclination considering Rachel's sexuality was burgeoning, and with all the confusion of the last few weeks maybe it was completely understandable. Ruth herself was beyond confused. Even the simple act of breathing had become a chore, a chore she was tired of struggling through. She wanted it to be over, all the pain, all the uncertainty. Instead of finishing her question to Rachel, Ruth attempted to suck in a breath. She forced a smile at her sweet kids. "I need you guys to pack up. We're leaving."

The kids looked at each other confused.

"Where are we going?" JD asked.

"I don't know yet, but I need you all to get your things ready now."

There was silence. They knew this was not a good development. They knew this was only more drama and more confusion, and it would lead to only more hurt. But they were also good kids—amazing kids—and so they each softly stood up from the table and headed for the stairs to do as Ruth had told them.

As for Ruth, she kept waiting for the cabin door to open, for Sam to walk through it and tell her everything was okay, to ask her to give Naomi some time. But when she peeked through the window of the cabin door, he was nowhere in sight. She moved up the stairs to the bedroom in the loft of the cabin that she had shared with him on so many different occasions. It seemed severely old and rundown in a way Ruth had never noticed before. She was grateful they had only unpacked the essentials from the Cadillac. She need only gather what was originally in her suitcase and she would be ready to leave. It was that easy, she thought. Still, she waited for the sound of Sam stepping through the door of the cabin downstairs. Still, there was nothing.

By the time Ruth gathered what little she had unpacked, the kids were waiting in their room. "You guys ready?" she asked.

Somberly, they each nodded and grabbed their suitcases. Ruth didn't know what would happen when she led what was left of her family out of the cabin towards the Cadillac. She understood that she was supposed to leave, but would Sam let her take the kids? And if he didn't, what then? Would the sheriff be called? Would there be another yelling match? He had no more right to their kids than she did. In fact, she suspected she would have *more* of a right. After all, he hadn't *just* been caught with a prostitute; he'd been caught doing illicit drugs! But no one exited the house, and Ruth and the kids moved across the yard like a sad caravan of war-torn refugees unimpeded. Everyone in the house seemed to simply continue with their grieving or socializing or whatever it was they were supposed to be doing. *Surely, it wouldn't be this easy,* Ruth thought. *Surely, Sam would come running out after his family. Surely!* But as Ruth loaded the suitcases into the back of the Cadillac, and the kids buckled themselves into their seats, the world around Ruth carried on as though she didn't exist at all.

Over

Ruth sucked in a deep breath as she slid in behind the driver's seat of the Cadillac and turned on the ignition. A scrapyard like arrangement of vehicles were parked everywhere, but Ruth performed a three-point turn, and the farm disappeared behind the cloud of dust the Cadillac kicked up in its wake.

Adrenaline coursed through Ruth as she pulled out onto the blacktop of the highway. For all she knew she was leaving the Christianson farm forever. But it felt good—this rebel alertness—like her naked body had been tossed into an icy pool and had gone into instant, satisfying survival mode. The fog had lifted, at least temporarily, and she wanted to take advantage of the adrenaline, to use it to her benefit, to make the correct next moves. She had the kids; that was the main thing. The next was to make sure she had cash. Surely Sam wouldn't close her out of their only banking account, but she couldn't risk it. He was capable of anything under the influence of his mother. And gas—the Cadillac was almost on empty. She needed gas in order to drive as far away from Conway as possible. For all Ruth knew Naomi would call the sheriff on her. For all she knew the sheriff was at the farmhouse already, paying his respects, and he had witnessed Ruth's escape with the kids first hand. She had to get out of the state.

Luckily, the children sat like beautiful hostages in their seats, not even playing with their cell phones or interacting with each other. They knew what was going on, and perhaps they had been waiting for this moment too. Ruth wondered if they had been wanting it. None of them had put up any fight or questioned her for a moment, not like they had when she made them pack up to leave Charleston. Ruth considered trying to say something heartening. Instead, she drove towards Conway where she would stop at Casey's General Store to top off the tank, purchase snacks for everyone, and withdraw money from the ATM. She would only be able to withdraw six hundred bucks from her and Sam's account, but that would be enough for now. She would take more the next day and the day after that and the day after that until Sam caught on to what she was doing or until their shared account was empty.

For a moment, Ruth wondered if it was some sort of crime to leave the state with her and Sam's kids in tow. But what alternative was there? It was over—everything. Suddenly, the word "over" stole Ruth's breath, and she almost slammed on the breaks. But it *was* over. There was no going back to Sam or their church or their former life. There was no going back to the farm or to Naomi or to all that had been. There was no going back to being the woman she once was, because she wasn't just leaving Sam. She knew as she sped away from the Christianson farm that she was leaving . . . *God*. It was as though a veil that blurred her sight since she was a little girl had simply vanished, and she could see with new hi-def clarity what she'd never been able to see before—what Florence had tried so desperately to impart to her. The Almighty God, Allah, Jehovah, El Shaddai, Elohim, Vishnu, all the supreme beings that made up all the religions of the world were to adults what imaginary friends were to children, a way of coping, of working through an existence that was confusing and hurtful and eventually lead to the unthinkable—death. But just like one day a child realizes he no longer needs that make-believe companion to guided them any longer through their tender years, the deity that had once commanded Ruth's every attention suddenly turned out to be merely a crutch she had unexpectedly cast off with the simultaneous escape from her marriage. And while she imagined herself crippled without Sam or God or the church, the real surprise was that she could not only walk by herself, she could run! Not one time had she thought to pray as she and her children made their getaway. Not once had she racked her mind for some proverb that would mask the reality that this world here in front of her was all she and her children had. For years she had lived with her head in the clouds. But, all of that was . . . *over*.

There was only one other vehicle sitting by the pumps when Ruth pulled the Cadillac up under the florescent awning that covered the Casey's filling station. "Go inside and pick out whatever you want to eat. We're going to be in the car for a while," she told the kids.

Without hesitation, Rachel, JD, and Tim all climbed out of their seats and went inside the general store to snack-food nirvana.

Ruth walked over to the ATM that sat next to the "ICE" freezer on the side of the building. Six hundred dollars—she wondered how far that could get her? She puzzled over where she planned to go anyway? Nonetheless—

"Ruth?"

Ruth turned to the voice that had spoken her name, but she knew who it was before she saw him.

There stood Delmer Green in all his lumberjack glory. "You might want to get inside; your kids are buying out half the store," he said with a wink.

Ruth couldn't help but smile. It was a relief, someone treating her like a human especially at this moment. The way Delmer's eyes sparkled at her, Ruth also remembered what it was like to feel like a woman. "I told them they could get whatever they wanted," Ruth sighed.

The ATM spit out her six-hundred-dollar allotment of twenty-dollar bills, and she saw Delmer register how large the stack of cash was. Sheepishly Ruth pulled the fat green tongue of money from the black mouth of the cash machine, folded it, and shoved it into her pocket. "I can't believe the service charges on the ATMs around here," she said, trying to appear casual.

"You okay?" Delmer asked, his suspicion clearly piqued.

Ruth looked over at the Cadillac. She didn't know how to answer Delmer.

He followed her gaze to the Cadillac, and then he turned back to her again. "Do you need some help, Ruth?"

Ruth still didn't answer. What could she say? How to say it? She peered into the general store where she could see the tops of her kids' heads bobbing through the aisles selecting junk food for their escape. That's what they were doing? They were escaping—all of them—now. Ruth turned to Delmer. "I'm leaving him, but I don't know where to go," Ruth said quietly.

Delmer understood exactly what Ruth was saying without her needing to explain more. "Will you let me help you?" he asked.

"Why would *you* help *me*?"

Delmer smiled. "Why *wouldn't* I help you?"

Ruth shook her head. "I don't know what I'm doing."

Delmer grew serious. He moved closer to Ruth and put his hands on her arms reassuringly. "It's okay."

"Mom, we're waiting for you!" JD yelled, leaning out from the door of the store.

"It's getting late. Come to my place for the night. You can figure things out there," Delmer offered.

"I don't know."

"Well, *I do*," Delmer assured her.

"I'm scared," Ruth stated matter-of-factly.

"Please, let me help you," Delmer said. "I've wanted to help you from the moment I saw you."

Honestly, Ruth didn't need to think about it. As soon as Delmer laid his hands on her, she knew she would accept anything he offered. It wasn't that she needed him to help, but that she wanted him to help. She wanted to feel like she wasn't the only one holding up the whole world for a moment. "Let me corral the kids," Ruth said.

Delmer pointed to the other vehicle next to the gas pumps. It was only now Ruth recognized his truck. "Follow me," he said.

"Okay," Ruth whispered. She headed for the doors of the store. Then she stopped and looked back. "Thank you."

Delmer lived ten miles outside of Conway on the opposite end of the county line from where the Christianson farm lay. As she followed

Delmer's truck down the blacktop, Ruth realized she knew the area where they were headed. There was a swimming hole somewhere nearby that she and Sam had visited years ago one summer when Rachel was first born. Delmer turned onto a well-maintained gravel road where a sign read "Baptist Campgrounds 5 miles," and a red arrow pointed towards the distant hill. Yes, that was it—the swimming hole was by the old Baptist campgrounds. But a mile before the campgrounds, Delmer's truck turned again onto an even smaller and more rutted road that wound its way deeper into the forest.

Gnarled tree limbs seemed to reach out across the lane for a piece of the Cadillac as Ruth maneuvered the thicket, and she considered perhaps she should be careful following someone who was basically a stranger into the darkest parts of the backwoods. But she was hardly vulnerable. Just let someone try and mess with her or her children right now; she would kill them with a single blow like a lioness protecting her cubs.

Another half mile down Delmer's small, private drive, a clearing appeared. In the middle of it set a beautiful log house wrapped all the way around by a large porch. A few lamps glowed through the windows of what looked like the nicely kept up home. Ruth breathed a sigh of relief. An older French woman named Odette once told Ruth, after she gave Ruth and Sam keys to their first apartment, that she knew they would be good renters because she had seen their car, and she could always tell how someone would treat their home by how well they kept up their vehicle. Sure enough, over the years Ruth had known this wisdom to be true. She never imagined Delmer living like some conventional bachelor, given his clean-cut appearance and his shiny truck. Then again, so many things Ruth had leaned on as fact had become fiction as of late.

Just down the hill from the house was the Gasconade River. Its surface reflected the last bits of dusk and looked like a slick of mercury quietly slipping through the black shadows of cedar and birch trees that bejeweled its banks. The kids were mostly quiet as they climbed out of the Cadillac.

"This is home," Delmer stated, opening his arms wide. "I want you to make yourselves comfortable. Whatever you need, you go for it."

None of the kids responded to Delmer's offer, but they followed him into the cabin acquiescing to his leadership. Ruth watched after their little caravan, and for a moment, surrounded by the tranquility of the place, she forgot she was a fugitive on the run from her marriage and God. Through the window, she saw Delmer introducing her kids to an exceptionally large yellow tomcat. The feline stretched and yawned and seemed eager to accept the scratch behind the ears that Delmer gave him. It was a dream in a way—a fantasy come to life: a beautiful house, a nice truck, a perfect man. Was Delmer Green gay? Suddenly, Ruth was sad. She didn't know what she expected from an evening in Delmer's presence, but whatever she had hoped for seemed to dim just slightly. She laughed at herself for caring about a man she barely knew. Then she laughed again because for the first time in what seemed like forever, she realized she still could laugh.

Delmer made venison burgers for the kids from a six-point buck he shot last deer season, and the kids scarfed down the juicy nourishment along with potatoes he sliced and cooked in a Fry Daddy with a seasoning he declared he made special and only shared with certain guests. For himself and Ruth, Delmer poured small tumblers of a red table wine he said was his favorite. Feeling like a rebel, Ruth didn't tell Delmer she was unaccustomed to drinking, and instead sipped at the bitter drink pretending to enjoy the pepper taste that soured her mouth and made her feel slightly lightheaded.

Over supper, there was no talk about Sam or Joe or anything that had occurred in the last few days or months. Instead, Delmer asked each of the kids about their favorite subjects in school, what kinds of music they liked, and who they would have dinner with if they could meet anyone from history? Then, to keep the kids entertained while he and Ruth cleaned up dishes, he let them select a movie to stream, and by the time the Fry Daddy was put away, Rachel, JD, and Tim were all soundly passed out in the living room.

"I was gonna offer to make them popcorn, but I guess that's kinda out of the question now, huh?" Delmer whispered to Ruth as he refilled his glass with more wine.

Ruth smiled. "It's been . . ." Ruth didn't finish her thought, instead she shook her head as though she didn't even have the words for what their little lives had been through the last couple months and especially the last few days.

"You want some more?" Delmer offered to pour Ruth more wine.

"I'm good. Thank you."

"Follow me," he said, and he headed for a door just off the kitchen that led to the covered porch.

A few moths fluttered madly around the antique porch light, and in the distance, Ruth relished the wild concert being performed by all the other insects swept up in the night's passions. She allowed herself to be cradled in the warmth of the summer evening as she settled into an Adirondack chair next to Delmer.

"This is heaven," she said.

"My sentiments exactly," Delmer smiled, and he sipped his wine.

"Why aren't . . ." Once again, Ruth stopped herself.

"Why aren't, what?" Delmer prodded.

"It's so nosey of me."

"I'm from a small town in Missouri. I'm used to nosey."

"Why aren't you married?" Ruth asked with an ashamed grimace.

Delmer took another sip of his wine and sighed. "I was with someone for quite a few years. Then we broke things off, and I . . . I don't know. I guess, I kinda liked being single. I just wanted to breathe a little, find myself. So, I moved out here and next thing I know, I'm single for a good four years now."

"Why did you break things off?"

Delmer smiled. "You really are nosey."

"You get to ask me anything you want next, I promise."

Delmer sighed again. "Why did we break things off? Well, I guess it was because we just didn't love each other anymore. We didn't hate each other either. We just . . . knew we'd be better off going our separate ways."

"Wasn't that hard?"

"Hey, I thought I got to ask the next question?" Delmer smiled.

"Sorry. Sorry. Yes, that's right."

"It wasn't easy, but at the same time, it was. It's difficult to explain to people. Everybody wants you to break up and hate one another and have only terrible things to say about each other. But that's not the way it was for us. Even after she got engaged and married a couple years ago, I never felt anything but happy that Katie was happy."

Ruth couldn't help but notice Delmer had said the word "she" and "Katie" when mentioning his ex, and Ruth was relieved in a way to know that he was heterosexual. Then again, maybe he wasn't. She had certainly been fooled once by a prince charming. Honestly, who really cared? What did she think she was going to do, bed him? Before her thoughts about Delmer's sexuality could become more protracted, Delmer cleared his throat.

"So, do you need to talk about things? If not, I'm totally not one to pry, but if you do, I want you to know I'm a good listener." He smiled sweetly at her in a way that truly was soothing and open and full of kindness.

"I don't know where to begin," Ruth said. "I've spent so much time the last few days reflecting on my life and how I arrived at this point, and there's no answer I have to make sense of it all—except for one thing. But that one thing is so far afield of all that I've ever known to be true that it literally wipes the whole experience of my existence clean. It's wondrous and terrifying, like realizing you've been looking at the world through a mirror, a mirror you've now put down, and you're seeing everything for the first time in a way that actually makes sense."

"Wow. I can't wait to hear what this thing is," Delmer beamed.

"I don't believe in God anymore," Ruth said flatly. "I . . . suddenly . . . don't believe in any of that stuff at all. I can't. I don't know how it happened exactly. But, I just . . . I don't."

"You think maybe you're having a reaction to . . ."

"No," Ruth said almost curtly. Then, she smiled. "No. I know it's not a reaction. Or maybe it is. It's an awakening. I'm being awakened to life—to *real* life, to what life *actually* is. And I'm . . . I'm in disbelief on many levels, but mostly, I'm in disbelief that I didn't get this before, that this was right in front of me all this time—this truth—and I looked right past it at what I wanted to see, what I was more comfortable seeing." Ruth shook her head, felt like she wasn't making sense. "I know what you must be thinking. *I know. I get it.* And please, convince me I'm wrong. But I don't think you can. I just . . . I know what I know and now there's no unknowing it."

Ruth looked at Delmer hopeful he wouldn't be appalled at what she had just shared. Instead of seeming shocked, his eyes were filled with even more understanding than she had previously perceived.

"Sorry to disappoint you, but what you just said, that's what I think too," Delmer shrugged. "I . . . I'm out here, and I'm looking up at the heavens, and I'm looking out at the glory around me, and I'm watching nature do its thing, and I think there isn't some big conspiracy. There isn't some big answer from on high. There is simply this, what we have in front of us, and I don't get why that can't be enough?"

"But you go to church. You go to Joe's church."

Delmer burst out laughing. "I go to all the churches in the area." Then he lowered his voice conspiratorially. "I'm a realtor. There's no better way to network in the Midwest than at church."

Now it was Ruth's turn to laugh out loud. "Scandal!"

"Isn't it?" Delmer smiled. "And it's a good thing I don't believe in heaven or hell either, 'cause if I did . . ." Delmer made a slicing motion across his neck.

Suddenly there was so much warmth between Ruth and Delmer, it was like he'd somehow lit a bonfire right there in front of them. As it stood, all that lit up the night was the bioluminescent glow of the fireflies that floated in the darkness just beyond the porch.

After a quiet moment, Ruth said softly. "I wondered if you were gay."

"I've gotten that before," Delmer smirked. "Personally, I don't know exactly what your views on homosexuality are considering your personal life at the moment, but I think being gay is just like being straight. It's just a physiological aspect of humanity that appears to differ from human to human. You got nothing to be sorry about. If I were gay, I'd be okay with that. And sometimes I've wondered if maybe there was something inside me I wasn't in touch with, but so far, nothing. I remain voraciously attracted to women, and when I'm lucky, I occasionally find a woman who's voraciously attracted to me, and we . . . voraciously enjoy one another."

Ruth raised her eyebrows. "Oh," she said, sounding much more judgmental than she meant to.

"Yep. I'm *that* carnal," Delmer sighed, as if he felt worthy of Ruth's condemnation.

"No. No. I didn't mean it that way. I . . . I'm not used to . . ."

"I get it."

"No, really. This is all new. Well, not really new. I mean, my mother was very, very . . . *carnal*," Ruth laughed. "It's just, I feel like I'm understanding so much for the first time in my life, *or* I don't know—I'm *seeing* it and *trying* to understand it."

"How far down the rabbit hole do you want to go?" Delmer asked, and he took another sip of his wine.

"What do you mean?" Ruth ventured cautiously.

"How much do you know about Joe and Naomi?" Delmer said, looking at Ruth pointedly.

Ruth suddenly felt nervous. She shrugged. "I mean, I was their daughter-in-law the last seventeen years, and I knew them a year before that."

"I know you spent a lot of time with them, but what do you know *about* them? Did Sam ever tell you anything?" Delmer asked.

Ruth shook her head. "It's sad to say. It's not that I didn't want to know them or Sam, but they never really talked about themselves. They just . . . railed about everybody else."

Delmer nodded as though he understood completely. Then he took another sip of wine, clearly contemplating whatever it was he was about to lay on her. Ruth shifted in her chair and decided maybe she should take another sip of her wine as well.

"Did you ever hear about Galen Fisher?"

"No."

"Galen Fisher was a really sweet kid who grew up in a wealthy family on a big farm a couple miles from here. His dad owned the Ford dealership in town and another one over in Rolla. You know, Fisher Ford?"

Ruth shook her head. She vaguely remembered the small Ford dealership in Conway that sat conveniently near the bank, but she didn't know its name, and she never knew anything about the family who owned it.

"Galen was a great kid. I only knew him the summer of our junior year when we would end up at parties together and down at the river doing bonfires and float trips. He was a lifeguard at the pool in Houston and was one of the best players on the football team. He knew everyone, or perhaps the truth is they knew him. Instead of being a prick about the money he was born into and the status of his family around Conway and Rolla, Galen was super down-to-earth. When we went on float trips, he would literally slug a person if they littered, and he always stood up for the weaker ones in the group if they got made fun of. I always kinda thought—damn—that's the way I wish I was. I think a lot of people thought the same way about him."

Ruth knew some tragic story was coming, and she braced herself for it.

"Anyway," Delmer continued, "one night about a week before our senior year, Galen was driving around a sharp bend over on Highway Z, and the brakes failed on his truck, or he was driving too fast, or he swerved to miss an animal—everyone has a different story. Point is, he rounded that corner, skidded off the road, and rolled his truck a few times crushing his legs and pinning him inside."

"Oh, my gosh," Ruth said quietly, imagining the horror of the scene.

"They had to get the Jaws of Life to pry him out." Delmer said, shaking his head. "Thing was, as they were trying to save him, Galen told the rescuers to be careful; he had HIV. Well, they thought he was kidding with them or out of his mind because of the loss of blood and the shock of the accident, but he said it again and again."

This was not the direction Ruth was imagining the story would take, and she sat there staring at Delmer wide-eyed with interest.

"Galen died in the ambulance on the way to the hospital, and when he was tested postmortem, it was true what he's told his rescuers, at some point in his life Galen had contracted HIV. Galen's parents, Jim and Donita, admitted they knew he was HIV positive, but they had kept quiet about it for fear of Galen being alienated by his friends. They said he'd contracted the disease when he was given a tainted blood transfusion after an accident the prior year playing football. Most people accepted this explanation because there was indeed an accident that had landed Galen in the hospital during one of Conway's first games against the Tigers.

"Well, suddenly all the paramedics and the farmers and even a choir lady who had been on the scene of the car accident were being tested to make sure they hadn't accidentally picked up the virus as they were helping him, and people everywhere were beyond upset. For folks around Conway, HIV was a gay disease, a disease that came from promiscuous, immoral, satanic behavior."

"So, what happened?" Ruth asked.

Delmer took a deep breath and continued, "As you can imagine, Jim and Donita were devastated, and despite their best efforts to maintain a strong front in the face of pretty intense vitriol and gossip, they soon sold both dealerships and moved out of town.

"Thing was, the mystery of how Galen Fisher got HIV didn't go away with the Fisher's perfectly plausible explanation, nor with their exodus. Then at long last, Joe Christianson got up in front of his church one Sunday morning and told everyone he knew *where* Galen had contracted HIV and *who* had given it to him."

Ruth needed Delmer to finish his story, but she had a forlorn sense of where it was headed.

"There was a particular pleasure palace on the outskirts of town—"

"Wheels Roller Rink," Ruth guessed.

"So, you *have* heard this story?"

"No," Ruth said. "But I know how Joe hated that place."

"Well, Joe told his congregation that it was Uncle Willie—the owner of Wheels that had given Galen HIV either because he had fornicated with him or had donated his tainted blood. Either way, Joe assured everyone that the rumors they had heard about Uncle Willie were true —that he was a homosexual, and it was high time they drove Uncle Willie and his house of reprobation out of their town. It was two nights after Joe's fiery sermon, Uncle Willie was found dead, bludgeoned to death by a roller skate."

Ruth let out a breath she didn't realize she'd been holding.

"Whether it was Joe who killed Uncle Willie or not, he was the one responsible for Willie's death. You don't say things like he said, you don't incite people to violence and maintain some sort of innocence."

"Do you think it was true—everything that was said about him and the roller rink?" Ruth asked.

"I think destroying lives is easy. I think if there was evidence against Uncle Willie, that should have been given to the authorities, and if there was only gossip, a man was killed in cold blood because someone decided they didn't like him."

Ruth didn't know what to make of this story except that Delmer was far more impressive than she had given him credit for. He was not just a man to be sexualized, but a human with wisdom and insight that was considerable given the environment in which he lived. She offered him her hand. He looked at it quizzically. Then, he took it. For a moment, they both sat with their fingers intertwined, looking into one another's eyes.

"How did you become like you are?" She asked. "You're not typical of this area."

Delmer smiled. "There are more of us around here than you realize. We just stay above the fray most of the time. We enjoy nature and all its bounty and don't get tangled up in all the little skirmishes people around here use to make their lives seem more important."

"That makes me profoundly happy," Ruth beamed. "I love this place.

It's so stunning and beautiful and wondrous, but I also feel this immense oppression here like a darkness has shadowed the beauty, and I've wished for so long that wasn't so."

"There's dark and light everywhere. Here, it's harder to hide, and for some folks, like your deceased father-in-law, darkness can be espoused without fear of retribution because he stands behind a pulpit."

"Do you think what Sam and I did with our lives—our ministry back in Charleston—that was darkness we were spreading?"

"Do you?" Delmer asked.

"There were good things. There were people who I know we helped. But the truth is, there were so many we hurt. I mean, look at my husband. Look at Uncle Willie."

"That's life, though, I think," Delmer said. "Unless we're perfect beings, even those of us who feel enlightened are bound to make mistakes, to do the wrong thing, to hurt people we want to love. That is the human experience. To deny that, to pretend that all people must be good and perfect at all times is the only hell any of us will ever truly know, and that feeling of letting others down, of not being enough just as you are, has destroyed good people since the dawn of time, with and without religion's help."

"You should have seen the way people came after me on social media once the story came out about Sam. People were vicious. I was called names I wouldn't reserve for my worst enemies by the very Christians who had exalted me mere days before. Of course, it was nothing compared to what happened to Sam." Ruth clinched her eyes recalling the pain of it. "Maybe he deserved it. Maybe I did too. I think all the judgment has to stop though. I think you're right. I think we all have to find our humanity again."

"That's why I think religion can be so destructive in particular," Delmer said. "If everyone knew that there was no heaven, that this—earth—is all there is, wouldn't we all behave differently?"

Ruth looked at Delmer and opened her mouth to say something, but no words came out.

"What?" he asked.

"If it's true this is all we have—this here, I've only been with one man my whole life, and I want to know what it feels like to kiss someone else," Ruth stated.

Delmer considered Ruth fully and completely. Then, he stood up from his chair and pulled Ruth up from her chair. Without comment, he pressed himself into her, wrapping her face in his hands, and holding her firmly, he kissed her.

The emotions that shot through Ruth's body from Delmer's kiss ran the gamut of everything from devastation for what she was doing to total elation for doing it. She opened her mouth to taste his tongue, and gently, he kissed her even deeper. Somehow her arms had found themselves wrapped around his body and the heat of him, the strength of him, the mass of all he had been to her that evening was a rock she was so enamored by she would have chained herself to it and thrown herself into the deepest ocean.

When they parted after kissing, Delmer looked Ruth sincerely in the eyes. "You are one of the most beautiful women I've ever met," he said.

"I wish all this was happening under different circumstances," she replied.

"Why? This is perfect. If it was anything different, it wouldn't be this."

Ruth knew he was right. This *was* perfect. It was one of those moments she would remember for the rest of her life. There was no heaven or hell, no future or past. There was just safety and love and life in this moment right in front of her.

Another Way

Ruth woke up in a guest room bed in Delmer's cabin. After their kiss the night before, he had shown her back into the house, and after checking on the kids, he had directed her down the hallway. They hugged and kissed again outside the door to the guest room. He told Ruth if she needed him, he would be just across the way. It was clear that he was inviting her to address him with all her needs if she wanted to. She felt the large, hard manhood in his pants when he pressed against her, and she was wet, so wet she was almost embarrassed. She was also exhausted, and she needed sleep more than she needed anything. So, she wrapped her arms around Delmer and let herself melt into the comfort of his embrace for a long moment, breathing in the smell of him, the freedom of him, and the safety of him. Then she told him good night, and they parted ways.

It was barely dawn now, and the rest of the house was silent. Clearly, no one else was awake, nor should they be. Ruth was still in her clothes from the night before having removed only her shoes before crawling into bed and passing out. She was used to only sleeping five to six hours a night, but she was not used to sleeping so soundly. So, she found herself surprisingly wide awake and feeling revitalized. She undressed and took a shower in the tiny bath that adjoined the guest room.

Normally Ruth would have completed her morning routine with a good thirty minutes to an hour of quiet time during which she would read her Bible and pray. No matter what was happening in her life, she could consistently achieve solace in God's word and intercession with Him. Finding a moment to take stock and consider the plates spinning in her life still seemed to be a good idea. Only now, there was no hocus-pocus involved. It was just her: her problems, her solutions. Instead of overwhelming her, this responsibility, that was now totally and completely hers alone, empowered her. There need be no deity fighting over her destiny. It was simply she herself who would oversee her life from this moment on. She was responsible for her own way. She had her own truth, and she emitted her own light. It was rebirth. It was salvation. It was the same refreshing feeling she had felt when she gave herself over to the Lord as a little girl, and just like when she was originally "saved" Ruth felt like she could do anything. Of course, what she *had* to do was talk to Sam. Somehow, they needed to decide on next steps for their lives, solid steps that were not based in fantasy but reality, steps that wouldn't destroy what little innocence was left of their children's adolescence and what little respect she and Sam might have for each other.

Ruth picked her cell phone off the nightstand next to the bed and exited the room. She padded down the hall towards the living room hoping not to disturb her kids. They were all still asleep, scattered about on pieces of the furniture just like they had been the night before. The tomcat had curled up next to Rachel, and when he saw Ruth, he began purring loud enough Ruth could hear him from the kitchen. She slipped out the back door and walked across the porch past the Adirondack chairs. There was a path just off the porch that led through the trees towards the river below, and she took it.

The trail was made of cut stone and wound down the hill in small switchbacks, so the drop off was navigated easily enough. This early in the morning the world was quiet, the sounds of the dark having disappeared with the sunlight and the resonance of the day not yet reaching full throttle. Ruth could sense that today would be a cool one. There was a wind rustling the needles of the pine trees that were tucked amongst the birch and live oak. Along the walkway, jack-in-the-pulpits, gayfeathers, and ferns relished the reprieve from the exhausting heat that had oppressed the region of late.

Ruth fingered her cell as she moved down the trail, and she

wondered what she should say to Sam *if* she managed to get him on the phone? How much information should she give him about where she was and what she planned to do? If for some reason he didn't answer, she wondered what she should say in her voicemail? She imagined that whatever it was, it might eventually be used against her in a court of law deciding the custody of her children. So, she needed to be wise like Solomon. She smiled. Maybe there were still some Bible stories that could come in handy. At this time of morning chances were Sam would be up. Just like she had done for years, he always spent time alone reading the Bible and praying in the wee hours of the day.

At the bottom of the hill there was a small landing built into the side of the bluff. It was made with the same rocks used for the path. Just like up at the house, two Adirondack chairs were sitting there waiting for someone to come snuggle up into them and fish or simply watch the deep water serenely slipping along the river.

Ruth told herself she needed to be honest. She would tell Sam she wanted to go back to Charleston with the kids. If she got Sam's voicemail instead of him, she would leave a message expressing the same thing. For a moment, she let her spirit settle. Then she hit Sam's name on the list of "Favorites" in her phone. The line rang three times before Sam answered.

"Hello?"

"Hey," Ruth said.

For a long moment, there was silence between them, that sort of peace that comes after a long hard fight is over, and negotiations for surrender are about to commence.

"I wanted to call and let you know I'm on my way back to Charleston," Ruth said.

"Why would you go back there?" Sam asked.

"Where else should I go?"

Sam was silent.

"Sam, if you . . . If you wanted to try to stay together but have an understanding between us about being with other people. Perhaps . . ."

"No," Sam said curtly.

"Well, I don't want you suffering, and I don't want to suffer either. You said before about Delmer—"

"I know what I said before. I was wrong. I've been scared."

"I've been scared too," Ruth said.

"But you would . . . stay with me?" Sam asked.

"Sam, I love you. I've loved you for as long as I've known you." Ruth was surprised at the words coming out of her mouth and the sincerity with which she was sharing them, but they were true, and that's what she had promised herself, that she would be honest with Sam.

"I love you too," Sam said quietly.

"I'm just suggesting maybe there's another way for us to be together that would make us both happy. We're great parents, and we've always been good partners. I hate to throw all of that away. And I'm not sure we should. But clearly, we can't do things the way we've been doing them. Too much has changed."

Sam sighed, "Yeah."

"I'm open to ideas," Ruth said.

"Well, just so you know I'm staying here. I talked to Mom about it, and we both think I should take over Dad's church. They need a pastor, and I need to find my footing again."

Ruth couldn't help but be surprised. "Your mom agreed to that?"

"Half of the congregation will probably leave in protest. But I know the work I need to do, and I know I can do it."

Ruth was not expecting to have this particular conversation with Sam, and she quietly chastised herself for not imagining this is exactly what would happen. *Of course, Naomi would want to keep Sam around at any cost now that Joe was gone,* Ruth thought.

"I could use your help," Sam said.

"Sam, I have to tell you something."

"Okay," Sam responded.

Ruth knew her future with Sam now spun precariously upon the words she was about to say, and for a moment she wanted to turn back, to see if she could close her eyes, once more, and believe. But she couldn't. So, matter-of-factly, she said, "I . . . I don't believe in God anymore."

There was silence on the other end of the line.

"If you're surprised by me saying that, well, it's been a surprise for me too," Ruth sputtered. Then suddenly, she couldn't help but smile. Right then and there, she felt the weight of the secret she had been trying to hide so desperately roll off her shoulders. She continued, "I can't help you with your dad's church, but I can be your wife and the mother to your children if you think—"

"Ruth, stop. Why are you saying this?" Sam suddenly shot back.

"I just realized this belief I had, it was all well and good . . . It was helpful for a long time but not anymore. I know beyond a shadow of a doubt everything I grew up telling myself about God and heaven and hell and all the rest of it, it isn't true. And I . . . I can't not know that."

"So, you're turning your back on God? Is this because of me?" Sam said in all seriousness.

"No. I'm not turning my back on anyone, because there's no one to turn my back on."

"Ruth, you need to take a deep breath—"

"That's just the thing," Ruth interrupted. "I haven't been able to breathe for forever. I've been suffocating and didn't even realize it. But Sam, I'm free now. I'm free, and I'm happy, and I—"

"You turn your back on God, there is no us!" Sam interrupted sharply.

"I'm sorry," Ruth said. "I'm just trying to be honest with you."

"Save your honesty for judgment day, Ruth," Sam shot back.

"There is no judgment day, Sam," Ruth countered.

"Stop. I'm serious. Stop, or I'm hanging up the phone," Sam said.

Ruth went silent.

Sam was quiet too. Then he seemed to find some resolution. "Where are you at? Come back to the farm. We'll call some elders, and me and my mom, we'll all lay hands on you and pray for you, Ruth."

"No."

"Ruth, you've let Satan into your heart. You've let him have control of your mind. He's fed you lies. He wants to destroy you, baby. He wants to destroy our family. I know what you're going through because I did it first. It was Satan who got inside of me, Ruth, who made me do what I did with those men," Sam said. "Please, don't go down this path. It's exactly what the devil wants. He wants to ruin us, Ruth. He wants to destroy all the good we're capable of."

"There's no devil, Sam," Ruth said.

"You're walking away from our family. You're letting Satan destroy everything."

"I'm here, Sam. I'm saying we can be together. You can believe however you want to. You can preach and pastor and do whatever you need to. I'm not trying to keep you from that. I'm just saying, I can't believe in God myself anymore. I'll be a mother. I'll raise our kids. Somehow, we can work out everything else if we're honest. That's all I want. I'm not walking away. I'm not."

"Get thee behind me, Satan," Sam said quietly.

"Sam, come on."

"GET THEE BEHIND ME, SATAN!" Sam yelled.

For a moment, Ruth froze. The voice coming from the other end of the line was not like anything she had ever heard come out of Sam's mouth before. It sounded eerily like his father. She started crying. "Sam, please don't do this."

"Don't you cry," Sam said. "Don't you dare cry! You don't get to cry, not when you are allowing Satan to rip your family apart!"

Despite his demands, more tears slipped down Ruth's cheeks as Sam continued to rail at her from the other end of the line. Clearly, the negotiations were done between them. There was no compromising at this point. Ruth had to simply head back to Charleston, file for divorce, and wait for the government to do its job of civilly and democratically dividing her and Sam's world. All hope of fantasy was gone. Reality would save the day now.

Ruth hung up on Sam's screams, and put her head in her hands and wailed out into the wilderness around her with a power she didn't know she possessed. Like vomiting out the final vestiges of some abominable sickness, Ruth moaned and shook and hurt like she had never hurt before from her head to her toes. Every atom that made up her being was in torment. It was devastating and awful, yet simultaneously it was wonderful and beautiful because she knew this was the only hell there really was, and she would survive it.

Ashes

Florence often reminded Ruth that she wanted to be cremated when she died, and she wanted to have her ashes scattered around the giant redwoods of Big Sur, California. Big Sur was her favorite place in the world, she would say. There was good energy in Big Sur. There was healing for the broken and life for the dead amongst the land where salt water met fresh water and humanity was constantly reminded of its insignificance above and below the prehistoric patronage of the vast flora and fauna. Florence told Ruth she had passed through Big Sur only two times when she was out traversing the country as a young woman, but both times had been magic. The first time she arrived in Big Sur was after being regaled about its existence by some hippies she had spent a few weeks with in the Castro of San Francisco. Florence was so enraptured by the stories they shared about the two-thousand-year-old redwoods and sequoias, she hitchhiked down Scenic Highway One the very next day. And yes, Florence said, *El Sur Grande* as the original explorers called it, was everything her hippy friends had assured her it would be and more. "The trees! The ancient trees of Big Sur!" Florence would sometimes say out of the blue. "They know more than any of us."

As a child, Ruth never knew how to react to Florence's wishes about being cremated. To Ruth the idea of throwing a loved one into a furnace and burning them to ash at the time of their passing seemed inconceivably evil. Ruth appreciated traditional funerals where a person's physical body could be admired one last time and laid to rest as though they had just fallen asleep on earth and would wake up in heaven. But Florence wanted nothing to do with church services and graveside grieving and headstones and caskets and lilies and all the rest of it. She wanted to be burned up and to have her ashes poured into a little green Frankoma pot she had "lifted" from a pawn shop in Oklahoma. "Then, I want my ashes scattered upon the earth where the nutrients of my dead body can give rise to new life," Florence mused dreamily. "But only in Big Sur," she finished, looking pointedly at Ruth.

Young Ruth rolled her eyes.

"What?" Florence scoffed.

"All you do is talk about dying." Ruth sighed.

"Are you kidding me with that?" Florence shot back.

"It's true," Ruth said. "We're going along, having a good day, and suddenly you start going on about dying and what you want me to do with your body and where you want your ashes scattered and all that."

"Pot calling kettle black," Florence scoffed. "You live for death. Literally. You live your life waiting for the moment you die. That's all your little Bible and your religion tells you to do—live for death, LIVE FOR DEATH!" Florence shook her hands in the air like she was wailing hallelujah. "How dare you be upset with me for bringing up my post-life wishes once in a blue moon. I bring up my death so you're prepared. I know that when your grandma died it wasn't exactly ideal, and I don't want you to suffer through my passing any more than you must. I'll be dead. That's it. There's no going to heaven or hell or any of that jazz. My time on earth will be complete, and I'll be gone. So, it really doesn't matter what you do with my body. But cremation is so much less expensive than a funeral, and truthfully, I want you to go to Big Sur. You won't go if I tell you to. But if it's my dying wish, I hope you'll feel like, in a way, you have no choice," Florence smiled.

It was one of the rare chaotic days at Holy Life Ministries when Ruth received the call from a hospital in DC that Florence was not much longer for this world. She'd been rushed to the emergency room earlier that morning after a neighbor who checked in on her found her in the craftsman unconscious on her couch. And while she shouldn't have felt so, Ruth resented Florence for the intrusion on her life at this particular moment. In fact, Ruth's first thought was to question whether Florence was dying at all or if she was simply putting on one of her overly dramatic shows to get attention. Neither of them had spoken since their meeting nine months before at the DC hotel, and Ruth imagined that Florence had probably spent those nine months concocting a plan to get Ruth's attention after Ruth hadn't called or written to try and patch things up. The doctor on the other end of the line assured Ruth that Florence was indeed in a precarious place and that her organs were starting to shut down. There was only a small window of time before she would leave this earth. The reality of the doctor's words dulled Ruth's anger, and she hoped the doctor hadn't sensed the depth of her previous condescension on the matter. To be certain there was no confusion about a now famous leader of the Christian faith and her concern for her decrepit mother's final hours, Ruth told the doctor she would fly to DC immediately.

It was the Saturday before Easter, the worst time in the world for Ruth to take leave from the church. The pageant planned for Sunday was dwarfed in size and price tag only by their lavish and renowned Christmas extravaganza. But the celebration of Christ rising from the dead was still going to be a grand spectacle. Attendance would be double last year according to their security team. An egg hunt was planned for the five hundred kids expected to attend. A passion play with over thirty performers—two from Broadway—was to be acted out live on stage as Sam told the story of Christ's death and resurrection before the regular congregation and hundreds if not thousands more visitors. Rehearsals had been going on for weeks. Committee meetings had hashed out every last detail from valet parking to making sure the bathrooms were stocked with enough toilet paper to having enough staff on hand for prayer and leading newcomers to the Lord.

Under normal circumstances, it wouldn't have been difficult for Sam to abscond from his duties as leader of the church for a few days. Even last minute, there was plenty of talent in their pool of associate pastors who could whip together a fine sermon. And at any other time, Ruth would have insisted her kids come pay their last respects to their grandma. But in this situation, there was no way she would force her family to drop everything they had planned for Easter Sunday to pay tribute to a woman they barely knew. Rachel was fulfilling a small but significant role in the passion play, a role she had been rehearsing for weeks. JD was giving his testimony at a special Promise Keeper's Easter pancake breakfast. Tim lived for the egg hunt the church put on; it was all he talked about the month before and the month after. No, Ruth would go to DC alone, and if Florence hung on past Easter, the rest of Ruth's family could follow later.

The mixed emotions Ruth felt upon hearing of Florence's impending demise followed her from her Saturday afternoon flight out of Charleston, into the cab she took from Dulles airport to the hospital at rush hour, and up the elevator to the fifth floor where she met the same man, Dr. Najibi, who had called her on the phone. Dr. Najibi was grey-haired and slim built but very handsome for his age, which Ruth guessed to be around fifty-five.

"Is she . . . still with us?" Ruth asked after Dr. Najibi introduced himself.

"She is. It's good you're here," Dr. Najibi said, and he guided Ruth down a hall away from the reception desk. "We've given her what we can in terms of pain management. She's comfortable."

"What happened exactly?" Ruth asked.

"It's a lot of things. Old age. Poor diet. Lack of consistency with taking her meds. Living conditions that don't appear to be ideal. She has an ear infection, an eye infection, and respiratory symptoms that appear to be the result of advanced fungal bronchitis. She also had a severe case of head lice, and given the delicacy of her condition we decided it would be best to shave her head."

All the self-righteousness Ruth had been so happily commiserating with fled her body, and she suddenly felt the present execrable moment swell up around her, making it difficult for her to breathe and belaboring her footsteps forward.

"Do you need a moment?" Dr. Najibi slowed down and looked at

Ruth intently as though he could see the turbulent reaction her body was putting her through.

"Do you have any water?" was all Ruth could get out.

"Certainly. Wait right here." Dr. Najibi turned and headed back in the direction they had just come from.

Ruth moved over to a chair in the hallway to sit and center herself. She prayed, *Dear Jesus, I need you to watch over me, right now. Please, Holy Father, bring comfort and light in my hour of need and give me strength in this moment of uncertainty.* Then she stopped short. Just down the corridor, she saw the thing she had only imagined up until now. Two rooms away and partially hidden by a half-closed door, lying in a hospital bed looking like a shriveled hairless child, was Florence. For a moment Ruth was horrified by the sight and didn't want to believe that the creature she was peering at was the woman who had given birth to her and raised her. As if to prove her eyes had deceived her, Ruth stood up and walked towards the room.

She expected to feel awful or perhaps even some sort of alleviation at the sight of Florence, but when she pushed the door open farther and saw the extent of her mother's trauma, Ruth felt nothing. All that registered in Ruth's mind was an image of IVs and tubes and flesh and bone that did not seem real.

Florence had been given a single room. Carefully and quietly, Ruth stepped into the dark space, moving over to Florence's bed like a thief fearful of hitting a tripwire. Florence looked a million years older than the woman Ruth had met in that hotel lobby nine months prior. It seemed impossible this frail soul before her was ever capable of being the person from whose existence Ruth had unspooled her own. How had this feeble mortal, Florence Kuhn, given rise to the spiritual giant, Ruth Christianson? Was it possible Ruth had imagined the power that Florence held? Under the warm light of the hospital bed her mother seemed like a mere wisp incapable of being the tyrant Ruth had made her out to be all these years. Ruth dared to reach out and touch Florence's hand, but she recoiled at the coldness of Florence's papery skin. Florence was still alive according to the monitors she was hooked up to, but that was the only evidence of her sentience. Ruth imagined she should be happy; she was almost free of the woman who had single-handedly tormented her directly or indirectly all her life. But this was not something to appreciate, the final decaying moments of human flesh. Where had the brown, carefree locks of her mother's hair gone? Where had the glowing, sun-kissed skin disappeared to? When had Florence's curves been replaced with angles so sharp just looking at them was painful? How had time managed to ravage Florence, and how had Ruth never recognized the total and complete plundering until now? The only answer was that this thing in front of her was not Florence. This was some likeness wheeled out to trick Ruth. Florence would surely appear at any moment laughing at Ruth's drawn face and serious gaze. Ruth had fallen for her trick. Ruth would be told she was a silly girl, just like she had always been, and for a moment Ruth wished this was true.

When Ruth heard a shuffling behind her, she knew it was Dr. Najibi returning with the water she had asked for. He had a small, plastic bottle which he held out to Ruth with a doctor's half smile that couldn't be read as either accompanying good or bad news.

"Is she asleep, or . . .?" Ruth asked.

"She's been unconscious all day," Dr. Najibi said.

"Can she hear us?"

Dr. Najibi shrugged. "If it makes you feel better to believe she can, you can certainly try to talk to her."

Ruth nodded, feeling the rush of culpability she had so far managed to stave off. How had she let things come to this? Was it her pride or Florence's? Could she have done things differently? Could there have been another outcome?

"Like I said, we've made her as comfortable as we can," Dr. Najibi offered. "If you need me, the nurses will let me know. If you don't have any other questions, I'll let you be alone with her."

Ruth nodded again. Once more Dr. Najibi gave Ruth a half smile and left the room.

There was an empty vinyl chair next to the bed inviting Ruth to sit and begin the process of waiting, waiting for Florence to regain consciousness perhaps but probably more realistically waiting for Florence's departure from the living world. Ruth moved over to the chair and set her purse on the table next to Florence's bed. There weren't any flowers. There wasn't a view. There was just a murky hospital room. The thought that this plain grey chamber would be the last thing Florence would see of this earth seemed crushingly unfair given the voracity with which Florence had attempted to live her life in full-blown, untethered technicolor.

Ruth shooed away the responsibility she felt for Florence's state by gently reminding herself that this was the way her mom wanted it to be because this is the way she had chosen it to be. Florence was here slipping away to an unsettling death because she had preferred to do the opposite of all that was good and right. Certainly, things could have turned out differently for Florence, far differently. Yes, all people died, but it could have been better. This scene could have played out twenty years in the future with Florence's grandkids, and perhaps even great-grandkids, huddled around her in hospice at a beautiful nursing home down in Charleston. Sam and Ruth would have taken care of Florence if she had let them. Over the years, Ruth had written checks to Florence that would've covered any medicines and other comforts she needed for months on end, but not a single one of those checks had ever been cashed. Pride cometh before a fall, Ruth thought. Then the guilt flooded her again. Florence had never taken any handouts from Ruth because she knew the strings attached to them. She would have had to cower before Ruth's religious proclivities and prostrate her otherwise atheist soul before a God she had never believed in. But that was just it, Ruth reminded herself. God said, come to me and I will give you life! Florence had been given the opportunities over and over to find Jesus and she had refused to open her heart to eternal salvation.

With the word "salvation" pulsating along Ruth's brainwaves like a neon sign against a dark sky, Ruth's heart began beating faster. Florence needed to wake up. She needed to wake up and say the sinner's prayer so she would go to heaven! It didn't matter if she had lived her whole life as a degenerate, she could still repent, and all would be forgiven in heaven and on earth. There was still time.

"Mom," Ruth said. She reached out and took Florence's hand. "Mom, it's Ruth. I'm here."

There was no response from Florence, and if it was possible, Florence's hand felt even colder now than it had moments before.

Ruth softly rubbed the blotchy, crinkled skin and tried once more. "Mom, it's Ruth. Can you hear me?"

Ruth stared at Florence's face hoping for some miracle in Florence's eyes, a pulse of crimson warming the grey of her face. *Jesus, please,* Ruth prayed. *You have to wake her up. You can't let her die and go to hell. Please, have mercy on my mom. Don't let Satan take her away without giving her one last chance to believe in you.* Panic began to take over, and Ruth wondered what she should do. She wanted to scream out loud. She wanted to shake Florence violently enough she would come to. *Jesus, please. You have to save my mom!* Ruth prayed. *You can't let her die and go to hell. Please. Father God, I love her. Please!* Ruth prayed. *Unmmiiniiiii ianm msmmmiiiil lffuuu shumminnily iiiiii ummm nnennnnn metatbl lleit abllie shunnnidooniiililiiiii.* Tongues from the Holy Spirit flittered through Ruth's mind. Maybe that was what she needed to do, pray in tongues. *Oooooh mii guuuunn ggususguuu fuuuuliiii unnnmi tiiinomins hunnndoooo.* Ruth leaned closer to Florence. "Mom, if you can hear me, would you open your eyes? I have something *so* important we need to talk about. Mom, it's Ruth. I flew in from Charleston. Please, look at me. Please." Then, Ruth stopped. She began to float out of her own body and up above the room. From there she could see herself crouched next to her mother's fragile body in that little hospital room, begging like a crazy person for a miracle that would never come. She would never see Florence's eyes staring back at her again. Those deep orbs of curiosity filled with libraries of knowledge of worlds Ruth had only imagined, a vivid confetti of amber specs peppering interlaced browns and greens, were just jelly in sockets sealed shut for the rest of eternity.

Suddenly, Ruth understood how silly it was to be all consumed with "saving" Florence. No, it wasn't just silly; it was deranged. Ruth had taken one of the most important moments in her life and turned it into a fanatical quest when, if she was honest, deep inside all she really wanted was to simply tell Florence one last time that she loved her. In an instant, this stunning awareness of her egomaniacal zealotry split Ruth open, and for the first time Ruth understood the truth Florence had tried so desperately to relay to her in that DC hotel lobby—all that mattered in the end was love, and everything else was just fluff. This realization was so abruptly and indisputably evident, it felt to Ruth that Florence had spoken it out loud right there in the hospital room, but no, Florence simply laid there unresponsive. Yet it was in that moment a mirror was reflected back on Ruth revealing with aching clarity that her belief in God had gone far beyond some simple need for comfort in a world that was far too often cruel, her belief had become a tool for control and manipulation, inhospitable to genuine human existence. This reverie was such a terrifying realization Ruth found herself unable to breathe as though her chest had been stunned by a bolt of electricity powerful enough to stop a heart cold. Ruth grappled for balance, to find her old self, herself that had not been hit with a notion capable of upending her world. *Pray*, she thought! *PRAY!*

"Father God, help me in this hour to find my way through the darkness." Ruth spoke out loud. And with that simple locution of faith, Ruth found herself back inside her body holding Florence's hand. Yet while she believed she had staved off an internal rebellion undoubtedly led by Satan himself, in fact, Ruth had not. A small light had been shined into the darkness of her world and it had exposed the truth; she had become not just a member of an unholy cult, she had become one of its most fearsome leaders.

Eventually the seed that had been planted on that day would grow and produce fruit which would nourish Ruth when all seemed lost, when she believed she had breathed her own last breath in the face of her next great challenge—the loss of her marriage.

Heaven & Earth

Florence passed an hour after Ruth arrived in DC to say goodbye, and Ruth did as Florence requested long ago. Ruth had Florence cremated, and she put the ashes in the Frankoma pot Florence kept on the mantle in the small craftsman. Over the years, the neighborhood all around the craftsman had been rebuilt and restored and meticulously maintained with Florence's little, dilapidated craftsman the only eyesore impervious to neighborhood demands the yard be cut and the structure renovated. Ruth spent ten minutes in what could barely be called a house anymore, walking through it with a realtor who was determined to land the listing that was valuable in land only. Ruth picked out a few dusty items sitting on dirty shelves or hanging precariously on the cracked walls, small antiques that were holdovers from her time growing up with Trudy. But the rest would need to be donated or tossed.

Instead of taking Florence's ashes to Big Sur, as Florence had insisted, Ruth brought Florence's ashes home to Charleston with her and put them away on a top shelf in her study where they remained, mostly unnoticed, until the day on which Ruth was called out of the blue by Lillian Monroe to get Ruth's reaction to a story the *National Enquirer* was about to release with videotaped evidence showing Ruth's husband, Pastor Sam Christianson, smoking crystal meth and engaging in various sex acts with a male prostitute.

Oddly, Ruth never imagined the call from Lillian was some awful joke when it happened, not even for a moment. Instead, she knew when she hung up the phone without comment that she needed to prepare her house. She would have to track down her children immediately and pack their bags and ready them all for a change to their lives so drastic she could not even begin to imagine how it would play out. Within two weeks of the news spreading across every media platform that existed all over the world, Ruth thought perhaps the worst had come: she and her family had been driven out of the church they had founded, their house—which was owned by the church—had been taken away, and they were escaping to Conway, Missouri, a place she knew would hardly be a refuge.

Instead of storing the Frankoma pot that held Florence's ashes, along with the rest of the belongings she couldn't fit into their Cadillac, Ruth taped up the small, mint green vessel and secured it in her suitcase with a mishmash of clothes and toiletries. And she had almost forgotten about its existence in her luggage until the morning of her call with Sam in which she told him she was no longer a believer, and he told her if she no longer subscribed to "God's way" than she could no longer be a part of his life.

In the instance that Sam severed the intimate thread between them, Ruth found herself suddenly unencumbered from the piece of her life she thought had anchored her, but now she blissfully realized had only weighed her down. She realized, too, what she needed to do. She would wake the kids up and feed them breakfast. Then she would load them up in the Escalade, and they would head for California. There was no doubt saying goodbye to Delmer Green would be unfortunate considering the magnetic attraction that clearly existed between them, but there was also currently no *real* future for them, and they both knew that.

The journey from Conway to Big Sur would be two days of solid driving past Kansas City to Lincoln, Nebraska, then over to Cheyenne, Wyoming, and on to Salt Lake City before hitting Nevada and finally making their way across three hundred and fifty miles of California wilderness before Pacific Highway One would deposit them twenty-nine miles south of Monterey in a land of trees and ferns and ocean cliffs.

Over the course of the two-day trek, Ruth procured a credit card, withdrew twenty thousand dollars from her and Sam's shared account, and contacted an attorney in Charleston who had nothing to do with her and Sam's former church, but whom she had met at numerous social functions and who she knew would help guide her through the various and vast protocols required to end a marriage properly, especially considering how public her divorce was sure to become. She also found a tiny home in the heart of Big Sur, perched on a bluff with views of the Pacific Ocean and a trail leading down to the water. It would sleep four if Rachel took the couch in the cozy study off the kitchen. The price per night would not have seemed astronomical to her former self, but given her current financial concerns, Ruth was disheartened by the expense. So, she bargained with the owner for her and the kids to stay at a reduced rate so long as they promised to remain a full month. She would figure out next steps after that.

There was no mistaking Big Sur the moment they arrived in it. Trees, indeed. Her mother was right about the glory of the redwoods and sequoias when she exclaimed her praise for the sentries that guarded the entrance to this Elysium. The forests of Big Sur loomed like a fortress before them, sending sharp scents of terra firma up to their noses, while the crashing of ocean waves at the feet of the mighty cliffs on which those trees sat overwhelmed their eyes and ears. Every few miles there was a turn off from the twisted, two-lane blacktop that snaked under the arboreal canopy, and at each stop there was a path that could be found either heading up a mountain to eye-popping vistas or down towards the turquoise blue and green water that churned with the power of the incredible depths beneath it. Rocks the color of elephant skin and as big as buildings littered the shoreline, while pelicans and sea lions basked in the glory of Big Sur's pristine ecological effervescence. Life for the dead, and healing for the broken. Yes, this Valhalla was exactly what Ruth needed to make peace with the end of one chapter in her life's story and find the beginning of the next.

Ruth didn't immediately take Florence's ashes and spread them. Instead, she helped her kids unpack into their little cabin. The briny air that filtered up from the ocean, over the trees, and enveloped their new home was invigorating, like splashing one's face with chilled water first thing in the morning. Wildflowers abounded, and Rachel picked bouquets for every room, while JD played catch with Tim in the yard, and Ruth made pasta.

They were seated at dinner when Tim asked, "Mom, can we stay here forever?" Tim spoke as nonchalantly as though his voice, which none of them had heard in weeks, had been involved in conversation the whole time. Rachel and JD exchanged looks of dumbfounded surprise, and Ruth attempted to hide her own happy shock as best she could.

"Well, we'll see how everyone feels in a couple weeks. For now, let's just enjoy it—like the last days of summer vacation." Ruth said.

"I can't wait to go hiking tomorrow," JD said. "There's supposed to be a waterfall that drops right into the ocean."

"I just want to sleep," Rachel said. "For some reason, this place makes me so tired."

"Well, we've been driving for two days. It's nice to finally have some room to stretch out in." Ruth smiled. She was grateful her kids seemed content.

"Yeah, I want to go hiking too," Tim said. "I wonder if there are dinosaur bones around here?"

As Rachel helped Ruth dry and put away dishes that night, Ruth knew she would have to ask about the incident with Mike that Naomi had spit at her so violently right before they left the farm. Perhaps Naomi was telling the truth as relayed to her by Mike, that Rachel had indeed tried to know him intimately. But then, perhaps Mike had tried to take advantage of Rachel. The thought chilled Ruth's core, and she prepared herself for whatever answer Rachel might offer. No matter what it was, she just wanted the truth. The truth could be dealt with. The truth could provide whatever emotional shelter was needed. That's all she wanted—to shelter, to make safe, to secure the lives of her children.

"Sweetie," Ruth ventured.

"Yeah?" Rachel asked.

"Your grandma, she told me something before we left that I wanted to ask you about?"

Rachel turned to Ruth suddenly tense and worried. "What?"

"When you were with Mike gathering the honey, did anything inappropriate happen?"

Rachel's gaze remained frozen on Ruth, her mind flipping through the various answers she might give. Ruth did her best to look back at Rachel, open and understanding.

"I was stupid. I told him I was a virgin, and I tried . . . I kissed him on the lips." Rachel's whole body suddenly began shaking and a tear dripped down her cheek. "Do you hate me now?" Rachel asked. "Do you think I'm awful like Dad?"

Ruth touched Rachel's face tenderly and blinked back her own tears. "Do you want to talk about it, what happened?"

"I don't know what's wrong with me. I think these things. I get so angry, and I'm so confused." More tears dripped down Rachel's cheeks.

"I promise it's okay," Ruth said, wiping the tears off Rachel's cheeks.

"Do you think I'm like Dad?" Rachel asked.

"No." Ruth shook her head. "The part that should make you feel bad is not the mistake, because you are going to make many, many mistakes in this life. The only part you should feel bad about is knowing when you've done something inappropriate and choosing to do it again. And that's where your dad went wrong. That's where I've gone wrong. But, not you. Do you understand me?"

"Do I need to ask God to forgive me?" Rachel asked.

Ruth considered this answer; it would define so much of her and Rachel's relationship from this point forward—it would define both of their worlds for as long as they lived. She took Rachel in her arms. "No. We ask people we've hurt to forgive us, and then we have to forgive ourselves. That's all the forgiveness you need."

"You promise?"

Ruth mustered all the conviction inside of herself and said, "I promise."

For the first week, it felt like Ruth and her kids slept for impossible volumes of time. Many mornings they didn't get up until after ten, and they were all in bed by eleven or even earlier the following evening. This luxurious slumber felt sloven in the best way possible, like they were recovering the ebullience that had been sapped from their collective lives. Aside from her conversation with Rachel, no one talked about Sam, and Ruth was surprised to find no one asked to say grace either. None of her children referenced God, the Bible, or church at all. Ruth wondered if perhaps what had died in her had also somehow withered away in them too?

And indeed, so much *had* died. Ruth peered out at the world so differently now. Ideals that had once defined her existence were shattered and gone. The most surprising consequence of this rebirth was how easy it was to understand the world in this bright, clear light without the twisted molds that otherwise warped reality into strange shapes that depended on flights of fantasy in order to be explained. Maybe the world truly had evolved from spinning dust and atoms of energy as opposed to being formed by the hands of some omnipotent being. Maybe homosexuality was as natural as the endless variations of nature that appeared all around everyone all the time. Maybe abortion truly was each individual woman's right, just like fleeing one's country or marriage was sometimes necessary in order to simply survive.

The past had brought Ruth and all her kids to this place, and she realized one could regret all that had been, or one could simply learn from those memories and move forward. The greatest sin Ruth could imagine now—if there was such a thing as sin—was the transgression of not learning, of having the chance to grow outward into the world—into the universe—and to not take it. Perhaps her mother had been an extremist in the opposite direction of Joe, trying too hard to break out of the molds of societal conventions. And this was the real fight wasn't it—the extremism? Everything in moderation was the maxim du jour, as far as Ruth was concerned. Don't eat too much. Don't work too much. Don't sleep too much. Don't talk too much. On and on you could go. The idea remained: learn, expand, grow.

Ruth and her kids' first two hikes through the magnificent evergreens down towards the ocean didn't land them on sand. During their initial trips down the mountain, they ended up taking detours off the trail deep onto the spongy forest floor following butterflies and salamanders or looking for flowers or searching for birds emitting exotic sounding songs from the tree limbs hundreds of feet above. By the time their little convoy finally made it to the impossibly small stretch of sand that held back the enormous emerald waves of the great Pacific, Ruth and her kids had grown used to the steep descent down the mountain, a change of what Ruth suspected was at least a thousand feet in altitude.

It was on the beach, after a lunch of apples and chicken salad, basking under the white afternoon sun while her kids played in the surf, that Ruth finally took a moment to breathe another one of the incredible breaths she had been finding so frequently in this calming niche of her life, and she considered how she might spread Florence's ashes most respectfully. On every hike she had brought the little Frankoma pot with her just in case she and the kids stumbled upon the perfect moment. Ruth pulled the pot from her backpack now and placed it in the sand next to the blanket she was lying on. "Thank you for bringing me here, mom. It's everything you said it would be." Ruth spread herself out on the blanket soaking the sun into every pore possible.

They reached the clearing at the top of the mountain that afternoon just as the sky was turning bright pink over the unending ocean. Rachel was leading the pack with a bouquet of flowers. JD was using a stick like a swashbuckler, swiping at grasses, bursting their seed pods, and sending those seeds fluttering into the air. JD was bringing up the rear, singing a song to himself, lost in his own enchanted world.

Ruth stopped and admired her motley cavalcade, appreciating their lanky, little bodies and their wholesome faces, which seemed to have regenerated the innocence she could have sworn was lost for good. These were not sinners. They weren't angels either. They were just little human beings whom she had brought into this life and who would hopefully live on long after she was gone. They were cells and atoms and energy just like her, the dust of stars spun into a miracle that was only here for a moment like flowers and birds and yes, even the tremendous two-thousand-year-old redwoods.

Ruth swung her backpack around in front of her, unzipped the front pocket and removed the Frankoma pot that held Florence's ashes. "Kids," Ruth called to them.

Seeing the green pot in her hands, Rachel, JD, and Tim all gathered around Ruth curiously. "Why do you have a pot in your backpack?" JD asked.

"Is that Grandma's ashes?" Rachel asked.

Ruth was surprised Rachel knew what was in the pot. She had never explained fully what she had done with Florence's body when she returned to Charleston after Florence had passed. Ruth nodded. "Yes, these are your Grandma Kuhn's ashes," she said.

"Cool," JD exclaimed, wide-eyed. "Can we see them?"

"I don't want to see them," Tim said, bothered by the idea.

"I wish you guys had known your grandma better. She was a special woman. She loved life more than anyone I know. She wanted to be in it, feeling it, all of it."

"I thought you didn't like Grandma Kuhn?" Rachel questioned skeptically.

"The things I didn't like about your grandma, I didn't like for all the wrong reasons," Ruth said. She opened the lid of the pot and set it on the ground. Then she removed the small, plastic bag that was inside.

"That just looks like dirt." Tim sighed as if suddenly disappointed.

"This is all that's left of Grandma Kuhn. She's gone now, and there will never be a chance to change the relationship I had with her or the relationship I kept you kids from having with her. But moving forward, I want you to know I'm going to do better. We all have to do better." Ruth smiled.

"What does that mean?" Rachel asked.

"It means right now is all we have. There isn't anything after this. So, we have to appreciate each other and each moment as they come." Even as she said it, Ruth could see her kids' little minds working, processing what she had just told them.

"Do you not believe in heaven anymore?" Rachel asked, once again surprising Ruth with such a pointed question.

Ruth considered her answer. Then, she smiled. "I think this here is heaven." Ruth looked out at the stunning beauty around them. "And all I ever wanted was to be with your grandma and you kids in heaven. Now I am." Ruth smiled.

Ruth's kids looked at one another as if gauging each other's reactions before deciding whether to take kindly to Ruth's surprising pronouncement. When none of them raised any objections to this new line of thinking, Ruth held out the bag of ashes. "Now, I want everybody to each take a little bit of grandma's ashes from this bag, and we're going to do what she asked me to do a long time ago. We're gonna scatter her ashes to the wind."

"Cool," JD said pushing up his sleeves.

Tim was not so excited.

"Rachel, do you want to start?" Ruth asked, holding out the bag to her daughter.

Without a word, Rachel reached in and grabbed a handful of the ashes. "It feels like sand."

Next, JD reached in and grabbed two handfuls.

Then it was Tim's turn. "It's okay if you don't want to," Ruth said. Tim couldn't help eyeing his siblings' hands full of the grey mix. He wouldn't miss out on his chance to follow suit. He reached into the bag and pulled out a handful of ashes too.

"What do we do, now?" Rachel asked.

Ruth reached into the bag and pulled out her own handful of ashes. She set the remainder of the ashes down and stepped away from her kids. "We say goodbye." Ruth raised her arm in the air and let her handful of ashes slip through her fingers to be carried off by the wind towards the trees and the ocean in the distance.

Tim mimicked Ruth but not quite as skillfully, simply throwing his ashes up into the air and causing most of them to fly back onto both Rachel and JD. "Bye, Grandma," he said.

"Gross!" Rachel dusted off her clothes with her free hand.

Ruth laughed.

JD ran out into the grass beyond everyone and threw his ashes into the air next. "Goodbye, Grandma!"

Not wanting to miss out on the moment, Rachel walked over to another stretch of flowers and grass. "Goodbye, Grandma," she said, and she let her ashes go.

Tim hovered over the remaining ash. "Can I get some more?"

Ruth smiled. "Yes, we aren't done until all Grandma's ashes are scattered."

Tim dug into the bag pulling out so many ashes they slipped between his fingers despite his tight grip. This time he went running and then threw them up into the air in what looked like an explosion of smoke. "Goodbye, Grandma!"

With a few more handfuls, all that had remained of Florence's body was gone, and Ruth emptied the remainder of the ashes from the bag into the air. "Goodbye, mom," she said. The dust disappeared into the darkening sky, and Ruth turned to her kids. They were flush from the excitement of the moment. Ruth took a mental picture. Yes, if this was all there was, she needed to cherish it even more.

"All right, let's get ready for dinner," Ruth said, and she motioned for the kids to head for the cabin. They clamored up the remainder of the hill towards the house, and Ruth followed them. The sun was gone and the chill of a coastal evening swept in replacing the warmth that had just etched their silhouettes with gold. Ruth smiled and sucked in a soothing, deep breath. She would sleep soundly tonight, she thought. Then tomorrow, after breakfast was—But, she stopped herself. She would worry about tomorrow . . . tomorrow.

JOSHUA SENTER was born and raised in the Ozark Mountains of Missouri where he was homeschooled on a cattle farm. In 1997 he moved to Los Angeles, California, to pursue filmmaking at Art Center College of Design. It was at Art Center Joshua discovered his love of writing. After graduating with honors, he found a job working on the hit Showtime series *The L Word*. He later joined the international phenomenon *Desperate Housewives*. While there, the series was nominated for both Emmy and Golden Globe Awards, and he was nominated for a Writer's Guild of America Award for his episode "Don't Look at Me."

In 2013 Joshua joined the Freeform series *Chasing Life* as a writer and producer. His debut novel *Daisies* was published by Diversion Books in 2014, and he began work as a writer/producer for the hit series *Finding Carter* in 2015. Soon he was placed on the Tracking Board's Young and Hungry List as one of the "Top 100 Writers Working in Hollywood." He has written television pilots for ABC, FOX, and NBC and movies for Lifetime and Freeform. The Valentine's Day movie he co-wrote, *The Thing About Harry*, aired in 2020 and was nominated for GLAAD's "Outstanding TV Movie Award." Joshua is also an adjunct professor of TV writing for the School of Cinematic Arts at USC. His sophomore novel, *Still the Night Call*, was released in 2022 and was named *Kirkus Reviews* "Best Indie Book" as well as "Best Literary Fiction of 2022" by *Indie Reader* and *Readers' Favorite*.